RINGS AND RADICALS

RINGS AND RADICALS

by

N. J. DIVINSKY

Professor of Mathematics
University of British Columbia, Vancouver

London
GEORGE ALLEN & UNWIN LTD
RUSKIN HOUSE   MUSEUM STREET

FIRST PUBLISHED IN GREAT BRITAIN
IN 1965

PRINTED IN GREAT BRITAIN
BY WILLMER BROTHERS LIMITED
BIRKENHEAD

TO MY FATHER

INTRODUCTION

The wise man gratifies every appetite and every passion, while the fool sacrifices all the rest to pall and satiate one.

FIELDING

A SERIOUS INTRODUCTION to modern algebra used to be a first year graduate course. It has slowly moved down into the senior undergraduate year and today some of it is even taught to third year university students. Such a course introduces students to the three large bodies of algebra: Fields, Groups, and Rings. In many institutions there are subsequent courses in Field Theory and Group Theory, but as a person interested in Ring Theory, I feel that this phase of algebra has not received its full share of publicity. There are many active workers in Ring Theory, both here in North America and in Europe—particularly in Russia. It is an exciting theory and one that has great potential.

One of the difficulties seems to be an absence of books on Ring Theory that are sufficiently elementary. The present text is an attempt to fill this gap.

In the summer of 1960 I gave a graduate course at the University of Oregon and in attempting to connect the classical finite-dimensional algebra theory of the 1930's, the unconditioned Jacobson theory of the 1940's, the general radical theory of the 1950's, and the recent Goldie ascending chain results, I found that both the historical development and the most general development, which yields the special results as corollaries, left much to be desired. It was then that this text was given birth.

The material in this text has been taught successfully to first year graduate students at both the University of Oregon and the University of British Columbia.

I assume that the reader is familiar with the fundamental notions of Modern Algebra, as found in books such as those of Albert [1], Birkhoff and MacLane [16], and Van der Waerden [50]. A particularly good book that should be read is that of McCoy [42].

In particular, the reader should recall that a ring is a *set* of elements with two binary operations called addition $(+)$ and multiplication $(.)$ such that for every a, b, and c of the ring:

$$(a + b) + c = a + (b + c);$$
$$a + b = b + a;$$
$$(a.b).c = a.(b.c);$$
$$a.(b+c) = a.b + a.c;$$
$$(b + c).a = b.a + c.a;$$

there exists an element 0 such that $a + 0 = a$, for every a;
for every a there exists an element $(-a)$ such that $a + (-a) = 0$.

A subset B of a ring A is called a *subring* of A if $a.b$ and $a + (-b)$ are in B for every a and b of B. Thus, B is itself a ring with respect to the operations of A.

A subset B of a ring A is called a *right ideal* of A if B is a subring of A and $b.x$ is in B for every b in B and every x in A.

A subset B of a ring A is called a *left ideal* of A if B is a subring of A and $x.b$ is in B for every b in B and every x in A.

A subset B of a ring A is called a *two-sided ideal*, or simply *ideal*, of A if B is both a right ideal and a left ideal.

If B is an ideal of a ring A, then the set of cosets $x + B$, for all x in A, can, in a natural way, be made into a ring, by defining:

$$(x + B) + (y + B) = (x + y) + B,$$
$$(x + B).(y + B) = (x.y) + B.$$

This ring of cosets, denoted by A/B, is called the *factor ring* or difference ring.

A *homomorphism* from a ring A to a ring R is a mapping h which sends elements of A into elements of R. That is, for every x in A, $h(x)$ is in R, and

$$h(x + y) = h(x) + h(y),$$
$$h(x.y) = h(x).h(y),$$

for every x and y in A.

An *isomorphism* between two rings A and R is a homomorphism h onto R (i.e. every element in R is the image, under h, of some element of A) which is a one-to-one mapping.

Mathematicians would like to classify and categorize all rings. They would like to be able to say something about this large class of abstract mathematical systems. This is an extremely difficult question, but in 1908 J. H. Wedderburn [51] suggested an ingenious technique and showed that it worked for finite-dimensional algebras. His method was to discard or ignore a certain part of the structure, leaving only the "well-behaved" part, and then to describe this part in terms of well-known things, such as matrices.

The part that is discarded is called the *radical*. Structure theory has come a long way since Wedderburn's fundamental paper appeared. Many different radicals have been considered and studied, and many deep and surprising results obtained. Of course, the larger the radical, the more one discards, and the less there is left. In the extreme case one may call every ring a radical and then one is left with nothing. To reach a proper compromise, that is to discard as little as possible and yet be able to prove deep theorems, is of course a basic problem in all mathematics.

During the 1930's Wedderburn's work was modernized, and rings with the descending chain condition were classified. The main obstacle was lack of knowledge about division rings. Although the finest minds made a deep study of division rings, and profound theorems were obtained, the final solution was not found and to this day this problem remains essentially unsolved.

In the early 1940's, attempts were made to classify rings without the descending chain condition. In 1945 Jacobson made the major break-through. In the early 1950's, the general theory of radicals was developed and, in 1958, Goldie obtained exquisite results on rings with the ascending chain condition.

At present there are several radicals that play prominent roles and we shall consider each of them in some detail. However, we begin with a general study of radicals based on Kurosh's work of 1953 [36]. (Amitsur obtained similar results at about the same time [3].)

I should like to thank the secretarial staffs of the Universities of British Columbia and Oregon and of Reed College for their help in typing the manuscript.

N.J.D.

Vancouver
January, 1964

CONTENTS

RINGS AND RADICALS

CHAPTER ONE

THE GENERAL THEORY OF RADICALS

1.1. Definitions. Some rings have properties that differ radically from the usual number-theoretic properties we are familiar with and these somewhat strange properties make it difficult to classify these rings. It is from among these unusual properties that we seek a definition of the radical of a ring.

Let $\mathscr{S}$ be a certain property that a ring may possess. We shall say that the ring R is an $\mathscr{S}$-*ring* if it possesses the property $\mathscr{S}$. An ideal J of R will be called an $\mathscr{S}$-*ideal* if J is an $\mathscr{S}$-ring. A ring which does not contain any non-zero $\mathscr{S}$-ideals will be called $\mathscr{S}$-*semi-simple*.

We shall call $\mathscr{S}$ a *radical property* if the following three conditions hold:

(A)   *A homomorphic image of an $\mathscr{S}$-ring is an $\mathscr{S}$-ring.*
(B)   *Every ring contains an $\mathscr{S}$-ideal S which contains every other $\mathscr{S}$-ideal of the ring.*
(C)   *The factor ring R/S is $\mathscr{S}$-semi-simple.*

The maximal $\mathscr{S}$-ideal S of a ring R is called the $\mathscr{S}$-*radical* of R. When $\mathscr{S}$ is a radical property, it is clear from (B) that 0 is an $\mathscr{S}$-ring. Notice that (A) does not guarantee that 0 is an $\mathscr{S}$-ring, for there may be no $\mathscr{S}$-rings. Since 0 is an $\mathscr{S}$-ring, we may say that an $\mathscr{S}$-semi-simple ring is one whose $\mathscr{S}$-radical is 0. An $\mathscr{S}$-ring is its own $\mathscr{S}$-radical and we call it an $\mathscr{S}$-*radical ring*. Clearly, 0 is the only ring which is both an $\mathscr{S}$-radical ring and an $\mathscr{S}$-semi-simple ring.

The three defining conditions enable us to discard as much of property $\mathscr{S}$ as possible. Condition (B) ensures that property $\mathscr{S}$ can somehow be taken hold of, and condition (C) ensures that one can discard it. Condition (A) is included to avoid some extreme and non-useful radical properties. For example, let $\mathscr{T}$ be the property determined as follows: every ring is a $\mathscr{T}$-ring except one certain fixed simple ring R (recall that a simple ring is one which has no non-zero proper ideals). Then, clearly, conditions (B) and (C) hold. However, condition (A) does not hold, for one can easily find a ring R' which is different from R (and is therefore a $\mathscr{T}$-ring) and which maps homomorphically onto R. Thus, this property $\mathscr{T}$ is not a radical property.

Conditions (A), (B), and (C) are the ones we insist on, but if we are presented with a property $\mathscr{S}$ and want to determine whether $\mathscr{S}$ is a radical property, they are not always the conditions we can test most easily. The following theorem gives us conditions which are equivalent to (A), (B), and (C), but which are often easier to test.

Theorem 1. *Property $\mathscr{S}$ is a radical property if and only if:*

(A)   *A homomorphic image of an $\mathscr{S}$-ring is an $\mathscr{S}$-ring.*

(D)   *If every non-zero homomorphic image of a ring R contains a non-zero $\mathscr{S}$-ideal, then R is an $\mathscr{S}$-ring.*

Remarks. We want to combine all the $\mathscr{S}$-ideals of a ring and we must be quite clear about what is meant. By the union (not set-theoretic union) or sum of two subrings I and J of a ring R we mean the set of all $i + j$ where i is in I and j is in J. More generally, if $I_1, I_2, I_3, \ldots$ is any (not necessarily finite or even countable) class of subrings of R, then by $\cup I_k$ or $I_1 + I_2 + I_3 + \ldots$ we mean the set of all sums $i_1 + i_2 + i_3 \ldots$ where i_k is in I_k and where only a finite number of the i_k are non-zero. We take as established (the proof is straightforward and immediate) the following lemma.

Lemma 1. *The union of any set of ideals (left, right, or two-sided) is again an ideal (left, right, or two-sided).*

Condition (B) is then almost always true. For the sum of all the $\mathscr{S}$-ideals of a ring is, by Lemma 1, an ideal, and it clearly contains all the $\mathscr{S}$-ideals of the ring. The difficulty, and the reason that (B) is not universally true, is that this sum of all the $\mathscr{S}$-ideals may not have property $\mathscr{S}$. We are now ready to prove Theorem 1.

Proof. Assume that $\mathscr{S}$ is a radical property. Then (A) implies (A). To see that (B) and (C) imply (D), let R be a ring which is not an $\mathscr{S}$-ring. Then, by (B), it has an $\mathscr{S}$-radical S, and $S \neq R$. Then R/S is a non-zero homomorphic image of R which does not have a non-zero $\mathscr{S}$-ideal, by (C). This establishes (D) and thus conditions (A), (B), and (C) imply (A) and (D).

To prove the converse, assume $\mathscr{S}$ has conditions (A) and (D). First we observe that 0 is an $\mathscr{S}$-ring by condition (D) since 0 satisfies the first part of (D) in a vacuous sense. To establish (B), let J be the union of all the $\mathscr{S}$-ideals of R. We must establish that J is an $\mathscr{S}$-ring. If $J = 0$, then it is an $\mathscr{S}$-ring. If $J \neq 0$, let J/K be any non-zero factor ring of the ring J. Since $K \subset J$, there must exist in R an $\mathscr{S}$-ideal W such that W is not contained in K. By the second isomorphism theorem, $(W + K)/K \cong W/(W \cap K)$. The left-hand side of this isomorphism is a non-zero ideal of J/K, while the right-hand side is a homomorphic image of the $\mathscr{S}$-ring W and is therefore an $\mathscr{S}$-ring by (A). Therefore, every non-zero homomorphic image of J contains a non-zero $\mathscr{S}$-ideal and, by (D), J is an $\mathscr{S}$-ideal. This establishes condition (B).

Finally, we must establish (C). Take any ring R. We know that R has an $\mathscr{S}$-radical S since (B) is already established. Suppose that R/S is not $\mathscr{S}$-semisimple and let M/S be its non-zero $\mathscr{S}$-radical. Then M is an ideal of R, and M contains S. Let M/N be any non-zero factor-ring of the ring M. If $N \supseteq S$, then M/N is a homomorphic image of the $\mathscr{S}$-ring M/S and, by (A), M/N is an

$\mathscr{S}$-ring. If, however, $N \not\supseteq S$, then $N \cap S \subset S$ and, again, by the second isomorphism theorem, $(N + S)/N \cong S/(N \cap S)$. The left-hand side of this isomorphism is a non-zero ideal of M/N and the right-hand side is a homomorphic image of the $\mathscr{S}$-ring S and, therefore, by (A) it is an $\mathscr{S}$-ring. Thus, every non-zero homomorphic image of M contains a non-zero $\mathscr{S}$-ideal and, by (D), M is an $\mathscr{S}$-ring. Then M must be in S, a contradiction. This establishes (C) and finishes the proof of Theorem 1.

The following lemma is quite useful in establishing whether a ring is an $\mathscr{S}$-radical ring or not, by using the $\mathscr{S}$-semi-simple rings.

Lemma 2. If $\mathscr{S}$ is a radical property, then R is an $\mathscr{S}$-radical ring if and only if R cannot be mapped homomorphically on a non-zero $\mathscr{S}$-semi-simple ring.

Proof. If R is an $\mathscr{S}$-radical ring, then by (A) every non-zero homomorphic image of R is also an $\mathscr{S}$-radical ring and therefore it cannot be $\mathscr{S}$-semi-simple. Conversely, if R is not an $\mathscr{S}$-radical ring, then by (B) and (C) it can be mapped homomorphically on the non-zero $\mathscr{S}$-semi-simple ring R/S, where S is the $\mathscr{S}$-radical of R.

1.2. Construction of a radical property. In order to construct radical properties we require the following fundamental result.

Theorem 2. *The class $\mathscr{M}$ is the class of all $\mathscr{S}$-semi-simple rings with respect to some radical property $\mathscr{S}$ if and only if $\mathscr{M}$ satisfies the following conditions:*

(E) *Every non-zero ideal of a ring of $\mathscr{M}$ can be mapped homomorphically onto some non-zero ring of $\mathscr{M}$.*

(F) *If every non-zero ideal of a ring R can be mapped homomorphically onto some non-zero ring of $\mathscr{M}$, then the ring R must be in $\mathscr{M}$.*

Remarks. It is easy to find a class $\mathscr{M}$ which has condition (E): let $\mathscr{M}$ be a class of simple rings. After we prove this theorem, we shall show how to manufacture a class with both (E) and (F) from a class with just (E). Thus, starting with a class of simple rings, we shall be able to make good use of this theorem.

Proof. Suppose that we are given a radical property $\mathscr{S}$ and that $\mathscr{M}$ is the class of all $\mathscr{S}$-semi-simple rings. Let R be in $\mathscr{M}$ and let I be an ideal of R. Since R is $\mathscr{S}$-semi-simple, I is not an $\mathscr{S}$-radical ring. By Lemma 2, I can be mapped homomorphically onto a non-zero $\mathscr{S}$-semi-simple ring, i.e. a ring of $\mathscr{M}$. Thus, $\mathscr{M}$ has condition (E). To establish (F), take R to be a ring which is not $\mathscr{S}$-semi-simple. Then R has a non-zero $\mathscr{S}$-radical S. This ideal S cannot be mapped homomorphically onto a non-zero $\mathscr{S}$-semi-simple ring, by Lemma 2. This establishes (F).

Conversely, let $\mathscr{M}$ be any class of rings which has conditions (E) and (F).

We then define a property $\mathscr{S}_m$ as follows:

R is an $\mathscr{S}_m$-ring if it cannot be mapped homomorphically on any non-zero ring of $\mathscr{M}$.

We shall now prove that $\mathscr{S}_m$ is a radical property by showing that it has conditions (A) and (D). Condition (A) is clear, for whenever a homomorphic image of some ring R can be mapped homomorphically onto a non-zero ring of $\mathscr{M}$, then R itself can be mapped homomorphically onto this same ring of $\mathscr{M}$. In this case, then, R is not an $\mathscr{S}_m$-ring, and this establishes (A). To show that (D) holds, let R be a ring such that every non-zero homomorphic image of R has a non-zero $\mathscr{S}_m$-ideal. If R is itself not an $\mathscr{S}_m$-ring, then it can be mapped homomorphically onto a non-zero ring R' of $\mathscr{M}$. Then, by assumption, R' must have a non-zero $\mathscr{S}_m$-ideal I. By (E), I can be mapped homomorphically onto some non-zero ring of $\mathscr{M}$, which contradicts the definition of an $\mathscr{S}_m$-ring. Thus R must be an $\mathscr{S}_m$-ring and (D) holds. Thus $\mathscr{S}_m$ is a radical property.

It remains to prove that $\mathscr{M}$ is the class of all $\mathscr{S}_m$-semi-simple rings. If R is a ring of $\mathscr{M}$, then by (E) a non-zero ideal of R cannot be an $\mathscr{S}_m$-ring. Thus, every ring in $\mathscr{M}$ is $\mathscr{S}_m$-semi-simple. On the other hand, let R be any $\mathscr{S}_m$-semi-simple ring. Then every non-zero ideal of R is not an $\mathscr{S}_m$-ring and, therefore, can be mapped homomorphically onto a non-zero ring of $\mathscr{M}$. Then, by (F), R is itself in $\mathscr{M}$. Thus, $\mathscr{M}$ is precisely the class of all $\mathscr{S}_m$-semi-simple rings, and the theorem is proved.

If we can find a class of rings with (E) and (F), we shall then obtain a radical property as above. If we find a class of rings with only (E), we can build it up to a class with both (E) and (F) as the following lemma shows.

Lemma 3. *If a class $\mathscr{M}$ of rings has (E) and if the class $\overline{\mathscr{M}}$ is defined as the set of all rings R such that every non-zero ideal of R can be mapped homomorphically onto some non-zero ring of $\mathscr{M}$, then the class $\overline{\mathscr{M}}$ has (E) and (F).*

Proof. First we note that since $\mathscr{M}$ has (E), $\mathscr{M}$ is contained in $\overline{\mathscr{M}}$. Next take R in $\overline{\mathscr{M}}$. Then every non-zero ideal of R can be mapped homomorphically onto a non-zero ring of $\mathscr{M}$ and thus onto a non-zero ring of $\overline{\mathscr{M}}$. Thus $\overline{\mathscr{M}}$ has (E). On the other hand, let R be a ring such that every non-zero ideal I of R can be mapped homomorphically onto a non-zero ring R' of $\overline{\mathscr{M}}$. By the definition of $\overline{\mathscr{M}}$, R' can be mapped homomorphically onto a non-zero ring of $\mathscr{M}$, and therefore R is in $\overline{\mathscr{M}}$. Thus $\overline{\mathscr{M}}$ has (F).

Thus, if we start with a class $\mathscr{M}$ of rings which has (E), we can build it up to a class $\overline{\mathscr{M}}$ which has both (E) and (F), and by Theorem 2 we can then obtain a radical property $\mathscr{S}_{\overline{m}}$. This radical property will be called the *upper radical property determined by $\mathscr{M}$*. The rings in $\overline{\mathscr{M}}$ are all the semi-simple rings with respect to this upper radical property and, since $\mathcal{M} \subset \bar{\mathcal{M}}$, the rings in $\mathcal{M}$ are all semi-simple with respect to this upper radical property determined by $\mathcal{M}$.

To justify the use of the word "upper" we make the following definition. If $\mathscr{S}$ and $\mathscr{T}$ are two radical properties, then we say that $\mathscr{S} \leqslant \mathscr{T}$ if every $\mathscr{S}$-radical ring is also a $\mathscr{T}$-radical ring. It is clear that this is equivalent to the statement that every $\mathscr{T}$-semi-simple ring is $\mathscr{S}$-semi-simple. Still another way of looking at it is to say that for every ring R, the $\mathscr{S}$-radical S of R is contained in the $\mathscr{T}$-radical T of R. Now we justify the use of the word "upper."

Lemma 4. *If $\mathcal{M}$ is a class of rings which has* (E) *and if $\mathscr{S}$ is a radical property for which all the rings in $\mathcal{M}$ are $\mathscr{S}$-semi-simple, then $\mathscr{S} \leqslant$ the upper radical property determined by $\mathcal{M}$.*

Proof. Since the class of all $\mathscr{S}$-semi-simple rings has (F) by Theroem 2, this class contains all the rings of $\mathcal{M}$, and thus $\mathscr{S} \leqslant$ the upper radical property determined by $\mathcal{M}$.

Now we want to construct a radical property from a class $\mathcal{N}$ of rings in such a way that the rings in $\mathcal{N}$ will all be radical rings. Here we need no conditions on the class $\mathcal{N}$. However, the construction is transfinite and requires some knowledge of cardinal and ordinal numbers.

1.3. Ordinal numbers. G. Cantor developed the theory of cardinal and ordinal numbers just before the turn of the century and his definitions involve the notion of a set. Unfortunately, the intuitive notion of a set as any collection of objects is not precise enough, for it may lead to some famous paradoxes. Various methods have been developed to avoid these paradoxes and, consequently, there exist various systems of axioms for the Theory of Sets.

It is not customary for books on algebra to concern themselves with these matters, and we certainly do not intend to go into a detailed discussion of Set Theory. Suffice it to say that it is necessary to select one of the systems of axioms and to call a collection a "set" only if it is allowed as a set by the selected system. In our definition of a ring, the word "set" is used, and we shall henceforth assume that we have selected a system of axioms and that a ring is a set which is allowed by the system. This is not a serious restriction. It essentially means that we shall have to exclude extremely large collections and, in particular, the collection of all objects, from our "sets". We may talk about these large collections, but they are not sets. It is possible to allow such enormous collections into the permitted family of sets, but something else is usually lost. For a contemporary treatment of ordinal numbers which allows enormous sets see [46]. We shall follow the older treatment as given in [32]. We refer the reader also to Chapter 14 in [15].

It is curious that the entire body of ring theory (as well as group theory and other algebraic studies) should balance, so to speak, on this slender but important connection with Set Theory.

Two sets are said to be *equivalent* if there exists a one-to-one correspondence between them. This relation is clearly an equivalence relation, and we may then divide the collection of all sets into classes, such that two sets are in the same class if and only if they are equivalent.

A *cardinal number* is an arbitrary representative of a class of mutually equivalent sets.

For example, the cardinal number $\aleph_0$ will correspond to the class containing the integers while c will correspond to the class containing the real numbers.

The cardinal number of a set M will be the arbitrary representative of the class of mutually equivalent sets to which M belongs.

One can add cardinal numbers, multiply them, take powers, and define inequality. Although not all the usual algebraic laws hold, one can arithmetize with cardinal numbers quite comfortably. We shall not present this interesting theory, nor shall we give proofs for most of the propositions that follow. (They can be found in [32].)

Because very large collections are not sets in our system of axioms, we have the following propositions.

Proposition 1. *For every set M, the set of all subsets of M has a greater cardinal number than M itself.*

Proposition 2. *For every set W of cardinal numbers there exists a cardinal number which is greater than every cardinal number in W.*

The only connection between two sets with the same cardinal number is a one-to-one correspondence. Apart from this correspondence the sets may have quite different properties. For example, the positive integers and the set of all rational numbers have the same cardinal number but have different properties. In particular, the positive integers have a smallest element while the rationals do not.

We wish to obtain some more intimate connection between sets. To do this, we consider ordered sets or chains. First we define a *partially ordered set S* as a set with a binary relation $>$ satisfying the reflexive law: $x > x$; the transitive law: $x > y$ and $y > z$ implies $x > z$; and the antisymmetric law: $x > y$ and $y > x$ implies $x = y$. Given any two elements in S, they may or may not be comparable, i.e. either $x > y$ or $y > x$ or neither of these might hold.

An *ordered set* or *chain* is a partially ordered set in which every two elements are comparable. Furthermore, we say a chain is *well-ordered* if it itself as well as each of its non-empty subsets has a first element, i.e. an element x such that for every y in the subset, $y > x$.

Two chains S and T are said to be *similar* if there exists a one-to-one correspondence between them which preserves the orderings, i.e. if a and b are in S, and α and β are in T, such that a corresponds to α and b to β, then if $b > a$ in S, we must have $\beta > \alpha$ in T. Thus, if two chains are similar, they have the same cardinal number, but the converse is false. The positive integers and the rational numbers (with their usual orderings) have the same cardinal number but they cannot be similar, for there is no way of preserving the orderings since the rationals do not have a first element.

Similarity is clearly an equivalence relation and we may thus divide the collection of all chains into classes such that two chains are in the same class if an only if they are similar.

An *ordinal type* is an arbitrary representative of a class of mutually similar chains.

As for cardinal numbers, one can develop an arithmetic for ordinal types, obtaining sums, products, and powers.

For example, if S and T are disjoint chains, the set $S + T$ will denote the set-theoretic union of S and T, with an order defined as follows: if a and b are in S, then they are related just as they were in S; if α and β are in T, then they are related just as they were in T; if a is in S and α is in T, then $\alpha > a$. In other words every element of T is bigger than any element of S. This makes $S + T$ into a chain.

If we have two ordinal types u and v, we represent them by disjoint sets S and T respectively, and form the chain $S + T$. Then we define $u + v$ as the ordinal type represented by $S + T$.

For transfinite ordinal types u, v, it is clear that $u + v \neq v + u$. For example, if S is a chain with a countable number of elements, $S = \{s_1, s_2, s_3, \ldots\}$ and if T consists of just one element, $T = \{\alpha\}$, then $T + S = \{\alpha, s_1, s_2, s_3, \ldots\}$ has no last element, but $S + T = \{s_1, s_2, s_3, \ldots, \alpha\}$ does have a last element. Thus, $T + S$ is not similar to $S + T$. If u is the ordinal type of S (and 1 is the ordinal type of T), then we have $1 + u \neq u + 1$. In fact, $1 + u = u$, and $u \neq u + 1$.

Ordinal types, however, are too general, and we select only those chains which are well ordered, in order to make the following definition: An *ordinal number* is an ordinal type which is represented by well-ordered sets.

This makes sense because of:

Proposition 3. *Every ordered set which is similar to a well-ordered set is itself well-ordered.*

For finite sets, cardinal number and ordinal number coincide. But for infinite sets, many different ordinal numbers correspond to the same cardinal number. Thus, ordinal numbers form a finer grid, so to speak, than cardinal numbers.

In order to define an order relation among ordinal numbers, we must first define a *segment*. If S is a well-ordered set and x is in S, then the set of all s in

S such that $x \geqslant s$, without the element x itself, is said to be a segment of S, the segment determined by x.

If u and v are ordinal numbers represented by the well-ordered sets S and T, respectively, we shall say that $u < v$ if S is similar to a segment of T. We then have the following propositions.

Proposition 4. *For any two ordinal numbers u and v, precisely one of the following three conditions holds: $u < v, u = v, v < u$.*

Proposition 5. *If C_u is the set of all ordinal numbers less than the ordinal number u, and if C_u is ordered according to increasing magnitude of its elements, then C_u is a well-ordered set.*

Proposition 6. *Every set of ordinal numbers, if ordered according to increasing magnitude of its elements, is a well-ordered set.*

Proposition 7. *For every ordinal number u, there exists a successor ordinal number $u + 1$, such that $u < u + 1$, and there is no ordinal number properly between them.*

Proposition 8. *To every set W of ordinal numbers there exists an ordinal number which is greater than every ordinal number in W.*

We observe that Proposition 8 would be false if the collection of all ordinal numbers were allowed to be a set. In fact, we must not allow quite a few collections to be sets, e.g. the collection of all ordinal numbers omitting any segment. These are all considered to be very large collections and are ruled out as sets.

Although each ordinal number has an immediate successor (Proposition 7), not every ordinal number has an immediate predecessor. Thus, for a given ordinal number u, $u - 1$ may not exist. For example, if w is the ordinal number represented by the positive integers, then $w - 1$ does not exist. Each predecessor of w is finite and w can be thought of as the limit of all the ordinal numbers that precede it. It is called a *limit ordinal*. However, w is not the only limit ordinal. Any ordinal number which is represented by a well-ordered set which does not have a last element does not have an immediate predecessor and is therefore a limit ordinal.

The ordinal numbers form an enormous sequence. It begins with the finite ordinals, takes a jump, so to speak, to w, the first limit ordinal, and continues from w to $w + 1, w + 2, \ldots$, then takes another jump to the limit ordinal $w.2$, and continues on further.

By taking small steps of 1 and jumping to limit ordinals, we can thus traverse this weird and enormous world of ordinal numbers.

The cardinal numbers are exactly the same as the ordinal numbers for finite ordinals but, from w on, the cardinals are few and far between. Between any two infinite cardinals there are vast stretches of ordinal numbers. If we consider the set of all ordinals corresponding to a given cardinal, we may (by Proposition 6) pick out the smallest such ordinal number, call such an ordinal number an *initial ordinal*, and think of cardinal numbers as simply initial ordinals. Note that all infinite initial ordinals must be limit ordinals.

Induction can be carried out just as it is for the integers.

Proposition 9. *If a statement is true for the ordinal number* 1, *and if the statement is true for the ordinal number u whenever it is true for all ordinal numbers* $< u$, *then the statement is true for all ordinal numbers.*

Proof. Suppose the statement were false for some ordinal number v. Consider the set M of all ordinal numbers $< v + 1$ (notice how carefully we avoid working with the collection of all ordinal numbers). Consider the subset N of all ordinal numbers in M for which the statement is false. Since N is well-ordered by Proposition 6, there exists a smallest ordinal number u in N. Since the statement is true for 1, $u > 1$. Now the statement is true for all ordinal numbers $< u$ and thus it must also be true for u itself. This is a contradiction; therefore no such v exists, and thus the statement is true for all ordinal numbers.

Proposition 9 is often referred to as transfinite induction.

We now have all the results about ordinal numbers that we require, namely Propositions 6, 8, and 9, but before we leave ordinal numbers, we shall state two more interesting results.

Proposition 10. *Every decreasing sequence of ordinal numbers contains only a finite number of ordinal numbers.*

Proposition 11. *Every set can be well-ordered.*

This last proposition is a consequence of the *Axiom of Choice* (if M is a set, the elements of which are non-empty sets every two of which are disjoint, then there is a set N which contains exactly one element of each of these sets) and, conversely, it implies the Axiom of Choice. Thus, Proposition 11 is essentially an axiom itself. It is also equivalent to Zorn's Lemma (see Section 3.5).

1.4. Construction of a second radical property. Let $\mathcal{N}$ be any class of rings. A ring is said to be of first degree over $\mathcal{N}$ if it is zero or a homomorphic image of some ring in $\mathcal{N}$. Clearly all rings of $\mathcal{N}$ are themselves rings of first degree over $\mathcal{N}$ and every homomorphic image of a ring of first degree over $\mathcal{N}$ is itself a ring of first degree over $\mathcal{N}$. A ring R is said to be of second degree over $\mathcal{N}$ if every non-zero homomorphic image of R contains a non-zero ideal which is a ring of degree 1 or of first degree over $\mathcal{N}$. For any ordinal number β, *if $\beta - 1$ exists, a ring R is said to be of degree β over $\mathcal{N}$ if every non-zero* *homomorphic image of R contains a non-zero ideal which is a ring of degree* $\beta - 1$ *over* $\mathcal{N}$. If β is a limit ordinal, then R is of degree β over $\mathcal{N}$ if it is of degree α over $\mathcal{N}$ for some $\alpha < \beta$.

The following two conditions are then true:

(1) *Every homomorphic image of a ring of degree* α *over* $\mathcal{N}$ *is itself of degree* α *over* $\mathcal{N}$.

(2) *If* $\alpha < \beta$, *then every ring of degree* α *over* $\mathcal{N}$ *is also of degree* β *over* $\mathcal{N}$.

To prove (1) first note that when $\alpha = 1$, (1) holds. Next take α not a limit ordinal and $\neq 1$. If R is of degree α over $\mathcal{N}$ and if R' is a homomorphic image of R, then every homomorphic image R'' of R' is also a homomorphic image of R and, thus, R'' will contain a non-zero ideal of degree $\alpha - 1$ over $\mathcal{N}$ if $R'' \neq 0$. Thus R' will be of degree α over $\mathcal{N}$, and therefore (1) holds if α is not a limit ordinal. Now suppose that α is a limit ordinal. Then R is of some degree α' over $\mathcal{N}$ with $\alpha' < \alpha$. We may take α' to be the smallest ordinal such that R is of degree α' over $\mathcal{N}$ (Proposition 6). Clearly, then, α' is itself not a limit ordinal. Thus, every homomorphic image R' of R is of degree α' over $\mathcal{N}$ and therefore of degree α over $\mathcal{N}$. Therefore, (1) is true for all α.

To prove (2) first note that when $\beta = 1$ there is nothing to prove. Next, assume that β is not a limit ordinal. If R is of degree $\beta - 1$ over $\mathcal{N}$, then every homomorphic image of R will also be of degree $\beta - 1$ over $\mathcal{N}$ by (1). Therefore, R satisfies the definition of a ring of degree β over $\mathcal{N}$ and (2) holds in this case. Finally, suppose that β is a limit ordinal. Then if R is of degree α over $\mathcal{N}$ with $\alpha < \beta$, R is of degree β over $\mathcal{N}$ by definition. Therefore, (2) holds for all β.

Let $\bar{\mathcal{N}}$ be the class of all rings which are of any degree over $\mathcal{N}$. Clearly $\mathcal{N} \leqslant \bar{\mathcal{N}}$. Define a ring to be an $\mathscr{S}_{\bar{\mathcal{N}}}$-ring if it belongs to $\bar{\mathcal{N}}$. We now show that the property $\mathscr{S}_{\bar{\mathcal{N}}}$ is a radical property.*

Theorem 3. *The property* $\mathscr{S}_{\bar{\mathcal{N}}}$ *has* (A) *and* (D).

Proof. By (1) we clearly obtain (A). To establish (D), let R be a ring such that every non-zero homomorphic image R_σ of R has a non-zero ideal I_σ which is a ring of degree α_σ. We can assert that there exists an ordinal β which is not less than any of the α_σ (Proposition 8). By (2), all the ideals I_σ can be considered as rings of degree β over $\mathcal{N}$. Therefore, R is of degree $\beta + 1$ over $\mathcal{N}$ and thus R is in $\bar{\mathcal{N}}$. This establishes (D) and proves that $\mathscr{S}_{\bar{\mathcal{N}}}$ is a radical property.*

*ADDED IN PROOF: This construction can be somewhat streamlined and the separation between limit ordinals and non-limit ordinals avoided. Define rings of first degree over $\mathcal{N}$, as above. Assume that rings of degree α over $\mathcal{N}$ have been defined for every $\alpha < \beta$. Then define a ring R to be of degree β over $\mathcal{N}$ if every non-zero homomorphic image of R contains a non-zero ideal which is of degree α over $\mathcal{N}$, for some $\alpha < \beta$. This leads to precisely the same radical class $\bar{\mathcal{N}}$ as above.

Furthermore, it can be shown that the process terminates at the first infinite limit ordinal ω_0. Thus $\bar{\mathcal{N}}$ is precisely the class of rings which are of degree ω_0 over $\mathcal{N}$. This work (done during the summer of 1964) will appear as a research paper in the near future.

Thus, if we begin with any class $\mathcal{N}$ of rings and build it up to $\bar{\mathcal{N}}$ and define the property. $\mathcal{S}_{\bar{\mathcal{N}}}$, we obtain a radical property called the *lower radical property determined by* $\mathcal{N}$. The rings in $\mathcal{N}$ are all radical rings with respect to this lower radical property determined by $\mathcal{N}$. To justify the use of the word "lower" we prove the following lemma.

Lemma 5. *If* $\mathcal{T}$ *is a radical property and every ring in* $\mathcal{N}$ *is* $\mathcal{T}$*-radical, then the lower radical property determined by* $\mathcal{N} \leqslant \mathcal{T}$.

Proof. The class of all $\mathcal{T}$-radical rings has (A) and (D). By (A) all rings of first degree over $\mathcal{N}$ are $\mathcal{T}$-radical. We proceed by induction (Proposition 9). Assume that all rings of degree $\alpha < \beta$ are $\mathcal{T}$-radical. Let R be of degree β. If β is a limit ordinal, then R is of degree α for some $\alpha < \beta$ and hence is $\mathcal{T}$-radical. If $\beta - 1$ exists, then every non-zero homomorphic image of R contains a non-zero ideal of degree $\beta - 1$ and therefore is $\mathcal{T}$-radical. Then, by (D), R is itself $\mathcal{T}$-radical. Thus the class of all $\mathcal{T}$-radical rings contains $\bar{\mathcal{N}}$, and therefore the lower radical determined by $\mathcal{N} \leqslant \mathcal{T}$.

1.5. Partitions of the simple rings. We shall now make use of our two constructions. We consider the class of all simple rings. We allow a ring R to be simple even if R is trivial, i.e. if all products in R are zero, but we assume that a simple ring is itself not zero.

If $\mathcal{S}$ is a radical property, then every simple ring must declare itself, so to speak. A simple ring is either $\mathcal{S}$-radical or $\mathcal{S}$-semi-simple. Thus, a radical property $\mathcal{S}$ partitions the class of simple rings into two disjoint classes: the class of simple rings which are $\mathcal{S}$-semi-simple, called the *upper class*, and the class of simple rings which are $\mathcal{S}$-radical, called the *lower class*. We say that $\mathcal{S}$ corresponds to this partition.

It is not obvious that if we begin with a partition of the simple rings there exists a radical property that corresponds to this partition, but it is true.

Theorem 4. *If a partition of the simple rings into two disjoint classes (with isomorphic rings in the same class) is given, and one is called the upper class and the other is called the lower class, then there exists at least one radical property which corresponds to this partition.*

Proof. We shall use both of our constructions and exhibit two radical properties that correspond to the given partition.

Let P_1 be the upper class. Since P_1 consists only of simple rings, it has condition (E) and therefore determines an upper radical property $\mathcal{S}_1$. All the rings in P_1 are $\mathcal{S}_1$- semi-simple. If R is a simple, $\mathcal{S}_1$-semi-simple ring, then by the definition of the upper radical property $\mathcal{S}_1$ determined by P_1, R can be mapped homomorphically onto some ring in $\bar{P}_1$, and therefore onto some ring in P_1. However, since R is simple, R must be isomorphic to a ring in P_1 and therefore R is in P_1. Therefore, all the simple rings which are not in P_1, i.e. the ones in the lower class, are $\mathscr{S}_1$-radical, and therefore $\mathscr{S}_1$ corresponds to this partition. This ends the proof, but we exhibit another radical property which corresponds to the given partition.

Let P_2 be the lower class of the given partition and let $\mathscr{S}_2$ be the lower radical property determined by P_2. Then all the rings in P_2 are $\mathscr{S}_2$-radical. Now let R be a simple $\mathscr{S}_2$-radical ring. Then R is of some degree α over P_2. Let β be the smallest ordinal such that R is of degree β over P_2 (Proposition 6). Clearly β is not a limit ordinal. If $\beta > 1$, R must have a non-zero ideal of degree $\beta - 1$ over P_2. Since R is simple, R itself must be of degree $\beta - 1$, contradicting the minimality of β, unless $\beta = 1$. However, if $\beta = 1$, R is a homomorphic image of some ring R' in P_2. Since R' is simple, R' is isomorphic to R and thus R is in P_2. Therefore all the rings in the upper class are not $\mathscr{S}_2$-radical and are therefore $\mathscr{S}_2$-semi-simple, and thus $\mathscr{S}_2$ also corresponds to this partition.

By Lemmas 4 and 5, we know that $\mathscr{S}_2 \leqslant \mathscr{S}_1$. We shall refer to $\mathscr{S}_2$ and $\mathscr{S}_1$ as the *lower and upper radical properties of the given partition.*

It is clear that if $\mathscr{S}$ is a radical property and $\mathscr{S}_2 \leqslant \mathscr{S} \leqslant \mathscr{S}_1$, then $\mathscr{S}$ corresponds to the given partition; in fact, this is an "if and only if" relationship.

The question naturally arises as to when $\mathscr{S}_2 \neq \mathscr{S}_1$ or when $\mathscr{S}_2 = \mathscr{S}_1$. If we take an extreme example and consider the partition where the lower class P_2 is vacuous, we find that the lower radical property of this partition is trivial in that only the zero ring is $\mathscr{S}_2$-radical and all non-zero rings are $\mathscr{S}_2$-semi-simple. However, the upper radical property is not trivial, for although all simple rings are $\mathscr{S}_1$-semi-simple, there are $\mathscr{S}_1$-radical rings which are not zero. These are rings which cannot be mapped homomorphically on a simple ring, i.e. rings which do not have any proper maximal ideals. The following example is such a ring.

Example 1. *The zero ring on the additive group p^∞* [44].

Let p be a fixed prime and consider the set W of all rational numbers which are of the form a/p^n, where a is any integer and n is any non-negative integer. Then W is an additive group and W contains the integers I. Then the additive group p^∞ is defined as the difference group $W - I$. Thus p^∞ is the set of all rational numbers less than 1, of the form a/p^n, and addition is taken modulo 1.

We make the additive group p^∞ into a ring by defining all products to be 0. This is called the zero ring on p^∞. Then an ideal of the ring p^∞ is merely a sub-group of the group p^∞. There are not many subgroups. Let H be any non-zero proper ideal, i.e. subgroup, of p^∞. Then there exist some numbers of p^∞ which are not in H. Consider the set of numbers not in H. Each of them has a certain positive integral power p in its denominator. Consider the set of these integral powers and let m be the minimal such power.

Then there exists a number c/p^m with c relatively prime to p, which is not in H, but all numbers of the form d/p^r with $r < m$ are in H. Thus all the numbers

$$0, \frac{1}{p^{m-1}}, \frac{2}{p^{m-1}}, \ldots, \frac{p^{m-1} - 1}{p^{m-1}}$$

are in H, and we now show that there are no other numbers in H. Since c/p^m is not in H, it is clear that $1/p^m$ cannot be in H. Now suppose that s/p^t is in H, that $t \geqslant m$, and that this number is expressed in its lowest form, i.e. s is relatively prime to p. Then

$$\frac{p^{t-m}s}{p^t} = \frac{s}{p^m}$$

is in H. Since the greatest common divisor of p and s is 1, we can find integers a, b such that $as + bp = 1$. Now,

$$\frac{as}{p^m} \text{ and } \frac{b}{p^{m-1}} = \frac{bp}{p^m}$$

are in H, and therefore

$$\frac{as + bp}{p^m} = \frac{1}{p^m}$$

is in H, a contradiction. Therefore, s/p^t cannot be in H, and thus H consists of precisely the numbers

$$0, \frac{1}{p^{m-1}}, \ldots, \frac{p^{m-1} - 1}{p^{m-1}}.$$

We call this subgroup H_{m-1}. Thus, the only ideals of the zero ring on p^∞ are the ones in the following sequence:

$$0 \subset H_1 \subset H_2 \subset \ldots \subset H_n \subset \ldots \subset p^\infty.$$

Each proper ideal contains only a finite number of elements, while p^∞ itself has an infinite number of elements. Furthermore, p^∞ as a ring has no proper maximal ideals.

We shall make use of the ring p^∞ in the next theorem, and to do this, let us consider the non-zero homomorphic images of p^∞. Each one is of the form p^∞/H_n for some n. The surprising thing is that p^∞ *is isomorphic to each of its non-zero homomorphic images.* We map $1/p$ into $1/p^{n+1}$, and this gives us a 1–1 mapping between p^∞ and p^∞/H_n which preserves both ring operations.

Problem 1. Show that the 1–1 map between p^∞ and p^∞/H_n preserves both ring operations.

Problem 2. Consider Example 1 in the case when p is not a prime. Which properties of Example 1 remain and which do not hold?

Another useful example is:

Example 2. *The zero ring on the infinite cyclic additive group.*

Let C^∞ be the infinite cyclic additive group $\{0, \pm a, \pm 2a, \ldots, \pm na, \ldots\}$. As above, we make this into a ring by defining all products to be zero. Let I be any non-zero ideal of C^∞. Let m be the smallest positive integer such that ma is in I. Then it is clear that I consists of $\{0, \pm ma, \pm 2ma, \ldots, \pm nma, \ldots\}$ and that I is isomorphic to C^∞. Thus the zero ring on C^∞ has the property that *it is isomorphic to every non-zero ideal of itself.*

We can now answer the question regarding the relationship between the upper and lower radicals of a given partition.

Theorem 5. *For every partition of the simple rings,* $\mathscr{S}_2 < \mathscr{S}_1$, *where* $\mathscr{S}_2$ *is the lower radical property of the partition and* $\mathscr{S}_1$ *is the upper radical property of the partition.*

Proof. Let P_1 and P_2 be the upper and lower classes respectively of the given partition. Assume first that P_1 does not contain any simple ring in which all products are zero (such a ring must necessarily be a cyclic additive group of prime order for it cannot have any non-zero proper subgroups). In this case we shall show that the zero ring on C^∞ is an $\mathscr{S}_1$-radical ring and an $\mathscr{S}_2$-semi-simple ring and thus establish that $\mathscr{S}_2 < \mathscr{S}_1$.

To see that C^∞ is $\mathscr{S}_1$-radical, we must show that it cannot be mapped homomorphically onto a non-zero ring of $\bar{P}_1$. If it could be so mapped, then it could be mapped homomorphically onto a non-zero ring of P_1, for every ring in $\bar{P}_1$ has the property that every non-zero ideal, and in particular itself, can be mapped homomorphically onto a non-zero ring of P_1. However, C^∞ cannot be mapped onto a ring of P_1, for the only simple images of C^∞ are those simple rings in which all products are zero, and we have assumed that P_1 does not contain any of these. Thus C^∞ is $\mathscr{S}_1$-radical.

If C^∞ is not $\mathscr{S}_2$-semi-simple, then it contains a non-zero $\mathscr{S}_2$-ideal. Since C^∞ is isomorphic to each of its non-zero ideals, C^∞ would then have to be an $\mathscr{S}_2$-radical ring. Then it would be of some degree over P_2. Let α be the minimal ordinal such that C^∞ is of degree α over P_2 (Proposition 6). Clearly α is not a limit ordinal. If $\alpha > 1$, then C^∞ must have a non-zero ideal of degree $\alpha - 1$ over P_2. But C^∞ is isomorphic to this ideal, C^∞ would be of degree $\alpha - 1$ over P_2, contradicting the minimality of α, unless $\alpha = 1$. But C^∞ is not of degree 1 over P_2 since C^∞ is not simple. Therefore, C^∞ is $\mathscr{S}_2$-semi-simple.

Now we assume that P_1 does contain a simple ring in which all products are zero, a ring of prime order p. We shall show that the zero ring on p^∞ is an $\mathscr{S}_1$-radical ring and an $\mathscr{S}_2$-semi-simple ring and this will finish the proof of the theorem.

To see that p^∞ is $\mathscr{S}_1$-radical, we show that it cannot be mapped homomorphically onto a non-zero ring of $\bar{P}_1$. As for C^∞, this happens only if p^∞ cannot be mapped homomorphically onto a non-zero ring of P_1. This is true because every non-zero homomorphic image of p^∞ is isomorphic to p^∞, and since p^∞ is not simple, it cannot be isomorphic to a ring in P_1.

Finally, we show that p^∞ is an $\mathscr{S}_2$-semi-simple ring. Let H_n be one of the non-zero proper ideals of p^∞. Now H_n/H_{n-1} is a ring of prime order p in which all products are zero and this is, by assumption, in P_1. Thus, H_n can be mapped homomorphically onto a non-zero ring of P_1, i.e. an $\mathscr{S}_2$-semi-simple ring. Therefore, by Lemma 2, H_n cannot be an $\mathscr{S}_2$-radical ring. Thus, if p^∞ has a non-zero $\mathscr{S}_2$-ideal, it must be itself. Then p^∞ is of some degree over P_2 and we let α be the minimal ordinal such that p^∞ is of degree α over P_2 (Proposition 6). Clearly α is not a limit ordinal. If $\alpha > 1$, then p^∞ must have a non-zero ideal of degree $\alpha - 1$ over P_2. However, none of the proper ideals of p^∞ can be of any degree over P_2, and thus p^∞ would have to be of degree $\alpha - 1$ over P_2. This would contradict the minimality of α unless $\alpha = 1$. However, p^∞ cannot be a non-zero homomorphic image of a simple ring because p^∞ is not simple. Therefore, p^∞ is not an $\mathscr{S}_2$-radical ring and, therefore, p^∞ is $\mathscr{S}_2$-semi-simple, which ends the proof.

It is thus clear that we can construct many different radical properties. For each partition of the simple rings we obtain at least two distinct ones. The time has now come to consider some more specific properties before we carry on with this general abstract discussion.

CHAPTER TWO

RINGS WITH THE DESCENDING CHAIN CONDITION

2.1. Nil and nilpotent. The following properties are quite different from those satisfied by real or complex numbers. An element x is said to be *nilpotent* if there exists a positive integer n such that $x^n = 0$. A ring R is said to be *nil* if every element x in R is nilpotent, $x^n = 0$, where n depends on the particular element x of R.

By the product $I \cdot J$ of two subrings of a ring R we mean the set of all finite sums $\sum i_m j_m$, where i_m is in I and j_m is in J. In particular, we may speak of $R^2 = R \cdot R$ and of R^s for any positive integer s. We say that a ring R is *nilpotent* if there exists a positive integer n such that $R^n = 0$. Clearly, if the ring R is nilpotent, then R is nil. The converse is false, as we shall soon see.

We now take $\mathscr{S}$ to be the nil property, and a ring R is an $\mathscr{S}$-ring if it is nil. We shall show that $\mathscr{S}$ is a radical property. The following lemma is clear.

Lemma 6. *If R is a nil ring, so is every subring of R and so is every homomorphic image of R. If R is an ideal of the ring R' and both R and R'/R are nil, then so is R'.*

The proof follows immediately from the definitions.

It is clear, then, that the nil property $\mathscr{S}$ has condition (A) and as soon as we show that it has (B), then (C) will follow by Lemma 6. To establish (B), we shall, of course, take the union of all the nil ideals of any ring, and the problem is simply to prove that this union is itself a nil ideal. To this end, we prove the following results.

Lemma 7. *The sum of two nil ideals, I_1 and I_2, of a ring R is again a nil ideal.*

Proof. Since $(I_1 + I_2)/I_2 \cong I_1/(I_1 \cap I_2)$, by the second isomorphism theorem, and since the right-hand side is a homomorphic image of the nil ideal I_1, the left-hand side is a nil ideal by Lemma 6, and Lemma 1. Since both I_2 and $(I_1 + I_2)/I_2$ are nil, $I_1 + I_2$ is nil by Lemma 6.

By a simple induction we then have the following corollary.

Corollary. *The sum of any finite number of nil ideals of a ring is again a nil ideal.*

Finally, we prove:

Lemma 8. *The union of all the nil ideals of a ring R is a nil ideal.*

Proof. Let W be the union of all the nil ideals of R. If x is in W, then x is in some finite sum of nil ideals of R and thus, by the corollary to Lemma 7, x is nilpotent. Therefore, W is nil.

Thus, we have:

Theorem 6. *The nil property is a radical property.*

The partition of the simple rings that is determined by the nil property seems quite clear: all simple nil rings are in the lower class and all simple non-nil rings in the upper. Of course, all simple rings in which all products are zero are nil. In fact, they are nilpotent and they all belong to the lower class. An important question that is still open is whether there are any other simple nil rings, i.e. besides these nilpotent ones in which all products are zero. The best guess is that there are no others.

Next let us consider the nilpotent property and see whether it is also a radical property. Lemmas 6 and 7, with the corollary, go over with very little added proof and we state them for completeness.

Lemma 9. *If R is a nilpotent ring, so is every subring of R and so is every homomorphic image of R. If R is an ideal of the ring R' and both R and R'/R are nilpotent, then so is R'.*

Lemma 10. *The sum of two nilpotent ideals, I_1 and I_2, of a ring R is again a nilpotent ideal.*

Corollary. *The sum of any finite number of nilpotent ideals of a ring R is again a nilpotent ideal.*

However, Lemma 8 does not extend so easily. We can easily obtain:

Lemma 11. *The union of all the nilpotent ideals of a ring R is a nil ideal.*

Proof. Each nilpotent ideal is, of course, a nil ideal and therefore the union of all the nilpotent ideals is contained in W, the union of all the nil ideals. Since W is nil by Lemma 8, then by Lemma 6, the union of all the nilpotent ideals is a nil ideal (we make use of Lemma 1 also).

The following example shows that the union of all the nilpotent ideals, which we know is a nil ideal, may not be nilpotent. It also shows that nil and nilpotent are, in general, different.

Example 3. Consider the set of symbols x_α where α is any real number, $0 < \alpha < 1$. Let F be some field, and let A be the commutative algebra over F with these x_α as a basis. Multiplication of the basal elements is defined as

c

$$x_\alpha x_\beta = x_{\alpha+\beta} \qquad \text{if } \alpha + \beta < 1,$$
$$= 0 \qquad \text{if } \alpha + \beta \geq 1.$$

Thought of as a ring, A is the set of all finite sums $\sum a_\alpha x_\alpha$, where the a_α are elements in a field F. Addition is defined artificially as $a_\alpha x_\alpha + a_\beta x_\beta$ just written together, if $\alpha \neq \beta$; and if $\alpha = \beta$, then, of course, $a_\alpha x_\alpha + a'_\alpha x_\alpha = (a_\alpha + a'_\alpha)x_\alpha$. Multiplication is distributive and defined as above. The ring A is then commutative.

It is clear that every element in A is nilpotent, for if we let n be any integer $> 1/\alpha$, $(x_\alpha)^n = x_{n\alpha} = 0$ and for any finite sum, the term with the smallest x-subscript will yield an integer which as a power will yield zero. Thus, A is a nil ring.

However, A is not nilpotent, for $x_{1/2} \cdot x_{1/4} \cdot x_{1/8} \cdots x_{1/2^n} \cdots \neq 0$. In fact, $A^2 = A$, for given any α, there exists a β such that $x_\beta x_\beta = x_\alpha$.

Take any basal element x_α and consider the ideal (x_α) generated by it. This is a nilpotent ideal, for $(x_\alpha)^n = 0$ for any integer $n > 1/\alpha$. The union of all of the ideals (x_α) fills out all of A and, therefore, the union of the nilpotent ideals of A is not a nilpotent ideal.

Notice that A as an algebra has a very large dimension over the field F. This dimension is certainly not finite, and it is not even countable.

This same construction would work if we used only rational numbers α, $0 < \alpha < 1$.

Another nil but non-nilpotent example is:

Example 4. Let B be an algebra over the field of real numbers with a basis u, v, w having the following multiplication table:

	u	v	w
u	v	0	0
v	w	u	0
w	0	$-v$	0

i.e. $w^2 = uv = uw = vw = wu = 0$, $u^2 = v$, $vu = w$, $v^2 = u$, $wv = -v$. Clearly, $A^2 = A$, and therefore A is not nilpotent. However, if we take a general element $\alpha = au + bv + cw$, then $\alpha^2 = b^2u + (a^2 - cb)v + baw$, $\alpha^3 = (a^2 - cb)bu + (a^2 - cb)aw$, and $\alpha^4 = 0$. Thus A is nil.

This is, of course, a non-associative ring.

We have established, then, that for the class of associative rings, not every ring has a nilpotent ideal which contains every other nilpotent ideal.

Theorem 7. *The nilpotent property is not a radical property.*

The concept of radical was introduced in the hope that a suitable radical property $\mathscr{S}$ could be found such that for any ring R something significant could be said about $R/(\mathscr{S}$-radical of $R)$. Taking nil as our property, what can we say about $R/($nil-radical of $R)$? We can, of course, say that this factor ring has no nil ideals, for it is nil-semi-simple. This is then our starting point and we shall study rings that have no non-zero nil ideals.

Ideally one would like to be able to say that every ring without nil ideals is of a certain well-known and familiar type. For this, models are needed. Fields, matrix rings, and division rings are some that have been widely used, though our knowledge of these is not as complete as one would like.

There are many questions that remain unanswered in connection with nil and nilpotent rings. For example, we know that if I is a non-zero nilpotent right ideal of a ring R, then $I + RI$ is a non-zero two-sided ideal that is nilpotent (for the proof of this, see the beginning of Lemma 12). However, if I is a non-zero nil right ideal of R, then we do not know whether it generates a nil two-sided ideal or whether a ring R can have non-zero nil one-sided ideals and not have any non-zero nil two-sided ideals. This question was raised by Koethe.

Another important open question is connected with local nilpotence. We say that a ring R is *locally nilpotent* if any finite set of elements of R generates a nilpotent subring. Now suppose that R is a nilpotent ring. Then, of course, it is locally nilpotent. But, suppose only that R is a nil ring. Then any subring of R generated by *one* element is nilpotent, but no one knows whether R is locally nilpotent. And, so far, no one has constructed an example of a ring which is nil but not locally nilpotent.*

At this point it would seem, then, that we cannot make a great deal of progress unless we limit ourselves somewhat and study certain classes of rings rather than the large class of all rings.

2.2. The descending chain condition. A ring R is said to have *the descending chain condition on left ideals*, or D.C.C. on left ideals, if every descending sequence of left ideals $R \supseteq L_1 \supseteq L_2 \supseteq \ldots$ terminates after a finite number of steps, i.e. there exists an integer n such that $L_n = L_{n+1} = L_{n+2} = \ldots$. This clearly implies that any non-vacuous set of left ideals contains a minimal left ideal (there may be several such minimal left ideals, but there is at least one).

We shall now study rings with D.C.C. on left ideals. The following theorem is fundamental for such rings and shows that nil and nilpotent are more or less equivalent concepts for such rings.

First we make the following definition: An element e of a ring is *idempotent* if $e^2 = e \neq 0$.

*ADDED IN PROOF: As we go to press, we hear from Moscow that E. S. Golod, a student of Professor Shafarevitch, has found an example of an algebra that is nil, but is not locally nilpotent.

* or to be left Artinian

Theorem 8. *If R is a ring with D.C.C. on left ideals, then any left ideal L which is not nilpotent is not nil and, in fact, contains an idempotent element.*

Proof. Consider all the non-nilpotent left ideals of R that are contained in L. By D.C.C. we obtain a minimal non-nilpotent left ideal L_1, contained in L. Now $L_1{}^2$ is a non-nilpotent left ideal contained in L_1 and therefore $L_1{}^2 = L_1$. There may, of course, be other left ideals contained in L_1, but if they are properly contained they must be nilpotent. Now consider all the left ideals I of R that are contained in L_1 and such that $L_1 I \neq 0$. Such left ideals exist, for L_1 itself satisfies the conditions. By D.C.C. we obtain a minimal such left ideal I_1. Then $L_1 I_1 \neq 0$, and thus there exists an element $e_1 \in I_1$ such that $L_1 e_1 \neq 0$. Now $L_1 e_1$ is a left ideal and it is contained in I_1 and $L_1 . L_1 e_1 = L_1 e_1 \neq 0$. Thus, by the minimality of I_1, $L_1 e_1 = I_1$. Therefore, there exists an element e_2 in L_1 such that $e_2 e_1 = e_1$. Then $e_2{}^n e_1 = e_1$ and e_2 is not a nilpotent element, and therefore L is not a nil left ideal.

To actually construct an idempotent element we note that $(e_2{}^2 - e_2)e_1 = 0$. Let J be the set of elements x in L_1 such that $xe_1 = 0$. Then J is a left ideal of R, contained in L_1 and $\neq L_1$ since $L_1 e_1 \neq 0$. Thus J is nilpotent, and since $e_2{}^2 - e_2$ is in J, $e_2{}^2 - e_2$ is nilpotent. Let $x = e_2{}^2 - e_2$, with $x^n = 0$. Define $e_3 = e_2 + x - 2e_2 x$. Then e_3 is not nilpotent, for if it were, $e_2 = e_3 - x + 2e_2 x$ would be nilpotent. (Note that both e_2 and e_3 commute with x and with each other.) However, $e_3{}^2 - e_3 = 4x^3 - 3x^2 = x_1$ is nilpotent, $x_1{}^{n_1} = 0$, with $n_1 < n$. Then we define $e_4 = e_3 + x_1 - 2e_3 x_1$ and eventually we obtain $e_n = e$, which is not nilpotent and such that $(e^2 - e)^1 = 0$, and thus e is idempotent.

Since the nil radical of a ring is, in particular, a left ideal, we have the following corollary.

Corollary. *The nil radical of a ring with D.C.C. on left ideals is nilpotent.*

For rings with D.C.C. on left ideals we can say something about the nil left ideals. To do this, we require the following lemma.

Lemma 12. *The union of all the nilpotent ideals of a general ring R contains all the nilpotent left ideals and all the nilpotent right ideals of R.*

Proof. Let J be a nilpotent right ideal of R. Then $J + RJ$ is a two-sided ideal. Now $(J + RJ)^1 \subseteq J^1 + RJ^1$. If $(J+RJ)^n \subseteq J^n + RJ^n$, then $(J+RJ)^{n+1} \subseteq (J^n + RJ^n)(J + RJ) \subseteq J^{n+1} + RJ^{n+1}$ and therefore, by induction, $(J + RJ)^m \subseteq J^m + RJ^m$ for every positive integer m. Since J is nilpotent, say $J^m = 0$, then $J + RJ$ is nilpotent and therefore $J \subseteq J + RJ \subseteq$ the union of all the nilpotent ideals of R. Similarly, if I is a nilpotent left ideal, we can show that $I + IR$ is a nilpotent two-sided ideal, and therefore $I \subseteq I + IR \subseteq$ the union of all the nilpotent ideals of R.

Theorem 9. *In a ring R with D.C.C. on left ideals, the nil radical (which is nilpotent) contains all the nil left ideals and all the nil right ideals of R.*

Proof. Since a nil left ideal is, by Theorem 8, nilpotent, it is in the nil radical by Lemma 12.

In fact, every nil right ideal of a ring R with D.C.C. on left ideals must also be nilpotent, and thus the nil radical of such rings R also contains all the nil right ideals.

To prove that every nil right ideal is nilpotent or contained in the nil radical, we let L be any nil right ideal of R. Let N be the nil radical of R and consider R/N. Since N is nilpotent (corollary to Theorem 8), $L + N \supset N$ unless L is nilpotent. Then $(L + N)/N$ is a nil right ideal of R/N, and R/N has no non-zero nilpotent left, right, or two-sided ideals, and has no non-zero nil left ideals (for they are all in N).

We may, therefore, assume that R itself has no nil left ideals or nilpotent one-sided ideals. Take x in L. Then $xR \subseteq L$, and thus xR is nil. Consequently, Rx is nil, for if $(xy)^n = 0$, then $(yx)^{n+1} = y(xy)^n x = 0$. Thus, Rx is a nil left ideal, and thus $Rx = 0$. This holds for every x in L and thus $RL = 0$, and in particular $LL = 0$, i.e. L is nilpotent. Thus $L = 0$.

Returning to the general case, then, if L is a nil right ideal of R, then $L \subseteq N$, the nil radical, and thus the theorem is established.

Problem. If R is a ring with D.C.C. on left ideals and R has a unity element 1, prove that if $xy = 1$, then $yx = 1$.

2.3. Ideals in nil semi-simple rings with D.C.C. We are now in a position to obtain fruitful results about nil semi-simple rings. In the following, then, *let R be a nil semi-simple ring with D.C.C. for left ideals.*

Lemma 13. *Every non-zero left ideal L of R is equal to Re, where e is some idempotent element in L.*

Proof. Since the nil radical of R is 0 and since all nil left ideals are in the nil radical, we know that L is not nil and therefore, by Theorem 8, L contains an idempotent element e. Let M_e be the set of elements x in L such that $xe = 0$. This is a left ideal of R. There may be many idempotent elements in L and for each idempotent element we have a corresponding left ideal M_e. Consider the set of these left ideals M_e and by D.C.C. obtain a minimal one, call it M_e, and let e be the corresponding idempotent element. If M_e is a non-zero left ideal it must contain at least one idempotent element, say e_1, and $e_1 e = 0$. Define $e' = e - ee_1 + e_1$. Then $e'e' = e'$. Now $e_1 \neq 0$ (if $M_e \neq 0$) and thus $e' \neq 0$, for otherwise $e_1 e' = 0 = e_1{}^2 = e_1$. Thus e' is idempotent and $e' e = ee = e$. Therefore, anything that annihilates e' on the left also annihilates e on the left. Therefore $M_{e'} \subseteq M_e$. However, $e_1 e = 0$, whereas $e_1 e' = e_1 e_1 \neq 0$. Thus

$M_{e'} \subset M_e$. This contradicts the minimality of M_e and thus one of these M_e ideals must have been 0. That is, for this idempotent element e in L, $M_e = 0$. Now take any element x in L and consider $(x - xe)e = 0$. Thus $x - xe = 0$, $x = xe$. Therefore $L = Le$. However, $L = Le \subseteq Re \subseteq L$. Therefore $L = Re$.

Lemma 14. *Every non-zero two-sided ideal I of R is equal to $Re = eR$, where e is a unique unity element of I.*

Proof. Since I is, in particular, a left ideal, $I = Re$ by Lemma 13. Let V be the set of elements x in I such that $ex = 0$. Then V is a right ideal of R. Now $eV = 0$, whereas $Ve = V$. Therefore $V^2 = Ve . V = 0$. Therefore, V is a nilpotent right ideal. We know that R does not have any nilpotent right ideals. Therefore $V = 0$. Consider then $e(x - ex) = 0$, $x - ex$ in V, $x = ex$, for every x in I. Therefore $I = Re = eR$. Thus e is a unity element for I. If e' is another unity element for I, then $ee' = e' = e$ and thus e is unique.

Corollary. *Every non-zero nil semi-simple ring with D.C.C. on left ideals has a unity element.*

Proof. The ring R is a two-sided ideal of itself and, by Lemma 14, R has a unique unity element.

Recalling that the *centre* of a ring R is the set of all elements x such that $xy = yx$ for every y in R, we prove:

Lemma 15. *An idempotent element is in the centre of R if and only if it is a unity element for an ideal of R.*

Proof. If e is an idempotent element in the centre of R, then $eR = Re$ is an ideal of R with e as its unity element. Conversely, if $eR = Re$ is an ideal with e as unity element, then for any x in R, ex and xe are in the ideal and therefore $ex = ex . e = e . xe = xe$ and therefore e is in the centre of R.

In general, if I is an ideal of a ring R, and J is an ideal of the ring I, then J may not be an ideal of R. Thus, properties that hold for ideals of R may not hold for ideals of I. However, for the special class of rings we are now considering, nil semi-simple rings with D.C.C. on left ideals, we have:

Lemma 16. *Let $I = Re = eR$ be any ideal of R. Then any left, right, or two-sided ideal of I is a left, right, or two-sided ideal of R.*

Proof. If L is a left ideal of I, then $L = eL$ and $RL = Re . L = IL \subseteq L$, and therefore L is a left ideal of R. Similarly, for any right ideal Q of I, $Q = Qe$ and $QR = QeR = QI \subseteq Q$.

Corollary 1. *Every ideal of R also has D.C.C. on left ideals.*

Corollary 2. *Every ideal of R is also nil semi-simple.*

Problem. Let R be an arbitrary ring. Prove that an idempotent element e of R is in the centre of R if and only if e commutes with every idempotent element of R.

2.4. Direct sums. Before we state our first basic theorem we must remind the reader about various kinds of internal sums. If a ring R contains two subrings A and B such that R is the sum of A and B, then every element x of R can be expressed as $x = a + b$, where a is in A and b is in B. However, this expression may not be unique, and even if we know a good deal about A and B, this does not always give us as much information about R as we would like. If every x of R could be expressed uniquely as $a + b$, then our knowledge of A and B would carry over more completely to R. To ensure that every x can be expressed uniquely as $a + b$, it is sufficient to assume that 0 can be expressed uniquely as $0 = 0 + 0$. For, if

$$x = a_1 + b_1 = a_2 + b_2,$$

we have
$$0 = (a_1 - a_2) + (b_1 - b_2).$$

And if 0 is expressed uniquely as $a + b$, then since $0 = 0 + 0$, we have $a = b = 0$. Then

$$a_1 - a_2 = 0 = b_1 - b_2, \qquad a_1 = a_2, \qquad \text{and } b_1 = b_2,$$

and thus every x has a unique expression $a + b$. Another way of looking at this is to take $A \cap B = 0$. Then if $0 = a + b$, $a = -b$, a is in both A and B, and therefore $a = 0$, $b = 0$, and 0 is uniquely expressed. Conversely, if 0 is uniquely expressed as $0 + 0$, then $A \cap B = 0$, for if x is in both A and B, then $-x$ is in B and $0 = x + (-x)$, and therefore $x = 0$.

When $R = A + B$, with $A \cap B = 0$, or with the equivalent assumption that 0 is uniquely expressed, we say that R is the *supplementary sum* of the subrings A and B. Similarly, R is the supplementary sum of the subrings $A_1, A_2, \ldots, A_m$ if $R = A_1 + \ldots + A_m$ and 0 is uniquely expressible as $0 + 0 + \ldots + 0$. An equivalent condition is that

$$A_i \cap (A_1 + A_2 + \ldots + A_{i-1} + A_{i+1} + \ldots + A_m) = 0$$

for every $i = 1, \ldots, m$. The proof is a straightforward extension of the proof above for two subrings.

Supplementary sums are still not quite what we want to ensure full knowledge of R from knowledge of the A_i. We want the A_i to be multiplicatively separate, i.e., $A_i A_j = A_j A_i = 0$ if $i \neq j$. If this is so, then each A_i is an ideal of R, for

$$RA_i = (A_1 + \ldots + A_m)A_i = A_i A_i \subseteq A_i$$

and similarly $A_i R \subseteq A_i$. Conversely, if R is a supplementary sum of the subrings $A_1, \ldots, A_m$ and if each A_i is an ideal of R, then $A_i A_j$ and $A_j A_i$ are both in $A_i \cap A_j$ and this is 0 for $i \neq j$.

We say that R is a *direct sum* of $A_1, \ldots, A_m$ if it is a supplementary sum and if each A_i is an ideal of R. We write this as $R = A_1 \oplus A_2 \oplus \ldots \oplus A_m$.

To prove that a ring R is a direct sum of a class of subsets $B_1, \ldots, B_n$ it is sufficient to show that R is equal to the sum of the B_i, that the B_i are ideals of R, and that 0 is uniquely expressible as a sum of elements from the B_i.

We continue to assume that R is a nil semi-simple ring with D.C.C. on left ideals. An ideal I of R is said to be a *simple ideal* if it is a non-nilpotent simple ring, i.e. if it does not contain any proper non-zero ideals of itself—by Lemma 16 it is enough to assume that it does not contain any proper non-zero ideals of R.

Lemma 17. *If $I_1, \ldots, I_m$ are distinct simple ideals of R and if $A = I_1 + \ldots + I_m$, then A is the direct sum of $I_1, \ldots, I_m$, $A = I_1 \oplus \ldots \oplus I_m$.*

Proof. Since A is the sum of the I_j's and since each I_j is an ideal of R and therefore an ideal of A, the only thing to be proved is that 0 is uniquely expressed. Suppose, then, that $0 = x_1 + x_2 + \ldots + x_n$, where x_j is in I_j. We must show that $x_j = 0$ for every j.

Consider $I_i \cap I_j$. This is an ideal of R, contained in both I_i and I_j. Since I_j and I_i are both simple ideals, $I_i \cap I_j = 0$ or $I_i \cap I_j = I_i = I_j$. If $i \neq j$, I_i and I_j are distinct and therefore $I_i \cap I_j = 0$.

By Lemma 14, each $I_j = Re_j = e_j R$, where e_j is the unity of I_j and is in the centre of R (Lemma 15). Let x_i be any element in I_i, with $i \neq j$. Then $e_j x_i$ is 0, for it is in $I_i \cap I_j$.

Returning to $0 = x_1 + \ldots + x_n$, multiply it by e_j. Then

$$0e_j = x_1 e_j + \ldots + x_n e_j, \qquad 0 = x_j e_j = x_j.$$

Therefore, for every $j = 1, \ldots, n$, $x_j = 0$ and the lemma is proved.

2.5. Central idempotent elements. We must finally study idempotent elements rather carefully before we obtain our basic theorems. An idempotent element is said to be *central* if it is in the centre of R. An idempotent element e is said to be *semi-primitive* if it is central and if it cannot be expressed as $u + v$, where u and v are central, idempotent, and such that $uv = 0$. We say that two idempotent elements u, v are *orthogonal* if $uv = vu = 0$ and we say that a set of idempotent elements $u_1, \ldots, u_m$ is *pairwise orthogonal* if $u_i u_j = u_j u_i = 0$ for $i \neq j$.

Lemma 18. *The central idempotent element e is semi-primitive if and only if there does not exist a central idempotent element $u \neq e$ such that $eu = u$, i.e., e is the only central idempotent element in the ideal eR.*

Proof. If e is semi-primitive and if there exists a central idempotent element $u \neq e$ such that $eu = u$, then let $v = e - u$. Clearly v is idempotent, and it is central since both e and u are central. Also $uv = 0$ and $e = u + v$. This contradicts the assumption that e is semi-primitive. On the other hand, if e is not semi-primitive, then $e = u + v$, where u and v are orthogonal central idempotent elements. Then $u \neq e$ and $eu = u$. The final remark in the lemma is clearly equivalent to the statement that there does not exist a central idempotent $u \neq e$ such that $eu = u$.

Lemma 19. *The central idempotent element e is semi-primitive if and only if the ideal Re is simple.*

Proof. If e is semi-primitive, then the ideal Re contains no other central idempotent elements. If Re contained a non-zero ideal J, then J would be an ideal of R by Lemma 16, and $J = Ru$ where u is central idempotent by Lemma 14. Since u must then be equal to e, $J = Re$ and thus Re is a simple ideal. Conversely, if the central idempotent element e is not semi-primitive, then by Lemma 18, Re contains a central idempotent $u \neq e$. Then Ru is a non-zero ideal contained in Re. Furthermore, $Ru \neq Re$, for e is in Re but e is not in Ru because if $e = xu$, then

$$e - u = (e - u)e = (e - u)ux = (u - u)x = 0, \quad \text{and } e = u,$$

a contradiction. Thus, Re is not a simple ideal and the lemma is proved.

Lemma 20. *Every central idempotent element e which is not semi-primitive is a sum of a finite number of pairwise orthogonal semi-primitive idempotent elements.*

Proof. We consider all finite sums of distinct semi-primitive idempotent elements contained in the ideal Re. It is clear that since the ideal Re must contain a minimal and therefore simple ideal, it contains some semi-primitive idempotent element. Each such sum consists of pairwise orthogonal semi-primitive idempotent elements, for if u and v are distinct, semi-primitive, and idempotent, then by Lemma 19, both Ru and Rv are simple ideals. If $uv \neq 0$, then $Ru \cap Rv \supseteq Ru \cdot Rv \neq 0$, for it contains $uuvv = uv$. Since both Ru and Rv are simple, we must then have $Ru = Rv$. By Lemma 18, $v = u$, contradicting their distinctness.

If $\sum_1^n u_i$ is such a sum of pairwise orthogonal semi-primitive idempotent elements of Re, then $e - \sum_1^n u_i$ is idempotent, for $eu_i = u_i$ for each $i = 1, \dots, n$. It is clearly central and thus $R(e - \sum_1^n u_i)$ is an ideal. If we consider the set of all such ideals, we obtain by D.C.C. on left ideals (actually all we really need here is D.C.C. on two-sided ideals) a minimal such ideal, which we want to show is zero. If this minimal ideal is not zero, then it is equal to Re', where e' is the central idempotent element $e - \sum_1^m v_i$ and the v_i are pairwise orthogonal semi-primitive idempotent elements. Now Re' has D.C.C. on left ideals by Lemma 16, Corollary 1, and therefore it contains a minimal ideal which is also a mimimal ideal of R and thus has the form Rv_{m+1}, where v_{m+1} is central idempotent. All of this is in Re' and thus v_{m+1} is also in Re'. This minimal ideal Rv_{m+1} must be simple, for ideals of it are also ideals of R, by Lemma 16. Thus, by Lemma 19, the idempotent element v_{m+1} is semi-primitive. This v_{m+1} cannot be equal to any v_j, $1 \leqslant j \leqslant m$, for then

$$v_j = xe' = x(e - \sum_1^m v_j).$$

Multiplying by v_j, we get $v_j = x(v_j - v_j) = 0$, a contradiction. Therefore, the sum $\sum_1^{m+1} v_i$ is a sum of distinct semi-primitive idempotent elements of Re and we consider

$$R(e - \sum_1^{m+1} v_i) = R(e' - v_{m+1}).$$

Since $e' - v_{m+1} = (e' - v_{m+1})e'$, the ideal $R(e' - v_{m+1}) \subseteq Re'$. However, e' is in Re', but it is not in $R(e' - v_{m+1})$, for if $e' = x(e' - v_{m+1})$, multiplying by v_{m+1} we get $v_{m+1} = x(v_{m+1} - v_{m+1}) = 0$, a contradiction. Thus, $R(e' - v_{m+1}) = R(e' - \sum_1^{m+1} v_i)$ is an ideal of the type considered and is properly contained in Re'. This contradicts the minimality of Re' and proves that the minimal ideal of this type must be zero. Thus, there exists a finite sum of pairwise orthogonal semi-primitive idempotent elements $\sum_1^m v_i$, such that $R(e - \sum_1^m v_i) = 0$, and thus $e = \sum_1^m v_i$, which completes the proof.

2.6. First structure theorem. Now we can prove the following important structure theorem.

Theorem 10. *Every non-zero nil semi-simple ring R with D.C.C. on left ideals has only a finite number of simple ideals. These are non-nilpotent simple rings with D.C.C. on left ideals, and R is the direct sum of them. Thus, every non-zero nil semi-simple ring R with D.C.C. on left ideals can be expressed uniquely as $R = A_1 \oplus \ldots \oplus A_n$, apart from the order of the A_i, where the A_i are non-nilpotent simple rings with D.C.C. on left ideals.*

Proof. By the corollary to Lemma 14, R has a unity element which we shall call 1. Clearly 1 is central idempotent. By Lemma 20, $1 = e_1 + e_2 + \ldots + e_n$, where the e_i are pairwise orthogonal semi-primitive idempotent elements. Of course, it may be that 1 is itself semi-primitive, in which case R is a simple ring by Lemma 19. But, in general,

$$R = R.1 = R(e_1 + e_2 + \ldots + e_n) = Re_1 + Re_2 + \ldots + Re_n.$$

Since each e_i is semi-primitive, the ideals Re_i are simple ideals by Lemma 19. By Lemma 17, R is the direct sum of these simple ideals, $R = Re_1 \oplus \ldots \oplus Re_n$.

If J is any ideal of R, then $J = JR = JRe_1 + \ldots + JRe_n$. If $JRe_i \neq 0$, then $J \cap Re_i \neq 0$ and therefore $Re_i \subseteq J$, and thus every ideal of R is a direct sum of the simple ideals Re_i that it contains. If, in particular, I is a simple ideal of R, then $I = IR = IRe_1 + \ldots + IRe_n$. If $I \neq 0$, then at least one of the $IRe_i \neq 0$ and thus $I \cap Re_i \neq 0$. Since both I and Re_i are simple, we must have $I = Re_i$. Thus, the ideals Re_i are the only simple ideals of R. Therefore, R has only a finite number of simple ideals. Each of them is, of course, not nilpotent since R is nil semi-simple, and each of them has D.C.C. on left ideals by Corollary 1, Lemma 16. This ends the proof.

2.7. Idempotent elements. To obtain even deeper information we naturally ask what can be said about a non-nilpotent simple ring A with D.C.C. on left ideals. We know that A must be nil semi-simple and thus has a unity element. In order to proceed, we must analyse the non-central idempotent elements of A and obtain results corresponding to Lemmas 18, 19, and 20. There is only one central idempotent element in A, namely its unity element, but there may be many non-central idempotent elements.

We say that an idempotent element e is *primitive* if e cannot be expressed as $u + v$, where u and v are orthogonal idempotent elements.

Lemma 21. *An idempotent element e in A is primitive if and only if A does not contain an idempotent element $u \neq e$ such that $eu = ue = u$, that is, e is the only idempotent element in eAe.*

Proof. if e is primitive, then if there exists an idempotent element $u \neq e$ such that $eu = ue = u$, we let $v = e - u$. Clearly

$$v^2 = (e - u)(e - u) = e - u - u + u = e - u = v,$$

and $vu = uv = 0$. Thus, $e = u + v$, where both u and v are idempotent and they are orthogonal. This contradicts the primitivity of e, and therefore no such u can exist.

Conversely, if e is not primitive, then $e = u + v$, where u, and v are orthogonal idempotent elements. Then $u \neq e$ and $eu = ue = u$. The final remark is clearly equivalent to the statement that there is no idempotent element $u \neq e$ such that $eu = ue = u$.

Lemma 22. *An idempotent element e in A is primitive if and only if Ae is a minimal left ideal.*

Proof. If Ae is not a minimal left ideal, then it properly contains a left ideal of A and by Lemma 13 this left ideal is of the form Au, where u is idempotent. Since $u = u^2$ is in Ae, we must have $ue = u$. Define $u' = eu$ and $v = e - eu$. Both u' and v are not zero, for if $u' = 0$, then $0 = ueu = uu = u$, a contradiction. And if $v = 0$, then $e = eu$ and Au then contains $eu = e$ and $Au = Ae$, a contradiction.

Now $e = u' + v$ and we shall show that u' and v are orthogonal and idempotent, for

$$u'u' = eueu = euu = eu = u',$$

$$vv = (e - eu)(e - eu) = e - eu - eu + eu = e - eu = v,$$

$$u'v = eu(e - eu) = eu - eu = 0,$$

$$vu' = (e - eu)eu = eu - eu = 0.$$

Therefore e is, by definition, not primitive. This proves that if e is primitive, then Ae is a minimal left ideal.

Conversely, if e is not primitive, then $e = u + v$, where u and v are orthogonal and idempotent. Then $eu = ue = u$ and $Au = Aue \subseteq Ae$. However, e is in Ae but not in Au, for if $e = xu$, then $ev = v = xuv = 0$, a contradiction. Therefore, Ae properly contains the non-zero left ideal Au and Ae is not a minimal left ideal. Note that e, even though primitive, may not be the only idempotent element in Ae.

Lemma 23. *An idempotent element e in A is primitive if and only if eAe is a division ring.*

Proof. If eAe is a division ring (i.e. a non-commutative field), then e is its unity element and there are no other idempotent elements in eAe, for if u is idempotent and in eAe, then $uu^{-1} = e$ and $u \cdot uu^{-1} = ue = u = uu \cdot u^{-1} = uu^{-1} = e$. Therefore, by Lemma 21, e is primitive.

Conversely, if e is primitive, then Ae is a minimal left ideal by Lemma 22. Let exe be any non-zero element in eAe. Then $Aexe$ is a left ideal contained in Ae and $Aexe$ is not zero since it contains $e \cdot exe = exe$. Therefore, $Aexe = Ae$ since Ae is minimal. Since e is in Ae, it must also be in $Aexe$ and, therefore, there exists an element y such that $yexe = e$. Then

$$eye \cdot exe = e \cdot yexe = ee = e.$$

Thus, eye is the left inverse of exe in the ring eAe. Consider $exe \cdot eye = z$. Now

$$z^2 = exeeye \cdot exeeye = exe \cdot e \cdot eye = exeeye = z$$

and z is in eAe. Also $z \neq 0$, for if $exeeye = 0$, then

$$0 = exeeyeexe = exe \cdot e = exe \neq 0.$$

Thus z is idempotent and in eAe. Since e is primitive, it is the only idempotent element in eAe, by Lemma 21, and therefore $z = e$. Thus

$$eye \cdot exe = exe \cdot eye = e,$$

and thus every non-zero element of eAe has an inverse and eAe is a division ring.

Lemma 24. *Every non-primitive idempotent element e of A can be expressed as a finite sum of pairwise orthogonal primitive idempotent elements.*

Proof. If the idempotent element e is not primitive, then by Lemma 22, Ae is not a minimal left ideal of A. By applying the D.C.C. to $A \supset Ae \supset \ldots$ we obtain a minimal left ideal of A contained in Ae, and it is then clear that Ae contains some primitive idempotent elements. We consider all finite sums of pairwise orthogonal primitive idempotent elements contained in Ae. It may be that Ae contains only one primitive idempotent element or that no two are orthogonal, in which case we have only sums of one primitive idempotent element. We then consider all left ideals of A of the form $A(e - \sum u_i)$, where $\sum u_i$ is a finite sum of pairwise orthogonal primitive idempotent elements contained in Ae. By D.C.C. we obtain a minimal such left ideal, which we want to show is zero. If not, then let it be represented as Av, where $v = e - \sum v_i$. It is clear that since the v_i are all in Ae, $v_i e = v_i$ for every i. However ev_i may not be equal to v_i. Instead of working with the v_i's we shall work with the ev_i's. First we note that $ev_i \neq 0$; otherwise $v_i ev_i = v_i v_i = v_i = 0$, a contradiction. Secondly, $ev_i . ev_i = ev_i$ and therefore ev_i is idempotent. Thirdly, $Aev_i \subseteq Av_i$ and since v_i is primitive, Av_i is a minimal left ideal of A, and since $Aev_i \neq 0$, $Aev_i = Av_i$. Therefore, Aev_i is a minimal left ideal of A and, by Lemma 22, the idempotent elements ev_i are all primitive. Fourthly, the ev_i are pairwise orthogonal, for $ev_i . ev_j = ev_i . v_j = 0$ if $i \neq j$ because the v_i are pairwise orthogonal. Finally,

$$A(e - \sum ev_i) = Ae(e - \sum v_i) \subseteq A(e - \sum v_i) = Av$$

and since Av is a minimal left ideal of this type and $A(e - \sum ev_i)$ is of the same type, we must have $A(e - \sum ev_i) = Av$. Let $v' = e - \sum ev_i$ and note that v' is idempotent, for

$$(e - \sum ev_i)(e - \sum ev_i) = e - \sum ev_i - \sum ev_i + (\sum ev_i)^2 = e - \sum ev_i.$$

Since Av' is a non-zero left ideal of A, it must be a minimal left ideal of A or it must contain a minimal left ideal of A, and in either case it contains a primitive idempotent element w. Now $wv' = w$, since v' is idempotent, but, as above, $v'w$ may not be equal to w. We then work with $w' = v'w$. As above, w' is not zero, for otherwise w is zero; w' is idempotent; $Aw' = Aw$ since Aw is a minimal left ideal of A, and therefore w' is a primitive idempotent element. Also,

$$ev_k . v'w = ev_k(e - \sum ev_i)w = (ev_k - ev_k)w = 0,$$

and

$$v'w . ev_k = v'wv' . ev_k = v'w(e - \sum ev_i)ev_k = v'w(ev_k - ev_k) = 0,$$

for every k. Thus, the sum $w' + \sum ev_i$ is a finite sum of pairwise orthogonal primitive idempotent elements. Now

$$A(v' - w') = A(e - [w' + \sum ev_i]) \subseteq Av'$$

because $(v' - w')v' = v' - w'$, as can easily be computed. However, v' is in Av', but v' cannot be in $A(v' - w')$, for if $v' = x(v' - w')$, multiplying on the right by w' gives $w' = 0$, a contradiction. Therefore, $A(e - [w' + \sum ev_i])$ is properly contained in Av' and is of the type considered. This contradicts the minimality of $Av' = Av$, and thus the minimal left ideal of the type $A(e - \sum u_i)$ must be zero. Then $e - \sum u_1 = 0$, and e is a finite sum of pairwise orthogonal primitive idempotent elements.

We are interested in applying Lemmas 21, 22, 23, 24 to non-nilpotent simple rings with D.C.C. on left ideals, but they hold true in any nil semi-simple ring R with D.C.C. on left ideals, for we have not used the simplicity of A anywhere in the proofs.

2.8. Second structure theorem: Simple rings. Before we obtain our second basic theorem we prove the following curious result.

Lemma 25. *If R is a ring with a unity element, 1, and if R has D.C.C. on left ideals, then whenever there are two elements x, y such that $xy = 1$, we also have $yx = 1$.*

Proof. Consider the descending chain of left ideals $Rx \supset Rx^2 \supset \ldots \supset Rx^n \supset \ldots$. By D.C.C. there must exist a positive integer m such that $Rx^m = Rx^{m+1}$. Since $x^m = 1 . x^m$ is in Rx^m, it must also be in Rx^{m+1}, and therefore there exists an element z in R such that $zx^{m+1} = x^m$. Then $(zx - 1)x^m = 0$. Multiplying on the right by y^m, we have

$$(zx - 1)x^m y^m = (zx - 1).1 = zx - 1 = 0.$$

Thus $zx = 1$. Then $z.xy = z = zx.y = y$, and thus $yx = 1$.

Theorem 11. *A ring A is a non-nilpotent simple ring with D.C.C. on left ideals if and only if A is isomorphic to the set of all square matrices $\mathcal{M}$ of some order n, with elements in a division ring D.*

Proof. Assume first that A is a non-nilpotent simple ring with D.C.C. on left ideals. Then it has a unity element 1 which is, by Lemma 24, a finite sum of pairwise orthogonal primitive idempotent elements, $1 = e_1 + \ldots + e_n$. By Lemma 23, the rings $e_i A e_i$ are division rings for $i = 1, \ldots, n$. Also, $Ae_i A = A$ for every $i = 1, \ldots, n$, because $Ae_i A$ is an ideal (it is the set of all finite sums of elements of the form $a_i e_i b_i$) and is not zero for it contains $e_i^3 = e_i$.

Define $A_{ij} = e_i A e_j$. Then

$$A_{ij} A_{jk} = e_i A e_j A e_k = e_i A e_k = A_{ik}.$$

Also, $A_{ij} A_{hk} = 0$ if $j \neq h$. Furthermore, the A_{ij} are subrings, for $A_{ij} A_{ij} = 0$ if $i \neq j$ and $A_{ii} A_{ii} = A_{ii}$. If a_{ij} is in A_{ij}, then $e_i a_{ij} = a_{ij} = a_{ij} e_j$ and $e_h a_{ij} = 0 = a_{ij} e_k$ if $h \neq i$ and $k \neq j$. In particular, $A_{1j} A_{j1} = A_{11}$. Since $A_{11} = e_1 A e_1$ contains e_1, it is not zero. Thus e_1 is in $A_{1j} A_{j1}$, and therefore e_1 is equal to a finite sum of products of elements from A_{1j} with elements from A_{j1}. However, we want to show that e_1 can be expressed as a single product of one element from A_{1j} and one element from A_{j1}. To do this, we first observe that there exists an element e_{j1} in A_{j1} such that $A_{1j} e_{j1} \neq 0$. Thus, there exists an element a_{1j} in A_{1j} such that $a_{1j} e_{j1} \neq 0$. We call this element a_j and note that it is in the division ring A_{11}. Therefore, there exists an element b_j in A_{11} such that $b_j a_j = e_1$. Then $b_j a_{1j} e_{j1} = e_1$. We define $e_{1j} = b_j a_{1j}$. It is in A_{1j} and $e_{1j} e_{j1} = e_1$. We thus obtain for each $j = 1, \ldots, n$, elements e_{1j} and e_{j1} such that $e_{1j} e_{j1} = e_1$ and e_{1j} is in A_{1j}, while e_{j1} is in A_{j1}.

We now define $e_{ij} = e_{i1} e_{1j}$. This gives us n^2 elements. We propose to show that they behave exactly like elements in a total matrix ring with 1's in the ijth place and 0's elsewhere.

Now $e_{ij} e_{jk} = e_{i1} e_{1j} e_{j1} e_{1k} = e_{i1} e_1 e_{1k} = e_{i1} e_{1k} = e_{ik}$,

$e_{ij} e_{hk} = e_{i1} e_{1j} e_{h1} e_{1k} = 0$ if $j \neq h$,

e_{ij} is in $e_i A e_j$.

Consider the *subring $\mathcal{M}$ generated by these n^2 elements e_{ij}*. This subring has $e_{11} + \ldots + e_{nn}$ as its unity element. However, $e_{ii}^2 = e_{ii}$ is idempotent and in $e_i A e_i$, and since e_i is a primitive idempotent element, $e_{ii} = e_i$ by Lemma 21. Thus, $e_{11} + \ldots + e_{nn} = e_1 + \ldots + e_n = 1$. Thus, A contains a subring $\mathcal{M}$ whose unity element is the unity element of A and whose generators behave exactly like matrix generators.

Let D be the set of all x in A such that $xm = mx$ for every m in $\mathcal{M}$. Now let a be any element of A. Define

$$a_{ij} = \sum_{k=1}^{n} e_{ki} a e_{jk}.$$

Then $a_{ij} e_{rs} = e_{ri} a e_{js}$ and $e_{rs} a_{ij} = e_{ri} a e_{js}$. Thus, a_{ij} is in D. Also

$$\sum_{i,j=1}^{n} a_{ij} e_{ij} = \sum_{i,j,k} e_{ki} a e_{jk} e_{ij} = \sum_{j,k} e_{kk} a e_{jj} = 1 \cdot a \cdot 1 = a.$$

Therefore, $A = \mathcal{M} D = D \mathcal{M}$.

We now show that D is a division ring. Since

$$A = \sum_{k,l} e_{kl} D,$$

we have $e_i A e_i = e_i \sum_{kl} e_{kl} D e_i = e_{ii} D = e_i D$.

Since $e_i A e_i$ is a division ring for every $i = 1, \ldots, n$, so is $e_i D$.

Now let us map $D \to e_i D$. This is clearly a homomorphism, for if $d_1 \to e_i d_1$ and $d_2 \to e_i d_2$, then

$$d_1 d_2 \to e_i d_1 d_2 = e_i e_i d_1 d_2 = e_i d_1 e_i d_2$$

(remember that every d commutes with all e_{ij} and $e_i = e_{ii}$). What is the kernel of this homomorphism? That is, suppose that $e_i d = 0$. Then for every $j, e_j d = e_{ji} e_{ii} e_{ij} d = e_{ji} e_i d e_{ij} = 0$. Then $d = 1d = (e_1 + \ldots + e_n)d = 0$. Therefore, D is isomorphic to $e_i D = e_i A e_i$ for every i. Thus, all of the division rings $e_i A e_i$ are isomorphic to one another and, more important, D itself is a division ring.

Let B be the set of all $n \times n$ matrices with elements in the division ring D,

$$B = \{\textstyle\sum_{ij} E_{ij} d\},$$

where E_{ij} is the matrix with 1 in the ijth place and 0's elsewhere. We map $B \to A$ by $\sum E_{ij} d_{ij} \to \sum e_{ij} d_{ij}$. This is clearly a homomorphism. To see that the kernel is 0, suppose that $\sum e_{ij} d_{ij} = 0$. Then $e_k \sum e_{ij} d_{ij} \cdot e_l = 0 = e_{kl} d_{kl}$. Then $e_{lk} e_{kl} d_{kl} = 0 = e_l d_{kl}$ and then, as above, $e_i d_{kl} = 0$ for every i, and $d_{kl} = 0$. Therefore, this is an isomorphism. It is customary to write $A = \mathscr{M} \times D$.

Now, to prove the converse, let $A = \mathscr{M} \times D$. Then A has a unity element and thus is not nilpotent. To see that A is simple, let I be an ideal and let $x = \sum e_{ij} d_{ij}$ be a non-zero element in I. Then, for some u, v, the element $d_{uv} \neq 0$. Then I also contains

$$d_{uv}^{-1} \textstyle\sum_r e_{ru} x e_{vr} = d_{uv}^{-1}(\textstyle\sum_{i,j,r} e_{ru} e_{ij} e_{vr} d_{uv})$$

$$= d_{uv}^{-1} \textstyle\sum_r e_{rr} d_{uv} = \textstyle\sum_r e_{rr} = 1.$$

Therefore $I = A$ and A is simple.

Remark. The fact that $\mathscr{M} \times D$ is simple follows from a more general result and the fact that every division ring is simple.

Lemma 26. *If B is a non-nilpotent simple ring, then $\mathscr{M} \times B = B_n$, the set of all $n \times n$ matrices with elements in B, is also simple and non-nilpotent.*

Proof. Let I be a non-zero ideal of B_n. Let C be the set of all elements of B that appear in the matrices of I. If $z \neq 0$ is an element of C then it is in the ijth place of some matrix Z_n in I. Let A_{pi} be the matrix with the element a in the pith place and 0's elsewhere and let B_{jq} be the matrix with the element b in the jqth place and 0's elsewhere. Since $A_{pi} Z_n$ is in I, the element az is in C, and since $Z_n B_{jq}$ is in I, the element zb is in C. Furthermore, $A_{pi} Z_n B_{jq}$ is in I and it has azb in the pqth place and 0's elsewhere.

Now consider BzB. It is an ideal of B and thus is either 0 or B. Let G be the set of elements y of B such that $ByB = 0$. Clearly G is an ideal of B, and if it is equal to B, then $B^3 = 0$. However, B is not nilpotent and therefore $G = 0$. Since $z \neq 0$, we must have $BzB \neq 0$. Consequently, $BzB = B$ and therefore $z = \sum_i a_i\, zb_i$.

Since every element of the form $a_i\, zb_i$ can be obtained in the pqth position of a matrix in I, with 0's elsewhere, these can be added to obtain a matrix in I with z in the pqth position, with 0's elsewhere. Therefore, every matrix all of whose entries are in C belongs to I.

Finally, we show that C is an ideal of B. Multiplicatively we already know that az and zb are in C for any z in C and any a, b in B. Additively, we must establish that if z and w are in C, then $z - w$ is also in C. We can obtain z in the pqth position, 0's elsewhere, for a matrix of I and do the same for w. If we subtract these matrices, we again get a matrix of I, with $z - w$ as an entry, and therefore $z - w$ is in C and C is an ideal of B. Since B is simple and $C \neq 0$, $C = B$.

Therefore, I contains every matrix with entries in B and $I = B_n$. Thus, B_n is simple and the lemma is proved. The non-nilpotency of B_n is immediate.

We also know that a division ring D has no left or right ideals and therefore trivially has D.C.C.; however $D_n = \mathcal{M} \times D$ does have one-sided ideals, e.g. the set of all matrices with non-zero elements only in the first column, plus the zero matrix, is a left ideal. Thus, we cannot show that $\mathcal{M} \times D$ has D.C.C. on left ideals by this method of Lemma 26. Instead we shall use some group theory, in particular the Jordan–Hölder theorem.

Let M_{i+1} be the set of all matrices of D_n whose first i columns are 0. These are left ideals of D_n and $D_n = M_1 \supset M_2 \supset M_3 \supset \ldots \supset M_n \supset M_{n+1} = 0$ is a properly descending sequence of left ideals. Furthermore, there is no left ideal of D_n that is properly between two consecutive M_i. To see this, consider M_n and let J be any non-zero left ideal of D_n contained in M_n. Then J contains a matrix with $a_i \neq 0$ in the ith row and last column, and 0's in the first $n - 1$ columns. Multiply this on the left with the matrix having ba_i^{-1} in the jth row and ith column and 0's elsewhere. The result, which must be in J, has b in the jth row and last column and 0's elsewhere. Since this holds for any $j = 1, \ldots, n$ and for any element b in D, it is clear that J must be all of M_n. Thus M_n is a minimal left ideal of D_n. Similarly, if J is a left ideal of D_n such that $M_{i-1} \supset J \supset M_i$, then J contains a matrix with a non-zero element in the $(i - 1)$st column. As above, we get all possible $(i - 1)$st columns in J, and thus $J = M_{i-1}$. Similarly, M_2 is a maximal left ideal of D_n.

Suppose now that we are given a sequence of left ideals

$$D_n = N_1 \supseteq N_2 \supseteq N_3 \supseteq \ldots \supseteq N_n \supseteq N_{n+1} \supseteq N_{n+2} = 0.$$

We shall show that this cannot be properly descending and that there are at most $n + 1$ distinct left ideals in this sequence. This will prove that D_n has D.C.C. on left ideals (it actually proves much more).

We could say that, thinking of D_n as an additive group, with D_n as a left operator domain Ω, we consider all Ω-subgroups. These are precisely the left ideals of D_n. Then the sequences of M_i's is a *composition series* for Ω-subgroups and, by the Jordan–Hölder theorem for such composition series, we can state that any normal series has a refinement which is equivalent to this composition series and thus, in particular, the sequence of N_i's can have at most $n + 1$ distinct terms. Notice that since addition is commutative, every left ideal is a normal Ω-subgroup. However, let us actually work out this group-theoretic result in this special case.

Define $M_{ij} = M_{i+1} + (M_i \cap N_j)$ for $i = 1, \ldots, n$ and $j = 1, \ldots, n + 2$. And define $M_{n+1,1} = 0$. This gives us $n^2 + 2n + 1$ left ideals. Since $M_{i,n+2} = M_{i+1,1}$ (for they both $= M_{i+1}$), we identify these pairs and thus remove n terms, leaving us $n^2 + n + 1$ terms, which form a descending sequence of left ideals:

$$D_n = M_{11} \supseteq M_{12} \supseteq \ldots \supseteq M_{1,n+2} \supseteq M_{2,2} \supseteq M_{2,3} \supseteq \ldots$$

$$\supseteq M_{n,n+1} \supseteq M_{n,n+2} (= M_{n+1,1} = 0).$$

Note that each $M_{i,n+2}$ can also be referred to as $M_{i+1,1}$. But the important thing is that, of the $n^2 + n + 1$ left ideals appearing in this sequence, only $n + 1$ of them are distinct, for the sequence contains $M_1, M_2, \ldots, M_n, M_{n+1} = 0$ and no refinements of this chain are possible.

Similarly, we define $N_{ji} = N_{j+1} + (N_j \cap M_i)$ for $j = 1, \ldots, n + 1$ and $i = 1, \ldots, n + 1$, and define $N_{n+2,1} = 0$. This gives us $n^2 + 2n + 2$ left ideals. Since $N_{j,n+1} = N_{j+1,1}$ (for they both are equal to N_{j+1}), we identify these pairs and thus remove $n + 1$ terms, leaving us $n^2 + n + 1$ terms, which also form a descending sequence of left ideals:

$$D_n = N_{11} \supseteq N_{12} \supseteq \ldots \supseteq N_{1,n+1} \supseteq N_{2,2} \supseteq N_{2,3} \supseteq \ldots$$

$$\supseteq N_{n+1,n} \supseteq N_{n+1,n+1} (= N_{n+2,1} = 0).$$

Here each $N_{j,n+1}$ can also be referred to as $N_{j+1,1}$, and this sequence contains the $n + 2$ left ideals $N_1, N_2, \ldots, N_{n+1}, N_{n+2} = 0$.

The sequence of M_{ij}'s has n^2 repeats, i.e. places where $M_{i,j} = M_{i,j+1}$. Whenever such a repeat occurs,

$$M_{i+1} + (M_i \cap N_j) = M_{i+1} + (M_i \cap N_{j+1}),$$

and these are then both equal to either M_{i+1} or M_i. We then consider the adjacent pair $N_{j,i}$ and $N_{j,i+1}$ in the other sequence and show that they must be equal. In this case

$$M_i \cap N_j \subseteq M_{i+1} + N_{j+1}.$$

Thus, for every element x in $M_i \cap N_j$, we have $x = m + n$, where m is in M_{i+1} and n is in N_{j+1}. Then $m = x - n$ and since x is in N_j and n is in $N_{j+1} \subseteq N_j$, the element m is in N_j and therefore m is in $M_{i+1} \cap N_j$. Thus

$$M_i \cap N_j \subseteq (M_{i+1} \cap N_j) + N_{j+1}.$$

Then $\qquad N_{j+1} + (M_i \cap N_j) \subseteq (M_{i+1} \cap N_j) + N_{j+1},$

but this is $\subseteq N_{j+1} + (M_i \cap N_j)$ and therefore these are equal, i.e. $N_{j,i} = N_{j,i+1}$. This covers all the cases, for if $M_{i,n+2} = M_{i+1,2}$, we use $M_{i+1,1}$ as the symbol for $M_{i,n+2}$, and then show that $N_{1,i+1} = N_{1,i+2}$.

Thus, the sequence of the N_{ji}'s has a repeat whenever the M_{ij} sequence has a repeat, and thus the N_{ji} sequence also must have n^2 repeats and therefore only $n + 1$ distinct left ideals. Thus, the set of $n + 2$ left ideals $N_1, N_2, \ldots,$ $N_{n+1}, N_{n+2} = 0$ has only $n + 1$ distinct left ideals. Therefore, D_n has D.C.C. on left ideals. This finally ends the proof of Theorem 11.

Remark. It is clear that all the results for nil semi-simple rings could have been obtained with D.C.C. on right ideals instead of on left ideals. However, starting with D_n, it is easy to see that by considering the right ideals $W_{i+1} =$ the set of matrices of D_n whose first i rows are 0, one can show that D_n has D.C.C. on right ideals as well as on left ideals. Then every ring which is a direct sum of different D_n's also has D.C.C. on both right and left ideals, for every right ideal of such a direct sum is clearly a direct sum of right ideals from each simple component. Thus, *every nil semi-simple ring which has D.C.C. for one kind of one-sided ideals also has it for the other side as well.*

If a ring is not nil semi-simple, then it may have D.C.C. on, say, right ideals and not on left ideals, as the following example illustrates.

Example 5. Let A be the set of all $\alpha x + \beta y$ where α, β are real numbers and $x^2 = x, yx = y, xy = 0, y^2 = 0$. This is an associative ring, or an algebra over the real field, if one prefers to think of it that way. We do not prefer to think of it as an algebra and there is a fundamental difference, particularly in the definition of an ideal. If we think of this just as a ring, then A has D.C.C. on right ideals, for if I is a non-zero right ideal and contains $c_1 x + c_2 y \neq 0$, then it contains $x + c_1^{-1} c_2 y$ and all real multiples of this, if $c_1 \neq 0$, or it contains all multiples of y. In either case, if $I \neq A$, I is a one-dimensional vector space over the reals, for

$$(c_1 x + c_2 y)\alpha x = \alpha c_1 x + \alpha c_2 y.$$

Thus, A has D.C.C. on right ideals.

However, the ring A does not have D.C.C. on left ideals, for if S is any additive subgroup of the reals, the set of all sy is a left ring ideal of A, since anything multiplying sy on the left gives 0. Since one can easily find an infinitely descending chain of additive subgroups of the reals, one obtains an infinitely descending chain of left ideals.

If we think of A as an algebra over the reals, then by a left ideal L we mean a left algebra ideal, i.e. L must be closed under scalar multiplication by elements of the base field. Thus, $\{sy\}$ would not be an algebra left ideal, for it would have to contain $s^{-1}.sy = y$ and thus all multiples of y. Since an algebra left ideal must be a vector space, A as an algebra does have D.C.C. on both left and right ideals, but as a ring A does not have D.C.C. on left ideals.

Of course, if a ring has a unity element, then algebra ideals and ring ideals coincide, but otherwise it requires much more for a subring to be an algebra ideal than to be a ring ideal.

Remark. In proving that D_n has D.C.C. on left ideals, the following is an attractive but false simplification. Let H_i be the set of all matrices with 0's everywhere except in the ith column. Then it is true that these are all minimal left ideals and that $D_n = H_1 + H_2 + \ldots + H_n$. Then, if I is any left ideal, one would like to say that

$$I = D_n \cap I = H_1 \cap I + H_2 \cap I + \ldots + H_n \cap I,$$

and since the H_i are minimal, each $H_i \cap I = 0$ or H_i, and thus the only left ideals are those built up from the H_i. Then, clearly, D_n would have D.C.C. on left ideals. But this is false. If we consider two by two matrices, D_2, then

$D_2 = H_1 + H_2$ where $H_1 =$ the set of all $\begin{pmatrix} a & 0 \\ b & 0 \end{pmatrix}$ and $H_2 =$ the set of all $\begin{pmatrix} 0 & c \\ 0 & d \end{pmatrix}$. Let I be the set of all $\begin{pmatrix} k_1 & k_1 \\ k_2 & k_2 \end{pmatrix}$. This is a left ideal. Yet, $I \cap H_1 = 0$ and $I \cap H_2 = 0$. What we can say is that $I = D_2 I = H_1 I + H_2 I$, and $H_1 I$ is in I but not necessarily in H_1. Thus, this sort of argument works for direct sums, but D_n is only a supplementary sum and thus the argument is false.

Finally, we want to prove that the representation of a non-nilpotent simple ring as matrices over a division ring is in some strong sense unique.

Theorem 12. *If $A = \mathscr{M} D$, where $\mathscr{M}$ is the matrix-like subring of A generated by elements e_{ij}, $i, j = 1, \ldots, n$ as in Theorem 11, and where $D = \{x$ in $A: xy = yx$ for every $y \in \mathscr{M}\}$, and if also $A = \mathscr{M}_1 D_1$, where $\mathscr{M}_1$ is a matrix-like subring of A generated by elements f_{ij}, $i, j = 1, \ldots, m$, with $1 = f_{11} + \ldots + f_{mm}$, and where $D_1 = \{x$ in $A: xy = yx$ for every y in $\mathscr{M}_1\}$, then not only is $m = n$, $\mathscr{M} \cong \mathscr{M}_1$, and $D \cong D_1$, but also there exists an element z in A which has a multiplicative inverse z^{-1} such that $\mathscr{M}_1 = z\mathscr{M} z^{-1}$ and $D_1 = zDz^{-1}$.*

Proof. We have $1 = e_{11} + \ldots + e_{nn} = f_{11} + \ldots + f_{mm}$, where each

$e_{ii} = e_i$ and $f_{jj} = f_j$ is primitive and idempotent. Assume without loss of generality that $n \leqslant m$. Now

$$f_1 = f_{11} = \sum_{ij} e_{ij} d_{ij}$$

and one of these d_{ij}, say d_{pq}, $\neq 0$. Define $x = d_{pq}^{-1} e_{1p} f_{11}$ and $y = f_{11} e_{q1}$. Then $xy = d_{pq}^{-1} e_{11} d_{pq} = e_{11}$. However, $yx =$ an element in $f_{11} A f_{11} = f_1 A f_1 \cong D_1$, a division ring. Also $yx \neq 0$, for otherwise $e_{11} = e_{11}^2 = xy \cdot xy = 0$, a contradiction. Furthermore, $yxyx = ye_{11}x = yx$, and thus yx is idempotent and in $f_{11} A f_{11}$, and, consequently, $yx = f_{11}$.

Now define $w = \sum_{i=1}^n e_{i1} xf_{1i}$ and $z = \sum_{j=1}^n f_{j1} ye_{1j}$. Then

$$wz = \sum_{i=1}^n e_{i1} xf_{1i} f_{i1} ye_{1i} = \sum_{i=1}^n e_{i1} xf_{11} ye_{1i} = \sum_{i=1}^n e_{i1} xye_{1i}$$
$$= \sum_{i=1}^n e_{i1} e_{11} e_{1i} = \sum_{i=1}^n e_{ii} = 1.$$

By Lemma 25 we then have $zw = 1$; but,

$$zw = \sum_{j=1}^n f_{j1} ye_{1j} e_{j1} xf_{1j} = \sum_{j=1}^n f_{jj} = 1.$$

Therefore, m must equal n, and not only is $\mathcal{M} \cong \mathcal{M}_1$ then, but also

$$ze_{pq} z^{-1} = ze_{pq} w = f_{p1} ye_{1p} e_{pq} e_{q1} xf_{1q} = f_{p1} ye_{11} xf_{1q} = f_{p1} f_{11} f_{1q} = f_{pq},$$

and therefore $\mathcal{M}_1 = z \mathcal{M} z^{-1}$. Finally, an element r commutes with every element in $\mathcal{M}_1$ if and only if $rzmz^{-1} = zmz^{-1}r$, i.e. $z^{-1}rzm = mz^{-1}rz$, or $z^{-1}rz$ commutes with every element in $\mathcal{M}$. Thus, r is in D_1 if and only if $z^{-1}rz$ is in D, i.e. $zDz^{-1} = D_1$.

The next natural question to arise is: What can be said about division rings. Much work has been done on this subject, particularly for division algebras over certain special fields [2]. However, no clear universal results are yet known. We shall pause to summarize what we have achieved up to this question about division rings.

Starting with any ring R which has D.C.C. on left ideals, we consider R/N where N is the nil radical. Then we can say that R/N is a direct sum of a finite number of matrix rings over division rings. This is unique apart from the order of the factors in the direct sum and apart from the limited choice of the matrix rings and division rings as given in Theorem 12. (See [2], [11], [29], [31].)

This is a remarkable success for the entire concept of radical; the only serious drawback is the assumption of D.C.C. Attempts have been made to weaken this condition somewhat while preserving the results obtained (see [6]).

2.9. Generalizations: Radical properties that coincide with nil on rings with D.C.C. Returning now to the general theory, it is clear that the nil radical corresponds to the partition of the simple rings for which the lower class consists of all nil simple rings and this includes all zero simple rings, $A^2 = 0$.

The upper class consists of all non-nil simple rings and this includes all matrix rings over division rings. If we consider only the simple rings with D.C.C. on left ideals, then we know that there are only the matrix rings over division rings and the zero simple rings. Since our nil radical is so successful on rings with D.C.C. on left ideals, it is natural to focus our attention on those general radical properties which in some sense coincide with the nil radical on rings with D.C.C. on left ideals. Since such a general radical property must correspond to a partition of the simple rings in which the zero simple rings are all in the lower class and in which the matrix rings over division rings are all in the upper class, it is clear that the general radical properties we seek are those that lie between the *lower radical property* $\mathscr{S}$ determined by the class of *all zero simple rings* and the *upper radical property* $\mathscr{T}$ determined by the class of *all matrix rings over division rings*, and $\mathscr{N}$, the nil radical property, lies between them: $\mathscr{S} < \mathscr{N} < \mathscr{T}$.

The difficulty in discussing or defining what we shall mean by *coinciding with the nil radical on rings with D.C.C. on left ideals* is that an ideal I of a ring with D.C.C. on left ideals may not have D.C.C. itself. Thus, we shall prove that every $\mathscr{T}$-radical ring with D.C.C. on left ideals is an $\mathscr{S}$-radical ring and also an $\mathscr{N}$-radical ring, but we shall not be able to prove that the $\mathscr{T}$-radical of any ring A with D.C.C. on left ideals is the same as the $\mathscr{S}$-radical of A. The reason for this difficulty, put in larger terms, is that the class K of all associative rings with D.C.C. on left ideals does not have the property that every ideal of a ring of K is itself a ring of K.

This difficulty does not arise between $\mathscr{N}$ and $\mathscr{T}$, for we can prove:

Lemma 27. *On rings with D.C.C. on left ideals,* $\mathscr{T} = \mathscr{N}$ *in the strong sense, i.e. not only is a ring with D.C.C. on left ideals $\mathscr{T}$-radical if and only if it is $\mathscr{N}$-radical but if A is any ring with D.C.C. on left ideals, the $\mathscr{T}$-radical of A coincides with the $\mathscr{N}$-radical of A.*

Proof. Let A be a ring with D.C.C. on left ideals. Since, in general, $\mathscr{N} < \mathscr{T}$, the $\mathscr{N}$-radical N of A is contained in the $\mathscr{T}$-radical T of A. By Theorems 10 and 11, A/N is a finite direct sum of matrix rings over division rings, say

$$A/N = D_1 \oplus \ldots \oplus D_n.$$

And T/N is then an ideal of A/N. However, any non-zero ideal I of A/N is a direct sum of some of the D_i, for as in the proof of Theorem 10,

$$I = I . A/N = ID_1 \oplus \ldots \oplus ID_n$$

and if $ID_i \neq 0$, then it is an ideal $\subseteq D_i$ and since D_i is simple, $ID_i = D_i$. Therefore,

$$I = D_{j_1} \oplus \ldots \oplus D_{j_r},$$

where $j_1, \ldots, j_r$ is some subset of $1, \ldots, n$. Thus, in particular, T/N (if it is non-zero) is a finite direct sum of matrix rings over division rings. Then T can be mapped homomorphically, via T/N, onto a non-zero matrix ring over a division ring and this is $\mathcal{T}$-semi-simple. This is in contradiction to the fact that T is a $\mathcal{T}$-radical ring. Thus T/N must be zero, $T = N$. In particular then, if A is a ring with D.C.C. on left ideals, it is $\mathcal{T}$-radical if and only if it is $\mathcal{N}$-radical.

In general, of course, $\mathcal{N} < \mathcal{T}$, for the set of all rational numbers of the form (even integer)/(odd integer) is clearly $\mathcal{N}$-semi-simple, but as we shall later prove, it is $\mathcal{T}$-radical.

For the relationship between $\mathcal{N}$ and $\mathcal{S}$ we have:

Lemma 28. *On rings with D.C.C. on left ideals, $\mathcal{N} = \mathcal{S}$ in the weak sense, i.e. a ring with D.C.C. on left ideals is $\mathcal{N}$-radical if and only if it is $\mathcal{S}$-radical; however, there exist rings with D.C.C. on left ideals whose $\mathcal{S}$-radical is not equal to their $\mathcal{N}$-radical.*

Proof. Let R be $\mathcal{N}$-radical and have D.C.C. on left ideals. Then R is nilpotent (Theorem 8), say $R^m = 0 \neq R^{m-1}$. Call $R^{m-1} = B$ and note that $RB = 0 = BR$. Consider any descending chain of left ideals of the form $R \supset B \supset \ldots \supset L$ and by D.C.C. we obtain a minimal ideal L of R. However, if J is any ideal of L, then J is also an ideal of R for $JR \subseteq BR = 0$. Thus L is a zero simple ring, i.e. it is $\mathcal{S}$-radical. Similarly, if R' is any non-zero homomorphic image of R, it has D.C.C. on left ideals and, as above, it must contain an $\mathcal{S}$-radical ring. Since every homomorphic image of R contains an $\mathcal{S}$-ideal, R itself must be $\mathcal{S}$-radical.

To obtain a ring whose $\mathcal{S}$-radical is smaller than its $\mathcal{N}$-radical, we cannot use an $\mathcal{N}$-radical which has D.C.C. on left ideals. In order to use one that does not have D.C.C. on left ideals we imbed it in a ring which has D.C.C. on left ideals in such a way that left ideals of the $\mathcal{N}$-radical are not left ideals of the ring. We do this in the following example.

Example 6. Let A be the set of all $\alpha x + \beta e$ where α and β are rational numbers and where $x^2 = 0$, $e^2 = e$, $ex = xe = x$. Since e is a unity element for A, the distinction between ring and algebra disappears and A is both a ring and an algebra (of dimension 2) over the rationals with every ring ideal an algebra ideal. Since every ideal of A is then a subvector space over the rationals, the only non-zero proper ideal of A is $N = \{\alpha x\}$, and since A is commutative, A has D.C.C. on left ideals. The ideal N is nilpotent, $N^2 = 0$, and is clearly the $\mathcal{N}$-radical of A.

We want to show that N is $\mathcal{S}$-semi-simple, and since A itself is clearly not $\mathcal{S}$-radical (for it can be mapped onto a field which is $\mathcal{S}$-semi-simple), we shall thus establish that the $\mathcal{S}$-radical of A is zero.

The ring N is isomorphic to the zero ring on the additive group of the rational numbers, and any additive subgroup of the rationals is then an ideal of N, but of course not of A. Clearly N does not have D.C.C. on ideals.

To see that N is $\mathscr{S}$-semi-simple, we assume that N contains some $\mathscr{S}$-ideals, each of them of some degree over the zero simple rings. Let α be the minimal ordinal such that N has an ideal I which is of degree α (Proposition 6 Section 1.3). Clearly α is not a limit ordinal. Since I is of degree α, every non-zero homomorphic image of I must contain a non-zero ideal of degree $\alpha - 1$ and, in particular, I itself must contain a non-zero ideal J of degree $\alpha - 1$. However, since $JN = 0$, J is then also an ideal of N and thus N contains a non-zero ideal of degree $\alpha - 1$, which contradicts the minimality of α, unless $\alpha = 1$. Thus, if N has any $\mathscr{S}$-ideals it must have one of degree 1 over the zero simple rings, i.e. N must contain a zero simple ideal. However, any ideal of N, i.e. any additive subgroup of the rationals, cannot be simple, for it must contain at least the infinite cyclic additive group generated by a non-zero element and this contains many additive subgroups, i.e. many ideals. Therefore, N has no $\mathscr{S}$-ideals and is therefore $\mathscr{S}$-semi-simple. This ends the proof of Lemma 28.

Remark. This discussion can be generalized to any ring R such that $R^2 = 0$. That is, it is easy to show that for any lower radical property determined by a class $\mathscr{P}$ of rings, a zero ring R, if it has any lower radical ideals, must have one of degree 1 over $\mathscr{P}$.

Remark. It is remarkable that although the zero ring N on the additive group of rationals is $\mathscr{S}$-semi-simple, every homomorphic image of N which is not isomorphic to N is $\mathscr{S}$-radical. Thus, the least definite homomorphic step away from N changes the picture from $\mathscr{S}$-semi-simple to $\mathscr{S}$-radical.

To see this we must recall some group theory, for all multiplication is trivial and we are concerned only with the additive properties. We claim that if H is any (additive) subgroup of the rationals, $H \neq 0$, then N/H is isomorphic to a direct sum of p^∞ groups for various primes p. Using results from Kaplansky's "Infinite Abelian Groups" [34, pp. 7–10], we see that N/H is a divisible group since N is divisible and every homomorphic image of a divisible group is divisible. Secondly, every divisible commutative additive group is a direct sum of groups isomorphic to the rationals or to p^∞ groups. Thirdly, N/H is a torsion group, for if $x \neq 0$ is in H and $y \neq 0$ is any element in N, then there exist integers m and n such that $my = nx$, and thus $my = 0$ in N/H. For torsion divisible commutative groups the direct sum has no groups isomorphic to the rationals and, thus, N/H is isomorphic to a direct sum of p^∞ groups. Clearly, then, N/H contains p^∞ for some p, as a subgroup, i.e. an ideal, and every non-zero homomorphic image of N/H contains p^∞ for some other p perhaps. Now p^∞ contains a minimal ideal, which is then a zero simple ring, and since every non-zero homomorphic image of p^∞ is isomorphic to p^∞, it also contains a zero simple ring. Therefore, for every prime p, p^∞ is of degree 2 over the zero simple rings and, in particular, is $\mathscr{S}$-radical. Thus, every non-zero homomorphic image of N/H contains an ideal of degree 2 and, thus, N/H is of degree 3 over the zero simple rings and N/H is $\mathscr{S}$-radical.

For algebras the situation is much clearer. The only zero simple algebras are the zero algebras of dimension one. For *finite-dimensional algebras the nil* (or nilpotent or, as it is often called, the classical) *radical is the only radical property that corresponds to the partition of the simple algebras for which the lower class consists of the one-dimensional zero algebra*, because every ideal of such an algebra is itself finite dimensional and thus Lemmas 27 and 28 apply, both in the strong sense.

For *rings* with D.C.C. on left ideals, however, there are several radicals that correspond to the zero simple–matrix over division, partition. We can, at least, state exactly where a general radical property must be if it is going to coincide with the nil (or classical) radical on rings with D.C.C. on left ideals. To do this, let $\mathscr{D}$ be the lower radical property determined by all nilpotent rings which are nil radicals of rings with D.C.C. on left ideals. Then we can prove (where "coincides" means "in the strong sense"):

Theorem 13. *A radical property φ coincides with $\mathscr{N}$ on rings with D.C.C. on left ideals if and only if $\mathscr{D} \leqslant \varphi \leqslant \mathscr{T}$.*

Proof. If φ is a radical property which coincides with $\mathscr{N}$ on rings with D.C.C. on left ideals, then we already know that $\mathscr{S} \leqslant \varphi \leqslant \mathscr{T}$. Every nilpotent ring which is the $\mathscr{N}$-radical of a ring with D.C.C. must then be φ-radical, and thus $\mathscr{D} \leqslant \varphi \leqslant \mathscr{T}$. Note that $\mathscr{S} \leqslant \mathscr{D}$.

To prove the converse, it is sufficient to show that both $\mathscr{D}$ and $\mathscr{T}$ coincide with $\mathscr{N}$ on rings with D.C.C. Lemma 27 tells us that $\mathscr{T} = \mathscr{N}$ in this case. To see that $\mathscr{D} = \mathscr{N}$, let R be any ring with D.C.C. on left ideals, let N be its $\mathscr{N}$-radical and D its $\mathscr{D}$-radical. Then $D \subseteq N$. However, N is nilpotent, and since it is the $\mathscr{N}$-radical of a ring with D.C.C. on left ideals, it is $\mathscr{D}$-radical. Thus $D = N$.

To round out the picture we consider one more radical property, $\mathscr{B}$, the lower radical property determined by all nilpotent rings. Clearly $\mathscr{D} \leqslant \mathscr{B} \leqslant \mathscr{N}$ in general. It is curious that $\mathscr{B}$ is identical with the lower radical property $\mathscr{B}'$ determined by the zero ring on C^∞, the infinite cyclic additive group. Clearly, if all nilpotent rings are radical, then the zero ring on C^∞ is radical. On the other hand, every nilpotent ring contains an ideal which is a zero ring on a cyclic additive group, for if $R^m = 0 \neq R^{m-1}$, any non-zero element in R^{m-1} generates a cyclic additive group which is a zero ring and an ideal of R. Since any zero ring on a cyclic additive group is a homomorphic image of the zero ring on C^∞, every nilpotent ring contains a non-zero ideal which is of degree 1 over the zero ring on C^∞ and, therefore, every nilpotent ring is of degree 2, and is $\mathscr{B}'$-radical.

Baer [13] constructed a radical which is known as Baer's lower radical and by considering his construction and observing that every ring which is a sum of nilpotent ideals must be of degree 3 over the zero ring on C^∞ (since every non-zero homomorphic image must contain a nilpotent ideal which we know is of degree 2), we shall show in the next chapter that $\mathscr{B}$ is precisely Baer's lower radical. We might also point out here that $\mathscr{N}$ is also known as the Koethe [35] radical and as Baer's upper radical. We thus have

$$\mathscr{S} < \mathscr{D} < \mathscr{B} < \mathscr{N} < \mathscr{T},$$

and we know that for rings with D.C.C. on left ideals, $\mathscr{D} = \mathscr{B} = \mathscr{N} = \mathscr{T} > \mathscr{S}$, where by equality here we mean coincidence in the strong sense. In view of Theorem 13, we shall seek only radicals between $\mathscr{D}$ and $\mathscr{T}$ in trying to obtain structure theorems for more general rings, to ensure that these at least coincide with the nil radical for rings with D.C.C. on left ideals. Before we leave this section, we wish to establish that the above five radicals are, in general, all different. We know that $\mathscr{S} \neq \mathscr{D}$ (Example 6) and that $\mathscr{N} \neq \mathscr{T}$, as referred to just before Lemma 28. We prove that $\mathscr{D} \neq \mathscr{B}$ in the following theorem. (See [21].)

Theorem 14. *The radical property $\mathscr{D} < \mathscr{B}$, Baer's lower radical.*

Proof. We propose to show that the zero ring on C^∞, which is $\mathscr{B}$-radical, is $\mathscr{D}$-semi-simple. This will prove the theorem. Suppose, then, that C^∞ contains some $\mathscr{D}$-ideals. Since every non-zero ideal of C^∞ is isomorphic to C^∞, if C^∞ has a non-zero $\mathscr{D}$-ideal, then C^∞ must itself be $\mathscr{D}$-radical. Let α be the minimal ordinal such that C^∞ is of degree α over the nilpotent rings that are nil radicals of rings with D.C.C. on left ideals (Proposition 6, Section 1.3). Clearly, α is not a limit ordinal. Every non-zero homomorphic image of C^∞ must contain a non-zero ideal of degree $\alpha - 1$ and, in particular, C^∞ must have such a non-zero ideal. Thus, C^∞ has degree $\alpha - 1$, which contradicts the minimality of α unless $\alpha = 1$. In that case there exists a ring R with D.C.C. on left ideals such that N, the nil radical of R, can be mapped homomorphically onto C^∞. Suppose, then, that $N/H \cong C^\infty$, where H is an ideal of N. Clearly $N^2 \subseteq H$. We then consider the ring R/N^2, which also must have D.C.C. on left ideals. Its nil radical must be N/N^2, for

$$(R/N^2)/(N/N^2) \cong R/N,$$

which is nil semi-simple, and N/N^2 is a nil ideal of R/N^2. Furthermore,

$$(N/N^2)/(H/N^2) \cong N/H = C^\infty.$$

Thus, we could just as easily work with the ring R/N^2 whose nil radical N/N^2 is a zero ring. We can then assume without any loss of generality that $N^2 = 0$ in the given ring R.

Every element of N is of the form $mx + h$, where m is an integer, h is in H, and x is a representative of the generator of the infinite cyclic additive group N/H. Then, if mx is in H, the integer m must be zero.

We have $R \neq N$, for if $R = N$, then N and N/H have D.C.C. on left ideals, in which case $N/H \cong C^\infty$. Therefore, R contains some idempotent elements, by Theorem 8. For every idempotent element e_i of R, let $M_i = \{y \text{ in } R: ye_i = 0\}$. The M_i are left ideals of R and by D.C.C. we select a minimal such left ideal $M = \{y \text{ in } R: ye = 0\}$. Then M is a nilpotent left ideal of R, for if it is not nilpotent it contains an idempotent element e', by Theorem 8. Then $e'e = 0$. Define $e^* = e + e' - ee'$. Then $e^* \neq 0$, for otherwise $0 = e^*e = e$, a contradiction. Also $e^* \cdot e^* = e^*$, as direct computation will show. Thus, e^* is idempotent, and we consider

$$M_{e^*} = \{y \text{ in } R: ye^* = 0\}.$$

If $ye^* = 0$, then $ye^*e = ye = 0$ and therefore $M_{e^*} \subseteq M$. However, e' is in M; but e' is not in M_{e^*}, for if $e'e^* = 0$, then $e' = 0$ for $e'e^* = e'$. This is not possible and thus $M_{e^*} \subset M$, contradicting the minimality of M. Thus M must be nilpotent.

Since all nilpotent left ideals are in N (Theorem 9), $M \subseteq N$ and thus $MN = 0$. Then every element y in R can be expressed as

$$y = ye + (y - ye),$$

where $y - ye$ is in M for $(y - ye)e = 0$. Thus $yx = yex$, or $y(x - ex) = 0$. Thus $R(x - ex) = 0$.

We consider the element ex. It is in N and therefore $ex = qx + h$ for some integer q. If $q \neq 1$ we consider

$$\{x - ex\} \supset \{2(x - ex)\} \supset \ldots \supset \{2^n(x - ex)\} \supset \ldots,$$

where $\{2^n(x - ex)\}$ is the additive group generated by $2^n(x - ex)$. These are all left ideals of R, for R annihilates them all on the left. None of them are zero, for if

$$2^n(x - ex) = 0 = 2^n(x - qx - h),$$

$2^n(1 - q)x = 2^n h$, which is in H. Thus $2^n(1 - q) = 0$, and this is impossible if $q \neq 1$. Also, this is a properly descending chain of left ideals, for if

$$\{2^n(x - ex)\} = \{2^{n+1}(x - ex)\},$$

then

$$2^n(x - ex) = k(2^{n+1})(x - ex) \quad \text{for some integer } k.$$

Then

$$2^n(x - qx - h) = 2^{n+1}k(x - qx - h)$$

and therefore

$$2^n(1 - q)(1 - 2k)x = (2^n - 2^{n+1}k)h,$$

which is in H. Thus $2^n(1 - q)(1 - 2k) = 0$, which is again impossible if $q \neq 1$. This then contradicts the D.C.C. for left ideals of R.

If, on the other hand, $q = 1$, $ex = x + h$, we consider

$$Rx \supset R.2x \supset R.2^2x \supset \ldots \supset R.2^nx \supset \ldots.$$

None of these left ideals are zero, for if $R.2^nx = 0$, then $e.2^nx = 2^n(x + h) = 0$. Thus $2^nx = -2^nh$, which is in H, and this is impossible. Finally, this is a properly descending chain, for if $R.2^n x = R.2^{n+1}x$, then $e.2^nx$ is in $R.2^{n+1}x$ and there must exist an element z in R such that

$$e.2^nx = z.2^{n+1}x.$$

Now $zx = mx + h_1$ and we have $2^n(x + h) = 2^{n+1}(mx + h_1)$. Then $(2^n - m2^{n+1})x$ is in H and this is impossible. Thus, in either case we get a contradiction to the D.C.C. on left ideals. Therefore, the zero ring on C^∞ is $\mathscr{D}$-semi-simple and the theorem is proved.

Finally to see that, in general, $\mathscr{B} < \mathscr{N}$ we consider the following example.

Example 7. Let G be the commutative group which is the supplementary sum of a countably infinite number of infinite cyclic additive groups $= \{\ldots, n_{-2}\, a_{-2},\, n_{-1}\, a_{-1}, n_0\, a_0, n_1\, a_1, n_2\, a_2, \ldots\}$, where the n_α are integers and the a_α are the generators of the components.

For $i = 1, 2, 3, \ldots$ let u_i be the mapping which sends a_α into 0 if $\alpha \equiv 0$ (mod 2^i) and sends a_α into $a_{\alpha-1}$ if $\alpha \not\equiv 0$ (mod 2^i). These u_i then send G into G, and they are homomorphisms of G into G (i.e. endomorphisms). We may add and multiply these u_i as follows: $g(u_i + u_j) = gu_i + gu_j$; $g(u_iu_j) = (gu_i)u_j$. Let U be the ring generated by the u_i, i.e. U is the set of all finite sums of finite products of these u_i.

It is clear that each u_i is nilpotent and $u_i^{2^i} = 0$, i.e. the endomorphism which maps everything into zero. And it is not too difficult to show that U is a nil ring even though it is not commutative. Then U is $\mathscr{N}$-radical. However, to see that U is $\mathscr{B}$-semi-simple involves a rather long computation and we refer the reader to Baer's paper [13, pp. 540–2].

CHAPTER THREE

RINGS WITH THE ASCENDING CHAIN CONDITION

3.1. Relationship between A.C.C. and D.C.C. A ring R is said to have the *ascending chain condition on left ideals*, or A.C.C. on left ideals, if every ascending sequence of left ideals $L_1 \subseteq L_2 \subseteq \ldots \subseteq L_n \subseteq \ldots$ terminates after a finite number of steps, i.e. there exists an integer n such that $L_n = L_{n+1} = \ldots$. This clearly implies that *any non-vacuous set of left ideals of R contains a maximal left ideal* (there may be several such maximal left ideals but there is at least one). In fact, these are equivalent properties, for if every non-vacuous set has a maximal left ideal, then the set of left ideals in any ascending sequence has a maximal left ideal, say L_n, and thus $L_n = L_{n+1} = \ldots$, which is precisely A.C.C. on left ideals.

Another equivalent formulation is that *every left ideal of R has a finite number of elements which generate it as a left ideal*. For if x_1 generates a left ideal L_1, we select x_2 not in L_1 and let L_2 be the left ideal generated by L_1 and x_2. We continue selecting x_i's until $L_1 \subset L_2 \subset \ldots \subset L_n$ and by A.C.C. this must stop after a finite number of steps. Consequently, if we begin with any left ideal L of R and consider $L_1 \subset L_2 \subset \ldots \subset L_n = L$, it is clear that L has a finite set of generators, namely $x_1, x_2, \ldots, x_n$. Conversely, if every left ideal has a finite set of generators, we take any sequence $L_1 \subset L_2 \subset \ldots$ and let $W = \cup L_i$. Then W is a left ideal and has generators $x_1, \ldots, x_n$. Now x_1 is in W and therefore is in some L_{i_1}. Similarly, x_j is in some L_{i_j}. Let m be the largest of the $i_1, \ldots, i_n$. Then L_m contains all the x_j and thus $W = L_m$. Consequently, $L_m = L_{m+1} = \ldots$, and thus we have A.C.C. on left ideals.

Notice that every nil semi-simple ring R with D.C.C. on left ideals has A.C.C. on left ideals, for every simple ideal of R can have at most a fixed finite number of distinct left ideals in any descending chain (namely the size of the matrices which represent the simple ideal) and thus cannot have an ascending chain of greater length; while R itself, being a finite direct sum of such simple ideals, can also not have an infinite ascending chain, for if L is a left ideal of R, then $L = RL = A_1 L + \ldots + A_n L$, where the A_i are the simple components of R. Then $A_i L$ is a left ideal of A_i and L is a supplementary sum of left ideals of the A_i. Since there are only a finite number of components A_i and since each component can only have a finite sequence of left ideals, it is thus clear that R has A.C.C. on left ideals.

Although A.C.C. and D.C.C. are related in some mysterious way, they are, in general, independent. The integers I have A.C.C., for given any ideal J (I is commutative and thus "the left" plays no role), it must be generated by some integer, m, for I is a so-called principal ideal domain. Then there are only a finite number of ideals that contain (m). Or since every ideal is finitely generated, I has A.C.C. However, I does not have D.C.C., for $I \supset (2) \supset (4) \supset \ldots \supset (2^n) \supset \ldots$, where (2^n) is the ideal generated by 2^n.

On the other hand, Example 1, the zero ring on p^∞, has D.C.C. but not A.C.C. For if $p^\infty > I > \ldots$, then $I = H_m$ for some m and H_m contains only a finite number of ideals. But $H_1 \subset H_2 \subset \ldots \subset H_m \subset \ldots$ is an infinite ascending chain of ideals.

What one can prove is the following theorem [28, p. 728].

Theorem 15. *If A has a left unity element and D.C.C. on left ideals, then it has A.C.C. on left ideals.*

Proof. Clearly $A \neq N$, its nil radical, since A has a left unity. Also N is nilpotent, $N^m = 0 \neq N^{m-1}$ (of course, if $N = 0$, A is nil semi-simple and has A.C.C. on left ideals as above). Now A/N is nil semi-simple and it has D.C.C. on left ideals. Therefore, by Lemmas 22 and 24 and the comment at the end of Section 2.7, it is not difficult to see that $A/N = L'_1 + \ldots + L'_t$, a finite supplementary sum of distinct minimal non-zero left ideals L'_i. There are then left ideals L_i^* in A such that each L_i^* contains N, $L_i^*/N = L'_i$, and thus there can be no left ideal of A properly between N and L_i^* for every $i = 1, \ldots, t$. Finally, we note that $A = L_1^* + \ldots + L_t^*$, although this is not a supplementary sum.

Take $x \neq 0$ in N^{m-1}. Then $Nx = 0$ and x is in $Ax = L_1^*x + \ldots + L_t^*x$ since A has a left unity element. We now prove that for every $i = 1, \ldots, t$, the left ideal L_i^*x is a minimal left ideal of A. Let I be a non-zero left ideal of A contained in L_i^*x. Then $I = Jx$, where $J = \{l$ in L_i^*: there exists an element y in I such that $y = lx\}$. Then J is a left ideal of A, $J \subseteq L_i^*$, and $N \subseteq J$ since $Nx = 0$. Since $I \neq 0$, $J \supset N$. Thus J must be all of L_i^* and $I = L_i^*x$. Therefore L_i^*x is a minimal left ideal of A. Note that L_i^*x is in N^{m-1}, for x is in N^{m-1} and N^{m-1} is an ideal of A.

Therefore, every element of N^{m-1} is contained in a sum of minimal left ideals of A which are contained in N^{m-1}, i.e. N^{m-1} is in the union of all the minimal left ideals of A which are in N^{m-1}, and therefore N^{m-1} is equal to this union.

We now show that this union is equal to a finite supplementary sum of such minimal left ideals. Let $L_{1,m-1}$ be any non-zero minimal left ideal of A contained in N^{m-1}. Let $L_{2,m-1}$ be any non-zero minimal left ideal of A contained in N^{m-1}, with $L_{2,m-1} \neq L_{1,m-1}$ if any such left ideals exist. Note that this implies that $L_{2,m-1} \cap L_{1,m-1} = 0$ because both are minimal left ideals. Define

$$\mathscr{L}_{11} = L_{1,m-1} \text{ and } \mathscr{L}_{12} = L_{1,m-1} + L_{2,m-1}.$$

Assuming that $\mathscr{L}_{1k}$ has been defined, let $L_{k+1,m-1}$ be any non-zero minimal left ideal of A contained in N^{m-1}, with $\mathscr{L}_{1,k} \cap L_{k+1,m-1} = 0$, if any such exist. Define

$$\mathscr{L}_{1,k+1} = \mathscr{L}_{1,k} + L_{k+1,m-1} \text{ and } \mathscr{C}_1 = \bigcup_{i=1}^{\infty} \mathscr{L}_{1i}.$$

It is clear that $\mathscr{C}_1$ and every $_{1i}$ are left ideals of A and that

$$\mathscr{L}_{1i} = L_{1,m-1} + \ldots + L_{i,m-1}$$

is a supplementary sum. Define

$$\mathscr{L}_{2,i} = L_{2,m-1} + \ldots + L_{i,m-1} \text{ and } \mathscr{C}_2 = \bigcup_{i=2}^{\infty} \mathscr{L}_{2,i}.$$

For $j \leqslant i$ define

$$\mathscr{L}_{j,i} = L_{j,m-1} + \ldots + L_{i,m-1} \text{ and } \mathscr{C}_j = \bigcup_{i=j}^{\infty} \mathscr{L}_{j,i}.$$

Then $\mathscr{C}_1 \supset \mathscr{C}_2 \supset \ldots \supset \mathscr{C}_j \supset \ldots$. This is a properly descending chain of left ideals if the $L_{r,m-1}$ are all non-zero, for $L_{r,m-1}$ is in $\mathscr{C}_r$; but it cannot be in $\mathscr{C}_{r+1}$, for if $L_{r,m-1}$ is in $\mathscr{C}_{r+1}$, then some non-zero element l in $L_{r,m-1}$ is in $\mathscr{C}_{r+1}$ and thus in some $\mathscr{L}_{r+1,p} = L_{r+1,m-1} + \ldots + L_{p,m-1}$. Then $l = l_{r+1} + \ldots + l_p$ with $l_p \neq 0$. Thus, $l_p = l - l_{r+1} - \ldots - l_{p-1}$ is in $\mathscr{L}_{1,p-1}$, and therefore $\mathscr{L}_{1,p-1} \cap L_{p,m-1} \neq 0$, a contradiction. However, A has D.C.C. on left ideals and thus the chain of $\mathscr{C}_j$ must terminate after a finite number of steps. But this can happen only if $\mathscr{C}_{n_1+1} = \mathscr{C}_{n_1+2} = \ldots = 0$. Therefore, $\mathscr{L}_{n_1+1,n_1+1} = 0 = L_{n_1+1,m-1}$. In that case $\mathscr{L}_{1,n_1} = L_{1,m-1} + \ldots + L_{n_1,m-1}$ has the property that it meets every non-zero minimal left ideal of A which is in N^{m-1}. However, this implies that every minimal left ideal W of A which is in N^{m-1} is contained in $\mathscr{L}_{1,n_1}$, for if $w \neq 0$ is in W and in $\mathscr{L}_{1,n_1}$, then the minimal left ideal generated by w (which must be W) is in $\mathscr{L}_{1,n_1}$ because $\mathscr{L}_{1,n_1}$ is itself a left ideal. Thus, $\mathscr{L}_{1,n_1}$ contains the union of all the minimal left ideals of A contained in N^{m-1} which is equal to N^{m-1} and therefore

$$N^{m-1} = \mathscr{L}_{1,n_1} = L_{1,m-1} + \ldots + L_{n_1,m-1}.$$

Note that this does not mean there are no other minimal left ideals of A in N^{m-1}; it merely means that all of them are contained in the finite sum $L_{1,m-1} + \ldots + L_{n_1,m-1}$. For example, with 2×2 matrices,

$$L_1 = \left\{ \begin{pmatrix} a & 0 \\ b & 0 \end{pmatrix} \right\} \text{ and } L_2 = \left\{ \begin{pmatrix} 0 & c \\ 0 & d \end{pmatrix} \right\}$$

are minimal left ideals and $\mathcal{M}_2 = L_1 + L_2$. However,

$$L_3 = \left\{ \begin{pmatrix} a & a \\ b & b \end{pmatrix} \right\}$$

is also a minimal left ideal contained in $L_1 + L_2$ and different from either one
  The chain

$$0 \subset L_{1,m-1} \subset L_{1,m-1} + L_{2,m-1} \subset \ldots \subset L_{1,m-1} + \ldots + L_{n,m-1} = N^{m-1}$$

is now a composition series for N^{m-1} in A because there can be no left ideal of A properly contained between $L_{1,m-1} + \ldots + L_{i,m-1}$ and $L_{1,m-1} + \ldots + L_{i,m-1} + L_{i+1,m-1}$, for

$$(L_{1,m-1} + \ldots + L_{i+1,m-1})/(L_{1,m-1} + \ldots + L_{i,m-1})$$
$$\cong L_{i+1,m-1}/([L_{1,m-1} + \ldots + L_{i,m-1}] \cap L_{i+1,m-1}) = L_{i+1,m-1},$$

a minimal left ideal of A.

We next consider A/N^{m-1} and consider the ideal N^{m-2}/N^{m-1}. Just as for N^{m-1} we obtain a composition series which gives us a chain of left ideals of A:

$$N^{m-1} \subset L_{1,m-2} \subset L_{1,m-2} + L_{2,m-2} \subset \ldots \subset L_{1,m-2} + \ldots + L_{n_2,m-2} = N^{m-2}.$$

We do this for each power of N until we obtain a finite chain of left ideals of A:

$$0 \subset L_1 \subset L_2 \subset \ldots \subset L_s = N$$

such that there are no left ideals of A properly contained between L_i and L_{i+1}.

Finally, we extend this composition series for N to one for A by adjoining the left ideals $N \subset L_1^* \subset L_1^* + L_2^* \subset \ldots \subset L_1^* + \ldots + L_t^* = A$ and we obtain a finite chain of left ideals between 0 and A which admits no refinements,

$$0 \subset I_1 \subset \ldots \subset I_v = A.$$

Then, just as in the last part of Theorem 11, we apply the Jordan–Hölder theorem and obtain the fact that no chain of left ideals of A can have more than $v + 1$ distinct members. This then finishes the proof of Theorem 15, for given any properly ascending chain of left ideals of A, its length is at most $v + 1$, and in particular finite.

This theorem gives us a hint that D.C.C. is stronger than A.C.C., for D.C.C. plus a left unity yields A.C.C., but A.C.C. with a left unity does not give D.C.C. (the integers). But at first the hint is only faint for we may begin in very much the same way in the A.C.C. case as in the D.C.C. case with the following remarkable result.

3.2. Nil and nilpotent.

Theorem 16. *If A is a ring with A.C.C. on left ideals, then every nil left ideal of A is nilpotent.*

Remark. Fate seems to have had a hand in suppressing this result. Levitzki [40] proved it in August 1939, but because of the war and other peculiar circumstances it did not appear in print until 1950, and then in a relatively obscure journal with a minor mistake in the proof! Rumours circulated that the theorem was true but it was not noticed until Jacobson put it into his 1956 book [31]. However, the minor flaw remained!

Proof. Let L be a nil left ideal of A. Since A has A.C.C. on left ideals, we know that L is finitely generated as a left ideal, but it may not be finitely generated as a ring. We consider L^2. Take a_1 in L; then $La_1 \subseteq L^2$. If $La_1 \neq L^2$ we can select a_2 in L such that $La_2 \nsubseteq La_1$. Simply take an element y in L^2 which is not in La_1. Then

$$y = \sum_{i=1}^{n} b_i c_i,$$

where the b_i and c_i are in L. One of these, say $b_1 c_1$, is not in La_1, for if all are in La_1, then so is y. Then Lc_1 is not in La_1 and we may take $a_2 = c_1$. We continue this process and at each step either $La_1 + La_2 + \ldots + La_j = L^2$ or we can select a_{j+1} in L such that La_{j+1} is not contained in $La_1 + \ldots + La_j$. We thus obtain a properly ascending chain of left ideals

$$La_1 \subset La_1 + La_2 \subset \ldots \subset La_1 + \ldots + La_j \subset \ldots.$$

By A.C.C. this chain must stop at, say, $La_1 + \ldots + La_n$. Then $L^2 = La_1 + \ldots + La_n$, for otherwise we can extend the chain.

Next we consider L^3 and show that every element in L^3 is of the form $\sum_{k=1}^{m} l_k b_k$, where the l_k are in L and the b_k are products of two of the a_i's. To see this, take z in L^3. Then $z = \sum l'_j y_j$, where the y_j are in L^2, and thus $y_j = \sum l''_i a_i$. Then $z = \sum l'_j l''_i a_i = \sum y'_i a_i$, where again the y'_i are in L^2, and thus $y'_i = \sum l_k a_k$. Then $z = \sum l_k a_k a_i = \sum l_k b_k$, where each b_k is a product of two of the a_i's.

It is then not difficult to see that every element in L^{t+1} is of the form $\sum_{i=1}^{q} l_i c_i$, where the l_i are in L and the c_i are products of t of the a_i's. To show that L is nilpotent, it is therefore sufficient to show that there exists an integer t such that the product of any t of the a_i's is zero. Since addition does not enter into this, we consider only the multiplicative properties of the finite set $a_1, \ldots, a_n$. Thus, we are interested only in the multiplicative semi-group (i.e. closed and associative only with respect to multiplication) generated by the a_i. Note that each a_i is nilpotent, for L is nil, and that S, the multiplicative semi-group generated by the a_i, contains the zero element. We want to prove that S is nilpotent, and to do this we require three lemmas. We note first that S is nil, for it is a subset of L.

E

Lemma 29. *If S is a multiplicative semi-group generated by a finite number of elements $a_1, \ldots, a_n$, and if S contains a zero element, then if S is nil but not nilpotent, S contains a proper semi-group S^* which is also nil but not nilpotent and S^* is generated by a finite set of elements $b_1, \ldots, b_m$, where $b_i = a_s^{r_i} c_i$, where a_s is fixed, r_i is a positive integer less than the index of the nilpotent element a_s, and the c_i are elements generated by the $a_j, j \neq s$.*

Proof. Let $a'_1, \ldots, a'_t$ be a subset of the a_j such that the semi-group S' generated by $a'_1, \ldots, a'_t$, is not nilpotent and t is minimal. It may be that $t = n$, but at least $t \geqslant 2$, for any single element generates a nilpotent semi-group since S is nil. Then the semi-group S_1, generated by $a'_2, \ldots, a'_t$, is nilpotent. Let u be the smallest positive integer such that $a'_1{}^u = 0$ (i.e. u is the index of a'_1) and let v be the smallest positive integer such that $S_1{}^v = 0$.

Consider all elements of the form

$$a'_1{}^r . a'_{i_1} a'_{i_2} \ldots a'_{i_p},$$

where $i_j \neq 1$ for $j = 1, \ldots, p$; where $1 \leqslant r < u$; and where $1 \leqslant p < v$. There are only a finite number of such elements. Call them $b_1, \ldots, b_m$, and let S^* be the semi-group generated by these b_i's. Since $S^* \subseteq a'_1 S$, we can show that S^* is a proper semi-group in S, i.e. $S^* \subset S$. For if $S^* = S$, then $a'_1 S = S$. In that case $S = a'_1 S = a'^2_1 S = \ldots = a''^u_1 S = 0$, a contradiction.

Of course, S^* is nil and it remains only to prove that S^* is not nilpotent. Since S' is not nilpotent, for every integer x there exist elements $d_1, \ldots, d_x$ such that $d_1 \ldots d_x \neq 0$, where each d_i is a certain a'_j (actually all one can say at first is that d_i is in S', but clearly if every product of x of the a'_j is 0, then $S'^x = 0$). If x is larger than both u and v, then at least one of the d_i is a'_1 and at least one of the d_i is not a'_1. Now let y be any integer and take $x > (u + v)(y + 2)$. As we read the non-zero product $d_1 \ldots d_x$ from left to right, it becomes clear that $d_1 \ldots d_x$ must equal $fg_1 \ldots g_y h$, where the g_i are in S^* and where f and h are either powers of a'_1 or elements of S_1. Thus $g_1 \ldots g_y \neq 0$. Thus, for every integer y there exist elements $g_1, \ldots, g_y$ in S^* such that $g_1 \ldots g_y \neq 0$. Consequently, S^* cannot be nilpotent and the lemma is proved.

Note that we can then obtain an infinite properly descending sequence of semi-groups, $S \supset S^* \supset S^{**} \supset \ldots$, all of them not nilpotent but nil.

For any set of elements T in S we define $Z(T) = \{a \text{ in } S : at = 0 \text{ for every } t \text{ in } T\}$.

Lemma 30. *If S and S^* are as in Lemma 29, then $Z(S) \subset Z(S^*)$.*

Proof. Clearly $Z(S) \subseteq Z(S^*)$, since $S^* \subset S$ and $Z(S) \subseteq Z(S') \subseteq Z(S^*)$. We shall prove that $Z(S') \subset Z(S^*)$. The element $a'_i{}^{u-1} . b_i = 0$ for every $i = 1, \ldots, m$ and therefore $a'_1{}^{u-1}$ is in $Z(S^*)$. If it is not in $Z(S')$, the lemma is true. On the other hand, if $a'_1{}^{u-1} . S' = 0$, then $a'_1{}^{u-1} . a_j' = 0$ for every $j = 1, \ldots, t$. In this case $u - 1 > 1$; otherwise $b_i = 0$ for every i and $S^* = 0$, which is a contradiction to its non-nilpotency. We may then consider $a'_1{}^{u-2}$. It must then be in $Z(S^*)$ for $a'_1{}^{u-2} \cdot b_i$ is in $a'_1{}^{u-1} S' = 0$. However, $a'_1{}^{u-2}$ is definitely not in $Z(S')$, for $a'_1{}^{u-2} \cdot a'_1 \neq 0$. Therefore, $Z(S') \subset Z(S^*)$ and consequently $Z(S) \subset Z(S^*)$.

Note that we can then obtain an infinite properly ascending sequence of semi-groups $Z(S) \subset Z(S^*) \subset \ldots$, for by working within S^* we can show, as above, that there is an element in S^* which left-annihilates S^{**} but does not left-annihilate S^*. Then it is clear that the set of elements of S which left-annihilate S^{**}, i.e. $Z(S^{**})$, properly contains $Z(S^*)$, the set of elements of S which left-annihilate S^*. Then by working within S^{**}, $S^{***}, \ldots$, we obtain this infinite ascending chain.

Finally, we can prove:

Lemma 31. *Every nil multiplicative semi-group generated by a finite number of elements of a ring A with A.C.C. on left ideals must be nilpotent.*

Proof. If S is the semi-group and it is not nilpotent, then by Lemmas 29 and 30, we obtain an infinite properly ascending chain of left annihilators $Z(S) \subset Z(S^*) \subset \ldots$. Then we define $Z'(T) = \{a \text{ in } A : at = 0 \text{ for every } t \text{ in } T\}$. For any set T of A, clearly $Z'(T)$ is a left ideal of A. Then $Z'(S) \subset Z'(S^*) \subset \ldots$. This chain of left ideals of A is also properly ascending, for if at any stage we have equality, then we must also have equality in the chain $Z(S) \subset Z(S^*) \subset \ldots$. Thus, if S is not nilpotent, we have a contradiction to the A.C.C. This proves the lemma.

Thus, for every left ideal L of A we express L^2 as LS, where S satisfies Lemma 31 and is therefore nilpotent, $S^t = 0$. Then $L^{t+1} = LS^t = 0$ and L is nilpotent. This ends the proof of Theorem 16.

Remark. The same proof holds, with the usual minor adjustments, for rings with A.C.C. on right ideals.

Herstein [27] recently produced a simpler proof of Theorem 16, and one of his students, C. Procesi, has simplified that. This proof was communicated to us verbally, and it seems to yield even more than Theorem 16.

Theorem 16*. *If A is a ring with A.C.C. on left ideals, then every nil left ideal is nilpotent and every nil right ideal is nilpotent.*

Proof. If L is a non-zero one-sided ideal of A, and L is nil but not nilpotent, then we can establish a contradiction. First we show that we can consider the case where A has no non-zero nilpotent ideals.

By A.C.C., we may select a maximal nilpotent left ideal I. Then $I + IA$ is a nilpotent two-sided ideal (Lemma 12). Since I is maximal, $I + IA$ is either I

or all of A. However, if A is nilpotent, then every one-sided ideal of A is also nilpotent and then no such L can exist. The only other possibility is $I + IA = I$. Then I is a maximal two-sided nilpotent ideal and A/I has no non-zero nilpotent ideals. Then A/I has no non-zero nilpotent one-sided ideals (Lemma 12) and we also observe that A/I has A.C.C. on left ideals. Since L is not nilpotent, $L + I \supset I$ and thus $(L + I)/I$ is a non-zero one-sided ideal of A/I. Then $(L + I)/I$ is nil but not nilpotent.

Thus, it is sufficient to consider the case where A has no non-zero nilpotent ideals (left, right, or two-sided). In this case if $xA = 0$ or $Ax = 0$, we can conclude that $x = 0$, because the right or left ideal generated by x is nilpotent and thus must be zero.

First we take L to be a nil right ideal of A. For each non-zero right ideal T of A which is contained in L, we consider $T_1 = \{x \in A: xT = 0\}$. These T_1 are clearly left ideals of A and by A.C.C. we can select a non-zero right ideal T such that T_1 is a maximal left ideal of this type. Note that $T_1 \neq A$, for if $AT = 0$, then $T = 0$, a contradiction.

Take a non-zero element a in T. Since $T \subseteq L$, a is a nilpotent element, $a^n = 0 \neq a^{n-1}$. Then, of course, $a^n T = 0$. Select an integer m such that $a^m T \neq 0$, but $a^{m+1}T = 0$. Since a is in T, $a^m T \subseteq T$. Therefore $T_1 \subseteq (a^m T)_1$. Since $a^m T \neq 0$, $(a^m T)_1 \neq A$. Then $(a^m T)_1 = T_1$, since T_1 is maximal of this type and $a^m T$ is a right ideal of A.

Now $a \cdot a^m T = 0$ and therefore a is in $(a^m T)_1$. Then a is in T_1 and therefore $aT = 0$. This is true for every a in T and therefore $T \cdot T = 0$. Since A has no non-zero nilpotent right ideals, $T = 0$.

The only possibility then is that L itself is 0. Thus A has no non-zero nil right ideals.

Now let L be a nil left ideal of A. Take any x in L. Then $Ax \subseteq L$ and therefore Ax is a nil left ideal. Then for every y in A, yx is a nilpotent element, $(yx)^n = 0$. Now consider xA. It is a right ideal. For any y in A, xy is also a nilpotent element for $(xy)^{n+1} = x(yx)^n y = 0$. Thus xA is a nil right ideal, and thus $xA = 0$. In that case $x = 0$ and thus $L = 0$. Therefore, A has no non-zero nil left ideals either.

Reverting back to the general case then, every nil right or nil left ideal is contained in a maximal nilpotent ideal and each of them is therefore nilpotent.

3.3. The Baer lower radical. With this fine and deep result our progress with A.C.C. begins to slow down. We may, of course, conclude that $\mathscr{N} = \beta$ on rings with A.C.C. but $\mathscr{D} < \beta$, for the zero ring on C^∞ has A.C.C., but, as we know, it is $\mathscr{D}$-semi-simple and β-radical. But, more seriously, one of our basic theorems with D.C.C. no longer holds. We unhappily present a non-trivial simple ring with A.C.C. which is not a matrix ring over a division ring.

Example 8. Let A be the set of all polynomials in $x, \alpha_0 + x\alpha_1 + \ldots + x^m\alpha_m$, where the coefficients α_i are rational functions in a variable y, with real coefficients. We define addition in the usual way, but multiplication is not so clear. We define the product of two polynomials in x in the standard way except that x does not commute with the coefficients α. If α' denotes the ordinary derivative of α, then we define $\alpha x = x\alpha + \alpha'$. We generalize this to:

$$\alpha x^n = x^n\alpha + x^{n-1}\binom{n}{1}\alpha' + \ldots + x^{n-r}\binom{n}{r}\alpha^{(r)} + \ldots + \alpha^{(n)}.$$

With these definitions A is a ring, though associativity is not trivial and must be checked carefully.

We may speak of the degree of a polynomial in the usual way and the degree $(f(x)g(x)) = \text{degree } (f(x)) + \text{degree } (g(x))$. Consequently, there are no zero divisors, but the only elements that have inverses are the non-zero elements α, i.e. polynomials of degree 0.

Given any two non-zero polynomials

$$f(x) = \alpha_0 + x\alpha_1 + \ldots + x^m\alpha_m$$

and
$$g(x) = \beta_0 + x\beta_1 + \ldots + x^r\beta_r$$

we may divide $f(x)$ by $g(x)$ on either side, for assuming that $m \geq r$,

$$f(x) - g(x) . x^{m-r} . \beta_r^{-1}\alpha_m$$

is a polynomial of degree less than the degree of $f(x)$. Carrying on in the usual remainder-theorem-like way, we obtain $f(x) = g(x)q(x) + r(x)$ with degree $(r(x)) < \text{degree } (g(x))$. Similarly, $f(x) = q_1(x)g(x) + r_1(x)$ with degree $(r_1(x)) < \text{degree } (g(x))$. We can now show that every right ideal of A is of the form $f(x)$. A and every left ideal of the form $A.h(x)$, i.e. A is a principal ideal domain. Let J be a non-zero right ideal and let $f(x)$ be a non-zero polynomial of minimal degree in J. Then, clearly, every polynomial in J must be of the form $f(x) g(x)$, and $J = f(x)A$. Similarly for left ideals. Since every right and left ideal is finitely generated as an ideal, A has A.C.C. on both right and left ideals.

To see that A is simple, let I be any non-zero ideal of A and $f(x)$ a polynomial of minimal degree in I. We may take $f(x)$ to be monic:

$$f(x) = \alpha_0 + x\alpha_1 + \ldots + x^{n-1}\alpha_{n-1} + x^n.$$

Let $\alpha = y$. Then $\alpha' = 1$ and higher derivatives are zero. Then $\alpha x = x\alpha + 1$ and $\alpha x^m = x^m\alpha + mx^{m-1}$.

Then $\alpha f(x) - f(x)\alpha$ must be in I; however, this is equal to

$$\alpha_1 + x.2\alpha_2 + \ldots + x^{n-2}(n-1)\alpha_{n-1} + x^{n-1}.n,$$

a non-zero polynomial of degree $n - 1$. This contradicts the minimality of the degree of $f(x)$ unless $n = 0$, in which case $f(x) = \alpha_0$. Then I contains 1 and must be all of A.

Finally we note that A contains only one (non-zero) idempotent element, namely 1. Consequently, if A is of the form $\mathcal{M}\mathcal{D}$, the matrices must be of dimension 1. For, if the matrices are of higher dimension, we obtain idempotent elements $e_{11}, e_{22}, \ldots$. Thus, if A is of the form $\mathcal{M}\mathcal{D}$, it must simply be a division ring. This is not so, for the only elements with inverses are the polynomials of degree 0. Therefore, A is simple with A.C.C., is not a zero ring, but is not of the form $\mathcal{M}\mathcal{D}$.

In spite of this example, recent work has given us deep results for rings with A.C.C. Example 8 turns out to have a quotient ring which *is* of the form $\mathcal{M}\mathcal{D}$ (see Sections 3.8, 3.9, and 3.10, in particular Theorem 31). To develop this material we shall first study general rings without any chain conditions, and we begin with the Baer lower radical, which was mentioned earlier but without details.

We already know that the union N_0 of all the nilpotent ideals of a ring R may not be nilpotent, although it must be nil. Furthermore, R/N_0 may have nilpotent ideals. Let N_1 be the ideal of R such that N_1/N_0 is the union of all the nilpotent ideals of R/N_0. In general, for every ordinal α which is not a limit ordinal, we define N_α to be the ideal of R such that $N_\alpha/N_{\alpha-1}$ is the union of all the nilpotent ideals of $R/N_{\alpha-1}$. If α is a limit ordinal, we define

$$N_\alpha = \bigcup_{\beta < \alpha} N_\beta.$$

In this way we obtain an ascending chain of ideals $N_0 \subseteq N_1 \subseteq \ldots \subseteq N_\alpha \subseteq \ldots$. If the set R has ordinal number v, then after at most v steps, this chain must terminate. We may then consider the smallest ordinal τ (Proposition 6, Section 1.3) such that $N_\tau = N_{\tau+1} = \ldots$. This ideal we shall call L, the Baer lower radical of R. It is characterized by the fact that R/L has no non-zero nilpotent ideals and L is the smallest ideal in our chain that gives such a factor ring. We may characterize L as follows:

Lemma 32. *The Baer lower radical L of a ring R is equal to the intersection of all ideals Q_i of R such that R/Q_i has no non-zero nilpotent ideals.*

Proof. Let $W = \cap\, Q_i$. Then, since R/L has no non-zero nilpotent ideals, $W \subseteq L$. Conversely, take any Q_i such that R/Q_i has no non-zero nilpotent ideals. Then $N_0 \subseteq Q_i$. By transfinite induction (Proposition 9, Section 1.3), assume that $N_\alpha \subseteq Q_i$ for every $\alpha < \beta$. If β is a limit ordinal, then

$$N_\beta = \bigcup_{\alpha < \beta} N_\alpha \subseteq Q_i.$$

If β is not a limit ordinal, then $\beta - 1$ exists and $N_{\beta-1} \subseteq Q_i$. If N_β is not in Q_i

then some nilpotent ideal $I/N_{\beta-1}$ of $R/N_{\beta-1}$ is not in $Q_i/N_{\beta-1}$. Then consider

$$\frac{I \cup Q_i}{Q_i} \cong \frac{I}{I \cap Q_i}$$

Some power $I^r \subseteq N_{\beta-1} \subseteq Q_i$, and therefore $I/(I \cap Q_i)$ is a nilpotent ideal. Thus, $(I \cup Q_i)/Q_i$ is a nilpotent ideal of R/Q_i. Since $I \nsubseteq Q_i$, this is a non-zero nilpotent ideal and this contradicts the fact that R/Q_i has no such ideals. Therefore, $N_\beta \subseteq Q_i$ and thus $L \subseteq Q_i$. Therefore, $L \subseteq W$ and $L = W$, which proves the lemma.

We shall say that a ring R is an L-ring if it is the Baer lower radical of some ring R', and we want to prove that this is a radical property. Note that the alternative definition for an L-ring, "R is an L-ring if it is equal to its own Baer lower radical," is perhaps more natural, but in the following proof of property (A) it becomes clear that the two are equivalent.

We begin with property (A) and show that every homomorphic image of an L-ring is an L-ring. Let R be an L-ring and assume that R/J is not an L-ring. Clearly, 0 is an L-ring, for it is the Baer lower radical of 0. Thus we may take $R/J \neq 0$. Since R/J is not an L-ring, it is not the Baer lower radical of any ring and, in particular, it cannot be its own Baer lower radical. Let M/J be the Baer lower radical of R/J. Then $M/J \neq R/J$ and $R/M \cong (R/J)/(M/J)$ has no non-zero nilpotent ideals, and is not equal to 0. Thus, M contains the Baer lower radical of R by Lemma 32, and, in particular, R is not equal to its own Baer lower radical, though it is the Baer lower radical of some ring R'. As such, (the Baer lower radical of R'), $R = \cup N_\alpha$. Let L be the Baer lower radical of R, $L \neq R$. Then not all the N_α are in L and, in particular, there must exist an ordinal α, not a limit ordinal, such that $N_\alpha \nsubseteq L$ but $N_{\alpha-1} \subseteq L$. Then $L/N_{\alpha-1}$ does not contain some nilpotent ideal $I/N_{\alpha-1}$ of $R'/N_{\alpha-1}$. Consequently, $I \nsubseteq L$, but some power $I^r \subseteq N_{\alpha-1} \subseteq L$. Then if we consider

$$\frac{L \cup I}{L} \cong \frac{I}{L \cap I},$$

the right-hand side is nilpotent since $I^r \subseteq L \cap I$. Therefore, the left-hand side is a nilpotent ideal in R/L. It is non-zero for $I \nsubseteq L$. But R/L has no non-zero nilpotent ideals and therefore I must be in L; thus $N_\alpha \subseteq L$ and therefore $L = R$. Thus, no such M can exist; in particular, R/J must be an L-ring and property (A) is established.

We next consider property (B): every ring contains an L-ideal which contains every other L-ideal of the ring. Thus, take any ring R and consider its Baer lower radical L. It is clear that every ring contains an L-ideal, but what is not clear is that this L-ideal does, in fact, contain every other L-ideal of R. To see this, let C be an ideal of R which is the Baer lower radical of some ring R^*.

We must show that $C \subseteq L$. Let $R' = R/L$. This ring has no non-zero nilpotent ideals. Let

$$C' = \frac{L \cup C}{L} \cong \frac{C}{C \cap L}.$$

If $C \nsubseteq L$, then C' is a non-zero ideal of R'. The right-hand side shows that this is a homomorphic image of C and therefore, by property (A), C' is an L-ring. In particular, C' must contain some non-zero nilpotent ideals, for if it has none it cannot be an L-ring. At first it seems quite possible for a ring R' to have no non-zero nilpotent ideals but to have an ideal C' which does have some non-zero nilpotent ideal (of C'). But this cannot happen!

Lemma 33. *If R' has no non-zero nilpotent ideals and C' is an ideal of R', then C' has no non-zero nilpotent ideals.*

Proof. Let J be a nilpotent ideal of C', with $J^n = 0$. Then the ideal $R'JR'$ of R' is nilpotent and $(R'JR')^{2n-1} = 0$. One can prove this by induction on n. If $n = 2$, then $(R'JR')^3 = R'J(R'R'JR'R')JR'$ and $R'R'JR'R' \subseteq C'$; therefore $(R'JR')^3 \subseteq R'JC'JR' \subseteq R'JJR' = 0$. Assume then that $(R'JR')^{2n-1} \subseteq R'J^nR'$ and consider

$$(R'JR')^{2(n+1)-1} = (R'JR')^{2n+1} \subseteq R'J^nR'(R'JR'R'JR')$$

$$\subseteq R'J^nC'JR' \subseteq R'J^nJR' \subseteq R'J^{n+1}R'.$$

Thus, for all n, we have $(R'JR')^{2n-1} \subseteq R'J^nR'$, and therefore, if $J^n = 0$, $R'JR'$ is a nilpotent ideal of R'. Since R' has no non-zero nilpotent ideals, $R'JR' = 0$. Thus, for any $x \in J$, $R'xR' = 0$. Let X be the ideal of R' generated by x. Then $X = \{ix + r_1x + xr_2 + \sum r_3 xr_4\}$, where i is an integer and the terms $\sum r_3 xr_4$ must be 0. Then $X^3 \subseteq R'xR' = 0$, as a straightforward computation shows. Thus X is a nilpotent ideal of R', and therefore $X = 0$. Thus $x = 0$ and $J = 0$. Therefore C' has no non-zero nilpotent ideals, and the lemma is proved.

Remark. C' may, of course, have many ideals, which are not ideals of R', but if it has a non-zero nilpotent one, then one can manufacture such an ideal of R'.

Returning to our examination of property (B), C' must be zero by Lemma 33 and therefore $C \subseteq L$, L contains all the L-ideals of R, and property (B) holds.

Finally, we observe that property (C) holds, for R/L has no non-zero nilpotent ideals and therefore is L-semi-simple.

Therefore, this L property is a radical property.

We stated earlier that this radical property L is equivalent to the lower radical property β determined by the class of all nilpotent rings, and we run through the proof again here. Since all nilpotent rings are L-radical, and since

β is the *lower* radical property with respect to these rings, $\beta \leqslant L$. On the other hand, if R is an L-ring, then every non-zero homomorphic image of R is also an L-ring and thus contains a non-zero nilpotent ideal. Thus, R is of degree 2 over the class of nilpotent rings and is therefore β-radical. Thus $L \leqslant \beta$, and therefore $L = \beta$. We thus have the following theorem.

Theorem 17. *The Baer lower radical* $L = $ *the lower radical property* β *determined by the class of all nilpotent rings.*

3.4. Prime rings. The building blocks for rings with D.C.C. were simple rings. Example 8 indicates that these may not do for more general rings. The more general tools which we shall use are prime rings and, accordingly, we make the following definition: An ideal P of a ring R is a *prime ideal* if $AB \subseteq P$ implies either $A \subseteq P$ or $B \subseteq P$, where A and B are ideals of R. In particular, R/P has no non-zero nilpotent ideals, for if $I^r \subseteq P$, then clearly $I \subseteq P$.

We shall call a ring R a *prime ring* if 0 is a prime ideal of R. That is, if A and B are ideals of R such that $AB = 0$, then either $A = 0$ or $B = 0$. In particular, then, R has no non-zero nilpotent ideals. We note that if R is any ring and P is a prime ideal of R, then R/P is a prime ring. We also note that every non-nilpotent simple ring is a prime ring. Thus, in using prime rings as our representation pieces, we are generalizing the older use of simple (non-nilpotent) rings.

To obtain a definition of prime ideal in terms of elements rather than ideals we prove:

Lemma 34. *The ideal P is a prime ideal of R if and only if $xRy \subseteq P$ implies either x or y in P.*

Proof. If P is a prime ideal and $xRy \subseteq P$, then $RxR \cdot RyR \subseteq P$ and by the definition of prime ideal we can conclude that either $RxR \subseteq P$ or $RyR \subseteq P$. Suppose that $RxR \subseteq P$ and let X be the ideal of R generated by x. Then

$$X = \{ix + ax + xb + \sum\nolimits_j c_j x d_j\},$$

where i is an integer and the elements a, b, c_j, d_j all belong to R. It is not difficult to see that $X^3 \subseteq RxR$, and thus $X^3 \subseteq P$. Since P is a prime ideal, $X \subseteq P$ and thus $x \in P$. Similarly, if we had assumed that $RyR \subseteq P$, we would have obtained $y \in P$.

Conversely, if $xRy \subseteq P$ implies x or y in P, let A and B be ideals of R such that $AB \subseteq P$. If $A \nsubseteq P$ and $B \nsubseteq P$, then we can select elements $a \in A$, $b \in B$ such that both a and b do not lie in P. Then aRb cannot be contained in P. However, since $aR \subseteq A$, $aRb \subseteq AB \subseteq P$, a contradiction. Therefore, either $A \subseteq P$ or $B \subseteq P$, and P is a prime ideal. This ends the proof of the lemma.

In the commutative case, the condition that $xy \in P$ implies x or y in P is used a great deal, particularly in connection with ideal decomposition theory [52]. This condition is equivalent, in the commutative case, to our condition that $xRy \subseteq P$ implies x or y in P. However, in the non-commutative case these conditions are different. For example, in 2×2 matrices, 0 is a prime ideal, but there exist non-zero elements x, y such that $xy = 0$. We say an ideal is *completely prime* if $xy \in P$ implies x or y in P, but this has, up to now, not been particularly useful.

A condition which seems slightly weaker can be used to define a prime ring.

Lemma 35. *R is a prime ring if and only if* $I.J = 0$ *implies* $I = 0$ *or* $J = 0$ *where I and J are one-sided ideals of R.*

Proof. If $I.J = 0$ implies $I = 0$ or $J = 0$ for left ideals, then the same thing certainly holds true for two-sided ideals, and therefore R is prime.

Conversely, suppose R is prime and let $I.J = 0$ for left ideals I and J. Then $IR.JR = I.RJ.R \subseteq IJ.R = 0.R = 0$. Since IR and JR are ideals, and since R is prime, one of them, say IR, is 0. Then I is a two-sided ideal of R. Since $R \neq 0$, we can conclude that $I = 0$, by the primeness of R. Similarly, if $JR = 0$ then $J = 0$. Therefore, if $I.J = 0$, then either $I = 0$ or $J = 0$.

The same sort of proof goes through for two right ideals.

Corollary. *R is a prime ring if and only if the left annihilator of every non-zero left ideal is 0.*

Proof. Let L be a non-zero left ideal of R and suppose that $xL = 0$. Then $xRLR \subseteq xL.R = 0.R = 0$. Then, by this lemma, either $xR = 0$ or $LR = 0$. If $LR = 0$, then, since $R \neq 0$, $L = 0$, a contradiction. Thus $xR = 0$. Then $x = 0$ by Lemma 34 applied to the prime ideal 0.

If the left annihilator of every non-zero left ideal is zero, then if $I.J = 0$ for left ideals, either $J = 0$ or if $J \neq 0$, then $I = 0$, since I is in the left annihilator of J.

The same result holds for right annihilators of non-zero right ideals.

3.5. Zorn's Lemma. Generally, if one has an element-wise definition, as given in Lemma 34, there is little more required. However, we need still another view on prime ideals and to get this we require the use of the famous "Zorn's Lemma." Following the clear exposition given in [34], we state it as follows (see also [15]):

"If S is a partially ordered set in which every chain has a least upper bound, then S has a maximal element."

We remind the reader that S is a *partially ordered* set if it has a binary relation $\geqslant$ satisfying: $x \geqslant x$ (reflexive); $x \geqslant y$ and $y \geqslant z$ implies $x \geqslant z$ (transitive);

$x \geqslant y$ and $y \geqslant x$ implies $x = y$ (antisymmetric). Given any two elements in S, they may or may not be comparable, i.e. either $x \geqslant y$ or $y \geqslant x$ or neither of these might hold.

A subset C of S is a *chain* if every two elements of C are comparable.

An element x is a *least upper bound* of a subset T of S if $x \geqslant t$ for every $t \in T$ and, if $y \geqslant t$ for every $t \in T$, then $y \geqslant x$. For a given subset T, no such x need exist, but if it does exist, then it is clearly unique. Furthermore, such an x may not belong to T itself.

An element m is *maximal* in S if there are no elements $\neq m$ in S which are $\geqslant m$. A set S may have many maximal elements or may have none.

Zorn's Lemma is not really a lemma at all, but an axiom. It is equivalent to the Axiom of Choice and to the Well-Ordering Proposition (see Section 1.3).

We would like to make use of Zorn's Lemma as follows: given an arbitrary set M of non-zero elements in a ring R, we want to find an ideal I in R which does not contain any elements of M, and we want I to be maximal with respect to this property. In other words, if J is any ideal of R which properly contains I, then J must contain some elements of M. The ideal I may not be a maximal ideal of R, but it is to be maximal with respect to exclusion of M. Again I may not be unique, but we are concerned with finding one such ideal I and we do not care whether it is unique or not.

To apply Zorn's Lemma, we consider the class S of all ideals of R which do not meet the set M. The ideal (0) belongs to S since M was restricted to contain only non-zero elements, so that S has at least some ideals in it. We make S into a partially ordered set by defining $\geqslant$ as the set-theoretic inclusion. Next we consider any chain $I_1 \subset I_2 \subset \ldots$ in S and let $W = \cup I_\alpha$, i.e. W is the set of all *finite* sums of elements from the I_α. Then W is the least upper bound of this chain. Everything is clear except perhaps the fact that W is also in S. To convince ourselves of this, assume that some element x of M lies in W. Then $x = a_{\alpha_1} + \ldots + a_{\alpha_t}$, where $a_{\alpha_i} \in I_i$. Let I_β be the largest of the ideals $I_{\alpha_1}, \ldots, I_{\alpha_t}$. Then $I_{\alpha_i} \subseteq I_\beta$ and thus $x \in I_\beta$. But I_β is in S and therefore does not meet M, and thus x cannot be in I_β. Therefore x is not in W, and W is in S. Thus, we have established that every chain has a least upper bound and by Zorn's Lemma, S contains a maximal element I. This is the ideal we want. It does not meet M, and every ideal which properly contains I cannot be in S and therefore must meet M.

From now on we shall simply say, for any set M of non-zero elements, pick an ideal by Zorn's Lemma, maximal with respect to the exclusion of M.

3.6. Prime ideals. We are now in a position to obtain our first fruitful result connected with prime ideals.

Theorem 18. *The β-radical of any ring is precisely the intersection of all the prime ideals of the ring.*

Proof. Let B be the β-radical of the ring R and let Q be $\cap P_i$, where the P_i run over all the prime ideals of R. For each prime ideal P_i, R/P_i has no non-zero nilpotent ideals, and therefore B, the intersection of all ideals Q_i such that R/Q_i has no non-zero nilpotent ideals, by Lemma 32, is contained in $Q = \cap P_i$.

Conversely, let x be any element not in B. We shall show that there exists a prime ideal which does not contain x. Then x will not be in Q; therefore $Q \subseteq B$. To do this, let X again be the ideal generated by x in the ring R. Then no power X^r can be in B, for $X \nsubseteq B$ and R/B has no non-zero nilpotent ideals. However, from the proof of Lemma 34, we know that $X^3 \subseteq RxR$ and therefore no power of RxR is in B.

In particular, the set xRx cannot be in B, for otherwise $RxR \cdot RxR$ would be. Therefore, there exists an element y_1 such that $x_1 = xy_1 x$ is not in B. We repeat this procedure for the element x_1 and obtain an element y_2 such that $x_2 = x_1 y_2 x_1$ is not in B. In this way we generate a sequence of elements $x, x_1, x_2, \ldots, x_n, \ldots$ all of which do not lie in B, and these elements are related as follows: $x_n = x_{n-1} y_n x_{n-1}$, for some elements y_n. Such a sequence of x_i's is called an m-sequence. Let M be the set consisting of the elements of this sequence. Then, of course, the ideal B does not meet M. By Zorn's Lemma we pick an ideal W which contains B, which does not meet M, and which is maximal with respect to the exclusion of M. We shall show now that W is a prime ideal.

Suppose that S and T are ideals of R such that $ST \subseteq W$ and assume that neither S nor T is contained in W. Let $S' = W + S$ and $T' = W + T$ Both S' and T' properly contain W and by the maximality of W with respect to exclusion of M, both S' and T' must meet M. Then some x_i is in S' and some x_j is in T'. Take $i < j$ and consider

$$x_{j+1} = x_j y_{j+1} x_j = x_{j-1} y_j x_{j-1} \cdot y_{j+1} x_j = \ldots = x_i k x_j,$$

for some k in R. Since x_i is in S', $x_i k$ is in S', and therefore $x_i k x_j$ is in $S'T'$. But

$$S'T' = (S + W)(T + W) \subseteq ST + W \subseteq W.$$

Therefore, $x_{j+1} = x_i k x_j$ is in W. However, W does not meet M, and thus we have a contradiction. Therefore, either S or T must be in W, and W is a prime ideal. But, x is not in this prime ideal and therefore x is not in Q. Thus, $Q \subseteq B$ and the theorem is proved.

The intersection of the prime ideals of a ring was first considered by N. H. McCoy (*Am. J. Math.*, **71**, 823–33 (1949)) and only later did Levitzki show (*Am. J. Math.*, **73**,, 25–9 (1951)) that this was equal to the Baer lower radical. This radical is often referred to as the Baer–McCoy radical. We shall use the single name of Baer, to avoid confusion with the Brown–McCoy radical of Chapter V, and not in any way to diminish McCoy's contribution.

3.7. Subdirect sums. We have discussed the direct sum of a finite number of rings and it is now necessary to generalize this notion. Let $\{A_i\}$ be a class of rings with no restriction on the index set $\{i\}$. Thus, we may have an uncountable number of rings in the class. Consider the set S of symbols $(a_1, a_2, \ldots)$ where a_i belongs to A_i. These are infinite vectors. Addition and multiplication are defined co-ordinate-wise:

$$(a_1, a_2, \ldots) + (b_1, b_2. \ldots) = (a_1 + b_1, a_2 + b_2, \ldots),$$

$$(a_1, a_2, \ldots) . (b_1, b_2, \ldots) = (a_1 b_1, a_2 b_2, \ldots).$$

Then S is a ring and it is called the *complete direct sum* of the rings A_i. This is a supplementary sum of ideals and thus it extends our previously defined direct sum.

The set of all elements of the form $(0, 0, \ldots, 0, a_i, 0, \ldots)$ is a subring (an ideal in fact) A'_i which is isomorphic to A_i, and the mapping

$$(a_1, a_2, \ldots, a_i, \ldots) \to (0, 0, \ldots, 0, a_i, 0, \ldots)$$

is a homomorphism of S onto A'_i.

This complete direct sum is somewhat too overwhelming to be really useful (except for counter-examples perhaps!) and it is to subrings of this complete direct sum that we give our attention. For example, the subring which consists of all elements of S which have only a finite number of non-zero entries is called the *weak direct sum* or *discrete direct sum* of the A_i. The natural homomorphisms of the weak direct sum to A'_i are still onto for every i. It is this property that we require, and we say that a subring S^* of the complete direct sum S is a *subdirect sum* of the rings A_i if the natural homomorphism of S^* to A'_i,

$$(a, a_2, \ldots, a_i, \ldots) \to (0, 0, \ldots, 0, a_i, 0, \ldots),$$

is an onto mapping for every i.

Of course, if we are given a subring B of S, and B is not a subdirect sum of the A'_i, then the natural homomorphisms of B to A'_j are at least into mappings and if we call the images of these homomorphisms A_i^*, then B is at least a subdirect sum of the rings A_i^*.

If B is a subdirect sum of the rings A_i, then for every i, $A_i \cong B/B_i$ where B_i is the kernel of the natural homomorphism from B to A'_i. Furthermore, $\cap B_i = 0$, for if $x = (a_1, a_2, \ldots)$ has the property that $a_i = 0$, the zero element of A_i, for every i, then $x = (0, 0, \ldots)$, the zero element of B. Thus, if B is a subdirect sum of the rings A_i, then B contains a class of ideals $\{B_i\}$ such that $\cap B_i = 0$ and $B/B_i \cong A_i$.

Conversely, suppose that B is an arbitrary ring and that it contains a class of ideals $\{B_i\}$ such that $\cap\, B_i = 0$. Define $A_i = B/B_i$ and consider the complete direct sum S of the A_i. For every element x in B, we may associate the element $(a_1, a_2, \ldots)$ of S, where a_i is the element $x + B_i$ of A_i that is determined by x. Then B is isomorphic to a subring $\bar{B}$ of S and B/B_i is isomorphic to A'_i. Thus, the natural homomorphism from $\bar{B}$ to A'_i is onto and B is isomorphic to a subdirect sum of the rings A_i. We then have:

Theorem 19. *A ring R is isomorphic to a subdirect sum of rings A_i if and only if R contains a class of ideals $\{B_i\}$ such that $\cap\, B_i = 0$ and $R/B_i \cong A_i$.*

We then have the following fundamental theorem.

Theorem 20. *Every β-semi-simple ring R is isomorphic to a subdirect sum of prime rings.*

Proof. If R is β-semi-simple, then by Theorem 18, the intersection of all the prime ideals P_i is zero. Then, by Theorem 19, R is isomorphic to a subdirect sum of rings $A_i \cong R/P_i$, each of which is a prime ring.

There is never any difficulty in representing any ring R as a subdirect sum, for given any class of ideals $\{B_i\}$ we may join in the ideal $(0) = B_0$ and then $\cap\, B_i = 0$ and Theorem 19 ensures a subdirect decomposition. In this case, however, one of the components is R itself and thus the decomposition is not particularly useful. For example, if we represent R by the isomorphism $r \leftrightarrow (r, r, r, 0, 0)$ or $r \leftrightarrow (r, 0)$ or $r \leftrightarrow (r, r, r, \ldots, r, \ldots)$ we have accomplished nothing. Thus, the only subdirect sums that we shall be interested in are those for which none of the kernels B_i are zero. Another way of putting this is to say that every natural homomorphism of R onto A'_i is not an isomorphism. This is not to say that A'_i may not be isomorphic to R by way of some other mapping (for example, Example 1 has the property that R/H_i, $H_i \neq 0$, is isomorphic to R) but the natural homomorphism

$$r = (a_1, a_2, \ldots) \to (0, 0, \ldots, 0, a_i, 0, \ldots)$$

must not be an isomorphism. Thus, Theorem 19 might be thought of as: a ring R is isomorphic to an interesting or significant subdirect sum if and only if R contains a class of *non-zero* ideals $\{B_i\}$ such that $\cap\, B_i = 0$. In connection with Theorem 20, if one of the prime ideals is zero, then R is itself a prime ring, and this would be much better than merely having R isomorphic to a subdirect sum of prime rings.

With this view, we shall say that a ring R is *subdirectly irreducible* if any set of non-zero ideals of R has a non-zero intersection, and this is equivalent to the assumption that the intersection of all the non-zero ideals of R is non-zero.

This intersection, called the *heart* of the ring, is then a minimal ideal which is contained in every non-zero ideal of R. Commutative subdirectly irreducible rings have been well analysed ([41], [20]), but our knowledge in the general non-commutative case is meagre. The importance of subdirectly irreducible rings is established in the following theorem.

Theorem 21. *Every ring R is isomorphic to a subdirect sum of subdirectly irreducible rings.*

Proof. For each $x \neq 0$ in R, by Zorn's Lemma, select an ideal I_x, maximal with respect to the exclusion of x. As x ranges over all non-zero elements of R, $\cap I_x$ must be zero, for if $y \in \cap I_x$, then if $y \neq 0$, y must be in I_y. But I_y excludes y and therefore $\cap I_x = 0$. Then, by Theorem 19, R is isomorphic to a subdirect sum of rings A_x, where $A_x \cong R/I_x$. Each of these is subdirectly irreducible, for any non-zero ideal J/I_x of R/I_x must contain the non-zero element $x + I_x$, since J is an ideal of R which properly contains I_x and therefore must contain x. Thus, the intersection of all the non-zero ideals of R/I_x is non-zero since it contains $x + I_x$, and thus R/I_x is subdirectly irreducible. This is true for every $x \neq 0$ of R and thus the theorem is established.

Theorem 20 is an interesting generalization of Theorem 10. The direct sum of a finite number of components has become a subdirect sum of a possibly infinite number of components. In the D.C.C. case the components were simple non-trivial rings and here they are prime rings. Without D.C.C. we cannot expect to release ourselves from some connection with infinity, but we should not be altogether satisfied with the notion of a subdirect sum. There is nothing unique about a subdirect sum representation and even if we can say that a certain ring can be represented as a subdirect sum of certain pleasant rings (e.g. prime or simple) the same ring may at the same time have a representation as a subdirect sum of rings with rather ugly properties.

For example, the even integers $2I$ can be represented as a subdirect sum of fields $2I/(2p_i)$, p_i an odd prime $\neq 1$, since the intersection of the ideals $(2p_i)$ is 0. To see that $2I/(2p)$ is a field, for any odd prime $p \neq 1$, we establish an isomorphism between $2I/(2p)$ and $I/(p)$. Map $1 \to p + 1, 2 \to 2(p + 1) \equiv 2 \pmod{2p}, 3 \to 3(p + 1) \equiv p + 3 \pmod{2p}, \ldots, p - 2 \to 2p - 2, p - 1 \to p - 1$, and $p \equiv 0 \pmod{p} \to 2p \equiv 0 \pmod{2p}$. This is a 1–1 map which preserves addition. It also preserves multiplication, for

$$a \cdot b \to a(p + 1) \cdot b(p + 1) = ab(p^2 + 1 + 2p) \equiv ab(p^2 + 1) \pmod{2p}.$$

Since $p^2 - p = p(p - 1)$ is divisible by $p \cdot 2$, $p^2 - p \equiv 0 \pmod{2p}$, or $p^2 \equiv p \pmod{2p}$. Therefore,

$$ab(p^2 + 1) \equiv ab(p + 1) \pmod{2p}$$

and thus

$$ab \to ab(p + 1) \equiv a(p + 1) \cdot b(p + 1) \pmod{2p}.$$

At the same time, $2I$ can be represented as a subdirect sum of rings $2I/(2 \cdot 2^i)$ since the intersection of the ideals $(2 \cdot 2^i)$, $i = 1, 2, \ldots$, must be zero. However, the rings $2I/(2 \cdot 2^i)$ are all nilpotent! Thus, one ring can have subdirect sum representations of both the best (fields) and worst (nilpotent) kinds.

Be this as it may, we shall, nevertheless, attempt to press our knowledge of Theorem 20 and try to discover something about prime rings. Our description of simple rings made use of matrix rings and division rings, but as we go deeper and study prime rings we should expect more complex models. But, in fact, we do not have any convenient models. Therefore, we cannot expect to say that a prime ring *is* something, but rather that it can be embedded in something known. Thus, our next topic is a preliminary study of embedding.

3.8. Quotient rings. If R is a ring with some regular elements (elements which are not right or left zero divisors), then Q is said to be a *left quotient ring* of R if Q is a ring such that: (1) $R \subseteq Q$; (2) every regular element of R has a two-sided inverse in Q; (3) every element of Q is of the form $y^{-1}x$, where x and y are in R, y is a regular element of R, and y^{-1} is the inverse of y.

Not every ring R with regular elements has a quotient ring. We determine the ones that do in the following theorem.

Theorem 22. *A ring R with some regular elements has a left quotient ring Q if and only if for every a, b in R with b regular, there exist elements c, d in R with c regular such that $ca = db$ (common left multiple property).*

Proof. If R has a left quotient ring Q, take any two elements a, b of R with b regular. Then b^{-1} exists in Q, and thus ab^{-1} is in Q. This element must be expressible as $c^{-1}d$, where c, d are in R with c regular. Thus $ab^{-1} = c^{-1}d$, or $ca = db$. Thus R has the common left multiple property.

Conversely, if R is a ring with regular elements, with the common left multiple property, we can construct a left quotient ring. To do this, consider the set Q^* of all pairs (a, b), where a, b are elements of R with b regular. Define $(a, b) \sim (c, d)$ if $xa = yc$, where x, y are regular elements such that $xb = yd$. The elements x, y are by no means unique. Since both b and d are regular, we first want to show that x, y can be chosen so that they are both regular themselves. By the common left multiple property, thinking of b as the regular element, we may find x, y such that $xb = yd$, with y regular. Since d is also regular, it is clear that yd is a regular element and therefore xb is regular. Therefore, if $fx = 0$, then $fxb = 0$ and thus $f = 0$. Thus x is not a right zero divisor. However, it is not clear why x cannot be a left zero divisor, $xg = 0$ with $g \neq 0$. To see that this cannot happen, select elements p, q with p regular such that $pb = qd$. We get such a pair by thinking of d as the regular element of the pair b, d. Then pb is regular. Now consider the pair pb and xb, thinking of xb as regular, and select elements α, β with β regular such that $\alpha xb = \beta pb$. Since b is regular, we have $\alpha x = \beta p$. Both β and p are regular; therefore βp is regular and therefore αx is regular. Now if $xg = 0$, $\alpha xg = 0$ and $g = 0$. Therefore, x is not a left zero divisor and thus x is a regular element of R.

Returning to our definition $(a, b) \sim (c, d)$ if $xa = yc$, where $xb = yd$, we now know that we may choose both x and y regular. But, we must now show that if there is another pair of regular elements x_1, y_1 such that $x_1 b = y_1 d$, then we must have $x_1 a = y_1 c$. Only then shall we be certain that the definition of $\sim$ is clearly defined. Accordingly, select elements γ_1, γ_2, both regular, such that $\gamma_1 y = \gamma_2 y_1$. Then $\gamma_1 yd = \gamma_2 y_1 d = \gamma_2 x_1 b = \gamma_1 xb$. Since b is regular, we have $\gamma_2 x_1 = \gamma_1 x$ and therefore $\gamma_2 x_1 a = \gamma_1 xa = \gamma_1 yc = \gamma_2 y_1 c$. Since γ_2 is regular, we have $x_1 a = y_1 c$, as desired. Thus, our definition of $\sim$ is well defined. Our next task is to show that $\sim$ is an equivalence relationship.

The proofs of both the reflexive and symmetric laws are immediate, for if $\alpha b = \alpha b$, then $\alpha a = \alpha a$, and thus $(a, b) \sim (a, b)$; while if $(a, b) \sim (c, d)$ and $\alpha b = \beta d$ with $\alpha a = \beta c$, then $(c, d) \sim (a, b)$ for $\beta d = \alpha b$ and $\beta c = \alpha a$. The proof of the transitive law requires somewhat more effort. If $(a, b) \sim (c, d)$ and $(c, d) \sim (e, f)$ and $\alpha b = \beta d$, $\alpha a = \beta c$, $\gamma d = \delta f$, $\gamma c = \delta e$, then select x, y both regular such that $x\gamma = y\beta$. Then $x\gamma c = y\beta c = x\delta e = y\alpha a$, and $x\gamma d = y\beta d = x\delta f = y\alpha b$. Let $\rho = x\delta$ and $\sigma = y\alpha$, both regular. Then $\rho f = \sigma b$ and $\rho e = \sigma a$. Therefore, $(a, b) \sim (e, f)$ and $\sim$ is an equivalence relationship.

We may then partition Q^* into equivalence classes and obtain a set Q whose elements are equivalence classes denoted by a/b (a representative of the class which contains (a, b)).

To make Q into a ring we first define addition and multiplication. Given two elements of Q, a/b and c/d, we can find x, y, both regular, such that $yd = xb$, because both b and d are regular. We then define

$$\frac{a}{b} + \frac{c}{d} = \frac{xa + yc}{yd}.$$

We can also find elements w, z such that $wa = zd$. We know that w must be regular because d is regular but we can say nothing about z. We then define

$$\frac{a}{b} \cdot \frac{c}{d} = \frac{zc}{wb}.$$

To show that these are well-defined operations we must check two things. First take $(a', b') \sim (a, b)$ and $(c', d') \sim (c, d)$ and consider

$$\frac{a'}{d'} + \frac{c'}{d'} \quad \text{and} \quad \frac{a'}{b'} \cdot \frac{c'}{b'}.$$

We must show that

$$\frac{a'}{b'} + \frac{c'}{d'} = \frac{a}{b} + \frac{c}{d} \quad \text{and} \quad \frac{a'}{b'} \cdot \frac{c'}{d'} = \frac{a}{b} \cdot \frac{c}{d}.$$

Accordingly, take regular elements α, β such that $\alpha b = \beta b'$ and $\alpha a = \beta a'$; and regular elements γ, δ such that $\gamma d = \delta d'$ and $\gamma c = \delta c'$. Now

$$\frac{a'}{b'} + \frac{c'}{d'} = \frac{x'a' + y'c'}{y'd'},$$

where $y'd' = x'b'$, and both x', y' are regular. Take regular elements e, f such that $ey'd' = fyd$. To establish that

$$\frac{xa + yc}{yd} = \frac{x'a' + y'c'}{y'd'}$$

we must merely show that $e(x'a' + y'c') = f(xa + yc)$.

Since $ey'd' = ex'b'$ and $fyd = fxb$, we have $ex'b' = fxb$. Select regular elements g, h such that $gfx = h\alpha$. Then $gfxb = h\alpha b = h\beta b' = gex'b'$. Since b' is regular, we have $h\beta = gex'$ and therefore $gfxa = h\alpha a = h\beta a' = gex'a'$. Since g is regular, we have $fxa = ex'a'$.

Similarly, select regular elements m, n such that $mfy = ny$. Then $mfyd = nyd = n\delta d' = mey'd'$. Since d' is regular, we have $n\delta = mey'$. Therefore $mfyc = nyc = n\delta c' = mey'c'$. Since m is regular, we have $fyc = ey'c'$.

Putting these together, we have $e(x'a' + y'c') = f(xa + yc)$ and therefore

$$\frac{a'}{b'} + \frac{c'}{d'} = \frac{a}{b} + \frac{c}{d}.$$

To establish the similar relation for multiplication take p, q regular such that $pwb = qw'b'$. To show that

$$\frac{a'}{b'} \cdot \frac{c'}{d'} = \frac{z'c'}{w'b'}$$

is equal to

$$\frac{a}{b} \cdot \frac{c}{d} = \frac{zc}{wb}$$

it is sufficient to show that $pzc = qz'c'$. To do this, select regular elements m, n such that $mpw = n\alpha$, where α is the element defined above, in connection with $(a, b) \sim (a', b')$. Then $mpwb = mqw'b' = n\alpha b = n\beta b'$. Since b' is regular, we have $mqw' = n\beta$. Then $mqw'a' = n\beta a' = n\alpha a = mpwa$. Since m is regular, we have $qw'a' = pwa$ and therefore $qz'd' = pzd$. Next select regular elements r, s, such that $rpz = s\gamma$. Then $rpzd = s\gamma d = s\delta d' = rqz'd'$. Since d' is regular, we have $s\delta = rqz'$ and therefore $s\delta c' = rqz'c' = s\gamma c = rpzc$. Since r is regular, we have $qz'c' = pzc$ and this proves that

$$\frac{a'}{b'} \cdot \frac{c'}{d'} = \frac{a}{b} \cdot \frac{c}{d}.$$

The second thing we must check is the case when we use regular elements x', y' instead of x, y. That is, suppose that $y'd = x'b$ and

$$\frac{a}{b} + \frac{c}{d} = \frac{x'a + y'c}{y'd}.$$

We must show that

$$\frac{x'a + y'c}{y'd} = \frac{xa + yc}{yd}.$$

Thus, take regular elements p, q such that $py'd = qyd$. We must show that $p(x'a + y'c) = q(xa + yc)$. However, $py'd = px'b = qyd = qxb$. Since b is regular, we have $px' = qx$, and therefore $px'a = qxa$. Since d is regular, $py' = qy$, and therefore $py'c = qyc$. Therefore,

$$\frac{x'a + y'c}{y'd} = \frac{xa + yc}{yd}$$

and addition is well defined.

For multiplication, if w', z' are elements such that $w'a = z'd$ with w' regular, then one may take

$$\frac{a}{b} \cdot \frac{c}{d} = \frac{z'c}{w'b} \text{ as well as } \frac{zc}{wb}.$$

To show that

$$\frac{z'c}{w'b} = \frac{zc}{wb},$$

take regular elements m, n such that $mw'b = nwb$. We must show that $mz'c = nzc$. Since b is regular, we have $mw' = nw$. Then $mw'a = nwa = mz'd = nzd$. Since d is regular, $mz' = nz$, and therefore $mz'c = nzc$. Thus multiplication is also well defined.

We shall leave the checking of associativity, distributivity, and additive commutativity to the reader. Closure is immediate and the existence of additive inverses is not difficult to establish. Then Q is a ring, and it remains to establish that it is a left quotient ring for R.

First we show that c/c is the unity element for Q. We consider

$$\frac{a}{b} \cdot \frac{c}{c} = \frac{yc}{xb},$$

where $yc = xa$, and we want to show that

$$\frac{yc}{xb} = \frac{a}{b}.$$

To do this, we take $\alpha xb = \beta b$ and we try to show that $\alpha yc = \beta a$. But $yc = xa$, and therefore $\alpha yc = \alpha xa$. Since b is regular, $\alpha x = \beta$, and therefore $\alpha xa = \beta a$, and thus $\alpha yc = \beta a$ and thus c/c is a right unity. On the other hand

$$\frac{c}{c} \cdot \frac{a}{b} = \frac{ya}{xc},$$

where $yb = xc$. To get

$$\frac{ya}{xc} = \frac{a}{b},$$

take $yb = \delta xc$. Then $\delta xc = \delta yb = \gamma b$, and since b is regular, $\delta y = \gamma$, and therefore $\delta ya = \gamma a$. Thus, c/c is also a left unity and Q has c/c as a unity element.

Let R^* be the set of all elements of Q of the form ca/c. Map $R \to R^*$ by $a \to ca/c$. This is well defined for $ca/c = da/d$, since if $\alpha c = \beta d$, then $\alpha ca = \beta da$. This mapping is 1–1 for if $ca/c = cb/c$, then clearly $a = b$. It preserves addition, for if $a \to ca/c$, $b \to cb/c$, $a + b \to c(a + b)/c$, then

$$\frac{c(a + b)}{c} = \frac{ca}{c} + \frac{cb}{c} = \frac{xca + ycb}{yc},$$

where $yc = xc$. Since c is regular, $x = y$, and thus

$$\frac{xca + ycb}{yc} = \frac{xc(a + b)}{xc} = \frac{c(a + b)}{c}.$$

This map also preserves multiplication, for

$$ab \to \frac{c(ab)}{c} = \frac{ca}{c} \cdot \frac{cb}{c} = \frac{ycb}{xc},$$

where $yc = xca$; thus

$$\frac{ycb}{xc} = \frac{xcab}{xc} = \frac{cab}{c}.$$

Therefore, R^* is isomorphic to R, and in this way we may say that $R \subseteq Q$, if we identify R^* with R. We shall thus write a for the element ca/c.

Now let b be any regular element of R, $b = cb/c$. Define $b^{-1} = c/cb$. Then

$$bb^{-1} = \frac{cb}{c} \cdot \frac{c}{cb} = \frac{yc}{xc},$$

where $ycb = xcb$. Since both b and c are regular, $y = x$ and $bb^{-1} = c/c = 1$. Similarly, $b^{-1}b = 1$, and thus every regular element of R has an inverse in Q. Finally, take any element a/b in Q. Consider

$$\frac{c}{cb} \cdot \frac{ca}{c} = \frac{yca}{xcb},$$

where $yc = xc$. Since c is regular, $y = x$, and therefore

$$\frac{yca}{xcb} = \frac{a}{b}.$$

Thus $a/b = b^{-1}a$, and therefore Q is a left quotient ring for R and the theorem is established.

It is clear that if $R_1 \cong R$, then $Q(R_1) \cong Q(R)$ and, in particular, if a ring R has a left quotient ring, then it is unique up to isomorphism.

To say that a given ring R can be embedded in some other ring does not tell us very much unless the over-ring is very intimately connected with R, i.e. unless the over-ring hugs R very closely, so to speak, and a quotient ring is quite satisfactory in this regard. Several extensions of these ideas to rings without regular elements have been studied ([37], [23], [49]).

There exist rings (not commutative, of course) which have some regular elements and which do not have left or right quotient rings. A more interesting question concerns the existence of a ring which has a right quotient ring but not a left quotient ring.

Example 9 [25]. Let F be the field generated by the real numbers and the infinite set of independent variables $x_1, x_2, \ldots, x_n, \ldots$. Thus, F is the set of all rational functions in $x_1, \ldots, x_n, \ldots$ with real coefficients. Let G be the subfield of F generated by the reals and $x_2, x_3, \ldots, x_n, \ldots$. Clearly G is a proper subfield of F, for it does not contain the variable x_1. We can set up a mapping from F to G which has no effect on the real coefficients but which sends x_i in F into x_{i+1} in G. This map is an isomorphism between F and G. This map is related to an automorphism, the difference being that the map is not onto F but into F.

Let z be an indeterminate over F and let R be the set of polynomials of the form $a_0 + za_1 + \ldots + z^n a_n$, with the a_i in F and the powers of z written on the left, as in Example 8. We define addition in the usual way, and we define the product of two polynomials in z in the standard way using the distributive law except that z does not commute with the coefficients. If a'_i is the image of a_i under the above isomorphism between F and G, then we define $a_i z = z a'_i$. With these definitions R is a ring.

Just as in Example 8, we may speak of the degree of a polynomial, and the degree $(f(z)g(z)) = $ degree $(f(z)) + $ degree $(g(z))$. Thus, there are no zero divisors, and all non-zero elements of R are regular.

Again as in Example 8, we may "divide" one polynomial into another on the right, for if

$$f(z) = a_0 + za_1 + \ldots + z^n a_n \qquad \text{and} \qquad g(z) = b_0 + zb_1 + \ldots + z^m b_m$$

with $m \leqslant n$, then let $\alpha = [((b'_m)^{(n-m)})']$, that is, the $(n-m)$th image of b_m under the isomorphism from F to G. Now consider $f(z) - g(z) z^{n-m} \alpha^{-1} a_n$. This is a polynomial of degree less than the degree of $f(z)$ and thus, after a finite number of steps, we obtain $f(z) = g(z)q(z) + r(z)$, where the degree of $r(z) <$ the degree of $g(z)$.

In Example 8 the same technique worked on both sides, but here it does not work on the left. To see this, let $f(z) = z^n a$, where a is a polynomial in F with some x_1's in it. For simplicity let $a = x_1$. Take $g(z) = z^m$ with $m < n$. Now if we multiply $g(z)$ on the left by $z^{n-m} \cdot b$, we get $z^n b^*$, where b^* is the $(n-m)$th image of b under the isomorphism from F to G. If, for example, $n - m = 1$, then $b^* = b'$ is in G and cannot have any x_1's in it and, in particular, cannot be equal to x_1. Thus, there is no way to divide $f(z)$ on the left by $g(z)$.

Since the technique does work on the right, we can conclude that every right ideal of R is principal and, in particular, is finitely generated, and therefore R has A.C.C. on right ideals. But, what is more important from our point of view, R has the common right multiple property. To see this, we first observe that any two non-zero polynomials $f(z)$, $g(z)$ in R have a right greatest common divisor $d(z)$, and that this right greatest common divisor can be represented as a right linear combination of the two polynomials:

$$d(z) = f(z) \cdot q_1(z) + g(z) \cdot q_2(z).$$

We also know that $d(z)q(z) = g(z)$, and thus

$$g(z) = f(z)q_1(z)q(z) + g(z)q_2(z)q(z).$$

Therefore

$$f(z) \cdot q_1(z)q(z) = g(z) \cdot [1 - q_2(z)q(z)],$$

which is not zero unless $d(z) = g(z)K$. For R has no zero divisors and, if this is zero, $1 = q_2(z)q(z)$, and therefore $q_2(z) = K$ is in F, $\neq 0$, and $q(z)$ is in F, $\neq 0$. Thus, $q_1(z) = 0$, and $d(z) = g(z) \cdot K$. In this case

$$f(z) = g(z) \cdot h(z) \neq 0.$$

Thus, R has regular elements and the common right multiple property, and therefore R has a right quotient ring, the right rational functions in z over F.

To see that R does not have a left quotient ring it is sufficient to show that R does not have the common left multiple property. To do this let $f(z) = z + x_1$ and $g(z) = z^2$. We claim that no $m(z)$, $n(z)$ exist such that $m(z) \cdot (z + x_1) = n(z) \cdot z^2$. Let

$$m(z) = a_0 + za_1 + \ldots + z^r a_r \quad \text{and} \quad n(z) = b_0 + zb_1 + \ldots + z^s b_s$$

with $a_r \neq 0$, $b_s \neq 0$. Then

$$m(z).(z + x_1) = a_0 x_1 + z[a_1 x_1 + a_0'] + z^2[a_2 x_1 + a_1'] + \ldots$$
$$+ z^r[a_r x_1 + a'_{r-1}] + z^{r+1}[a'_r],$$
$$n(z).z^2 = z^2[b''_0] + \ldots + z^{s+2}[b''_s].$$

For these to be equal, we must have $r = s + 1$ and $a_0 = a_1 = 0$. Then the proposed equality leads to:

$$b''_0 = a_2 x_1,$$
$$b''_1 = a_3 x_1 + a'_2,$$
$$\vdots$$
$$b''_i = a_{i+2} x_1 + a'_{i+1},$$
$$\vdots$$
$$b''_{s-1} = a_{s+1} x_1 + a'_s,$$
$$b''_s = a'_{s+1} \neq 0.$$

From $b''_s = a'_{s+1}$ we get $b'_s = a_{s+1}$. Therefore, from the second last equality we get

$$b''_{s-1} = b'_s x_1 + a'_s,$$
$$x_1 = b'_s{}^{-1}(b''_{s-1} - a'_s).$$

No matter which elements in F we select for a_s, b_s, and b_{s-1}, the elements a'_s, b''_{s-1}, b'_s, and $b'_s{}^{-1}$ will all be in G. However, x_1 is not in G and thus this equality can never be satisfied.

This proves that R does not have a left quotient ring.

3.9. Semi-prime rings. We shall say that a ring R is *semi-prime* if it has no non-zero nilpotent ideals. Such rings correspond to prime rings in much the same way as semi-simple rings with D.C.C. correspond to simple non-trivial rings with D.C.C. We recall that a ring R is prime if $xRy = 0$ implies that either $x = 0$ or $y = 0$. We obtain a similar element-wise characterization for semi-prime rings in:

Lemma 36. *R is semi-prime if and only if $xRx = 0$ implies $x = 0$.*

Proof. If R is semi-prime and $xRx = 0$, then $RxRRxR = 0$ and thus $RxR = 0$. Let $X = (x)$. Then $X^3 \subseteq RxR = 0$ and therefore $X = 0$, $x = 0$. Conversely, if $xRx = 0$ implies $x = 0$, let A be a non-zero nilpotent ideal of R with $A^n = 0 \neq A^{n-1}$ and let $B = A^{n-1}$. Then $B^2 = 0$. Take $x \neq 0$ in B. Then $xRx \subseteq xB \subseteq B^2 = 0$. Thus $x = 0$, a contradiction. Therefore, no such non-zero nilpotent ideals exist, and R is semi-prime.

Corollary. *If R is semi-prime, then $xR = 0$ or $Rx = 0$ implies $x = 0$.*

Proof. Clearly, if $xR = 0$ or $Rx = 0$, then $xRx = 0$ and $x = 0$ by Lemma 36.

Note that the converse of the corollary is false, for if R' is a trivial ring and we adjoin a unity element to R' to obtain a ring R, then $xR = 0$ or $Rx = 0$ implies $x = 0$. However, $R'^2 = 0$ and R' is a non-zero nilpotent ideal of R. Thus, R is not semi-prime. Note that in this case $xRx = 0$ implies only that x is in R'.

3.10. Prime and semi-prime rings with A.C.C.

Quotient rings, Theorem 20, and the structure of a non-nilpotent simple ring with D.C.C. have all been brilliantly joined together by Goldie [24, 25] to give us deep results in the A.C.C. case. We shall follow the work of Lesieur and Croisot [38] in developing this material.

In this section we shall henceforth assume that R is a *semi-prime ring with A.C.C.* on left ideals. Thus, all the results will hold in the case of a prime ring with A.C.C.

By $(x|$ we shall mean the left ideal generated by the element x.

Lemma 37. *If $(x| \cap (y| = 0$, where x and y are non-zero elements of R, then x and y are both right zero divisors, i.e. there exist non-zero elements a and b in R such that $ax = by = 0$.*

Proof. Define $I_n \equiv (xy| + \ldots + (xy^n|$. Then $I_1 \subseteq I_2 \subseteq \ldots \subseteq I_n \subseteq \ldots$, and by A.C.C. this chain of left ideals must terminate after a finite number of steps. Let n be the smallest integer such that $I_n = I_{n+1}$. Then

$$xy^{n+1} = x_1 y + \ldots + x_n y^n,$$

where all the x_i are in $(x|$. Either y is a right zero divisor or $xy \neq 0$ and in the latter case $xy^m \neq 0$ for every positive integer m. In particular, $xy^{n+1} \neq 0$, and then we have $(xy^n - x_1 - x_2 y - \ldots - x_n y^{n-1})y = 0$. Again either y is a right zero divisor or $x_1 = xy^n - x_2 y - \ldots - x_n y^{n-1}$. This element is in $(x|$ and in $(y|$ and therefore $x_1 = 0$ since $(x| \cap (y| = 0$. Therefore,

$$xy^n = x_2 y + x_3 y^2 + \ldots + x_n y^{n-1}$$

and thus $I_{n-1} = I_n$. This contradicts the minimality of n. Therefore y is a right zero divisor. Similarly, by defining $J_n \equiv (yx| + \ldots + (yx^n|$, we obtain the fact that x is a right zero divisor.

We now want to pick out a certain select class of left ideals of R and our first objective will be to establish that for these selected left ideals, R has the descending chain condition. This is an interesting idea with which to overcome the difficulty that R does not have D.C.C. on *all* left ideals. However, if we select just 0 and R itself, then for these two left ideals R has D.C.C. But this leads to little. The idea involved here is much more subtle than just getting around the absence of D.C.C. We shall show that R has a left quotient ring Q and that there is a one-to-one correspondence between the left ideals of Q and the selected left ideals of R preserving order by inclusion. In this way we shall show that R has a left quotient ring Q with D.C.C. on left ideals. Then it will be fairly easy to show that Q is a semi-simple ring. This is an ambitious programme and at first sight seems quite hopeless, or perhaps fantastic is a better adjective. But it works!*

We shall say that a left ideal X of R is *closed* if for every element b not in X, there exists a non-zero element c in $(b|$ such that $X \cap (c| = 0$.

We note that both 0 and R are closed left ideals.

Lemma 38. *If $\{X_\alpha\}$ is a class of closed left ideals of R, then $I = \cap X_\alpha$ is a closed left ideal.*

Proof. Take any element b not in I. Then there must exist some X_α such that b is not in X_α. Since X_α is closed, there exists a non-zero element $c \in (b|$ such that $X_\alpha \cap (c| = 0$. Then $I \cap (c| = 0$ and therefore I is closed. It is clear that I is a left ideal.

For any set $S \subseteq R$, we shall denote by S_l the set of left annihilators of S, i.e. $S_l = \{x \text{ in } R: xS = 0\}$. We remark that $S_l = \cap s_l$, where the intersection on the right ranges over all elements s in S. It is clear that for any set S, S_l is a left ideal. We shall show that for any set S, S_l is a closed left ideal, but first we must prove the following important result.

Lemma. 39. *For every non-zero element x of R, there exists a non-zero left ideal C such that $C \cap x_l = 0$.*

Proof. By A.C.C. select an element $z \neq 0$ in R such that $x_l \subseteq z_l$ and z_l is maximal of this type. Consider zRx. If $zRx = 0$, then $zR \subseteq x_l \subseteq z_l$. Therefore $zRz = 0$ and $z = 0$. Thus $zRx \neq 0$. Take an element r in R such that $zrx \neq 0$. Then $z_l \subseteq (zrx)_l$. Since z_l is maximal and since $zrx \neq 0$, we have $z_l = (zrx)_l$. Thus, if $wzrx = 0$, we can conclude that $wz = 0$. Take an element v in R such that $vzr \neq 0$ (this is possible since $Rzr \neq 0$) and let $C = (vzr| \neq 0$. Then $C \cap x_l = 0$, for if c is in C, $c = v'zr$, where v' is in $(v|$, and if at the same time $v'zrx = 0$, then $v'z = 0$ and thus $c = 0$.

Lemma 40. *For every set S, S_l is a closed left ideal.*

Proof. It is sufficient to show that s_l is a closed left ideal for every $s \in S$, for then, since $S_l = \cap s_l$, Lemma 38 tells us that S_l is closed. Consider, then, an arbitrary $s \in S$, and the left ideal s_l. Take b not in s_l. Then $bs \neq 0$. Then there exists a non-zero left ideal C such that $C \cap (bs)_l = 0$, by Lemma 39. Take a

---

* During the winter of 1957–58, as a joke, we carried a small bag of coals to Professor Goldie, at Newcastle. Perhaps this helped fire his mind. . . .

non-zero element c in C. Then $cbs \neq 0$. Consider the element cb. It is in $(b|$. We next show that $(cb| \cap s_l = 0$. If x is in $(cb|$ and in s_l, then $x = c'b$, where $c' \in (c| \subseteq C$ and $c'bs = 0$. Then c' is in $(bs)_l$ and in C and therefore $c' = 0$, $x = 0$. Thus $(cb| \cap s_l = 0$. What we have shown, then, is that for every element b not in s_l, there exists a non-zero element cb in $(b|$ such that $(cb| \cap s_l = 0$. This is precisely the definition of closure for s_l, and this proves the lemma.

If we are given a left ideal X, it may not be closed but it is contained in some closed left ideals, for example $X \subseteq R$. We can say more, for there exists a unique smallest closed left ideal which contains X. Define $\bar{X}$ to be the inter-section of all the closed left ideals that contain X. By Lemma 38, $\bar{X}$ is a closed left ideal. It certainly contains X and is contained in every closed left ideal which contains X. Thus $\bar{X}$, called the closure of X, is the unique smallest closed left ideal which contains X. We would like an element-wise character-ization of $\bar{X}$.*

Lemma 41. $\bar{X} = \{a \text{ in } R: \text{ for every } a' \in (a|, a' \neq 0, \text{ we have } X \cap (a'| \neq 0\}$.

Proof. Let $V = \{a \in R: \text{ for every } a' \in (a|, a' \neq 0, \text{ we have } X \cap (a'| \neq 0\} \cdot$ Then we shall show that V is a closed left ideal, and that it contains X and is contained in every closed left ideal that contains X. Then $V = \bar{X}$.

It is clear that $X \subseteq V$. Also, if $a \in V$, then $(r + i)a$, where $r \in R$ and i is an integer, is also in V since for every $b \in ((r + i)a| \subseteq (a|, b \neq 0$, we have $X \cap (b| \neq 0$. In particular, then, $RV \subseteq V$. Furthermore, V satisfies the closure property, for if d is not in V, consider $(d|$. Then there exists a non-zero element c in $(d|$ such that $X \cap (c| = 0$, for otherwise d would be in V. Then $V \cap (c| = 0$, for otherwise if $w \neq 0$ is in $V \cap (c|$, then $(w| \cap X \neq 0$. But $(w| \subseteq (c|$ and thus $(w| \cap X \subseteq (c| \cap X = 0$, a contradiction. Therefore, V is closed. Suppose now that F is a closed left ideal, and $X \subseteq F$. Take g not in F. Then there exists a non-zero element $h \in (g|$ such that $(h| \cap F = 0$. Then $(h| \cap X = 0$. Then the element g is not in V. Thus $V \subseteq F$. The only thing left to prove is that V is closed under subtraction. Take x, y in V and let $z = x - y \neq 0$. It is clear that 0 is in V and thus we need only consider the case $z \neq 0$.

To show that z is in V we must show that for every $z' \neq 0$ in $(z|$, we have $X \cap (z'| \neq 0$. We have $z' = x' - y'$, where $x' \in (x|$ and $y' \in (y|$. By Lemma 39, there exists a non-zero left ideal C such that $C \cap z'_l = 0$. Take a non-zero c in C. Then

$$cz' = cx' - cy' \neq 0.$$

Then either $cx' \neq 0$ or $cy' \neq 0$. Suppose that $cx' \neq 0$. Since x is in V, there exists a non-zero element x'' in $(cx'| \cap X$, because $x' = (r + i)x$ is also in V. Then $x'' = c'x'$ with $c' \in (c| \subseteq C$. Now if $c'y' = 0$, then

---

* Mr. R. G. Biggs has pointed out that $\bar{X}$ is the largest left ideal $\supseteq X$ with the property that if I is a left ideal and $X \cap I = 0$, then $\bar{X} \cap I = 0$.

$$c'(x' - y') = c'x' \neq 0$$

and is in X, and therefore $(z' | \cap X \neq 0$. On the other hand, if $c'y' \neq 0$, we observe that $y' = (r_1 + i_1)y$ is in V and therefore $(c'y' | \cap X \neq 0$. Take a non-zero element $c''y'$ in $(c'y' |$ and in X, where $c'' \in (c' | \subseteq C$. Then

$$c''z' = c\,(x' - y')$$

is non-zero, for if $c''(x' - y') = 0$, then c'' is in $z'_1 \cap C = 0$. Then $c'' = 0$, a contradiction. Furthermore, $c''x' - c''y'$ is in X because $c''x'$ is in $(c'x' | \subseteq X$ and $c''y'$ is also in X. Thus, again we have found a non-zero element in $X \cap (z' |$. This proves that V is closed under subtraction, and thus V is the minimal closed left ideal which contains X. Thus $V = \bar{X}$ and the lemma is proved.

Remark. It is clear that for any left ideal X, we have $\bar{\bar{X}} = \bar{X}$. Also, if $X \cap Y = 0$, where X and Y are left ideals and Y happens to be contained in $\bar{X}$, then $Y = 0$. For if $y \neq 0$ is in $\bar{X}$, then $X \cap (y | \neq 0$.

To obtain some feeling for the notion of closure, let us take a rather elementary example, namely two by two matrices with integers as entries. Let X be the left ideal which is the set of all matrices of the form $\begin{pmatrix} 0 & Kx \\ 0 & Ky \end{pmatrix}$, where K is some fixed non-zero integer $\neq \pm 1$. To see that X is not a closed left ideal consider $b = \begin{pmatrix} 0 & 1 \\ 0 & 0 \end{pmatrix}$. Clearly $b \notin X$. Now $(b |$ contains elements of the form

$$\begin{pmatrix} r & s \\ t & u \end{pmatrix} \begin{pmatrix} 0 & 1 \\ 0 & 0 \end{pmatrix} = \begin{pmatrix} 0 & r \\ 0 & t \end{pmatrix}.$$

Let c be any non-zero matrix of this type, say $c = \begin{pmatrix} 0 & r \\ 0 & t \end{pmatrix}$. Then $(c |$ contains

$$\begin{pmatrix} K & 0 \\ 0 & K \end{pmatrix} \begin{pmatrix} 0 & r \\ 0 & t \end{pmatrix} = \begin{pmatrix} 0 & Kr \\ 0 & Kt \end{pmatrix}$$

and this non-zero element also belongs to X. Thus $X \cap (c | \neq 0$ and therefore X is not closed.

Now what does the closure of X, $\bar{X}$, look like? It is the set of all matrices of the form $\begin{pmatrix} 0 & x \\ 0 & y \end{pmatrix}$, where x and y are arbitrary integers. To see that this $\bar{X}$ is closed, take $b \notin \bar{X}$. Say $b = \begin{pmatrix} r & x \\ s & y \end{pmatrix}$ with $r^2 + s^2 \neq 0$. Then take c in $(b |$ with

$$c = \begin{pmatrix} r & s \\ 0 & 0 \end{pmatrix} \begin{pmatrix} r & x \\ s & y \end{pmatrix} = \begin{pmatrix} r^2 + s^2 & rx + sy \\ 0 & 0 \end{pmatrix}.$$

Now $(c |$ consists of elements of the form

$$\begin{pmatrix} e & f \\ g & h \end{pmatrix} \begin{pmatrix} r^2 + s^2 & rx + sy \\ 0 & 0 \end{pmatrix} = \begin{pmatrix} e(r^2 + s^2) & e(rx + sy) \\ g(r^2 + s^2) & g(rx + sy) \end{pmatrix}.$$

If one of these also lies in $\bar{X}$, then $e(r^2 + s^2)$ and $g(r^2 + s^2)$ must both be 0. Since $r^2 + s^2 \neq 0$, we have $e = g = 0$. Then the only element of $(c|$ that lies in $\bar{X}$ is $\begin{pmatrix} 0 & 0 \\ 0 & 0 \end{pmatrix}$ and thus $(c| \cap \bar{X} = 0$. This proves that $\bar{X}$ is closed.

Summarizing this another way, in two by two matrices, a left ideal may be a matrix left ideal, so to speak, with entries from an ideal of the integers. Its closure extends the entries from the ideal of the integers to all the integers, but leaves the matrix structure alone.*

We now want to concentrate on the class of closed left ideals of R. If X and Y are closed left ideals, then $X \cap Y$ is also a closed left ideal (Lemma 38) but $X + Y$ may not be closed. We then become interested in $\overline{X + Y}$, and if we wanted to put a lattice view on our discussion, we could define $X \cup Y$ to be $\overline{X + Y}$. The next lemma, from a lattice point of view, is the condition for *modularity*.

Lemma 42. *If A, B, C are closed left ideals of R and $B \subseteq A$, then*

$$A \cap \overline{(B + C)} = \overline{B + (A \cap C)}.$$

Proof. Since $B \subseteq A$, it is obvious that $\overline{B + A \cap C} \subseteq A$. Also

$$\overline{B + (A \cap C)} \subseteq \overline{B + C}$$

and therefore $\overline{B + (A \cap C)} \subseteq A \cap \overline{(B + C)}.$

Conversely, take any element x which is in both A and $\overline{B + C}$. By Lemma 41 we know that for every $x' \neq 0$ in $(x|$, we have $(B + C) \cap (x'| \neq 0$. Take a non-zero element x'' in this intersection. Then $x'' = b + c$, with b in B, c in C, and x'' in $(x'|$. Now $c = x'' - b$ is in A because $b \in B \subseteq A$ and $x'' \in (x'| \subseteq (x| \subseteq A$. Thus, c is in $A \cap C$. Then x'' is in $B + (A \cap C)$. Thus,

$$(x'| \cap [B + (A \cap C)] \neq 0,$$

and this holds for every non-zero x' in $(x|$. We can then conclude, by Lemma 41, that x is in $\overline{B + (A \cap C)}$. Therefore

$$A \cap \overline{(B + C)} \subseteq \overline{B + (A \cap C)}$$

and the lemma is established.

Lemma 43. *If $X \cap Y = 0$, for ordinary left ideals X and Y, then $\bar{X} \cap Y = 0$. Then if C is a closed left ideal, $C \neq R$, there exists a non-zero closed left ideal C' such that $C \cap C' = 0$.*

* This example was communicated to me by Professor D. Murdoch.

Proof. Suppose that $X \cap Y = 0$, but $\bar{X} \cap Y \neq 0$. Take a non-zero element y in $\bar{X} \cap Y \neq 0$. Since y is in $\bar{X}$, $(y| \cap X \neq 0$ by Lemma 41. Then $Y \cap X \neq 0$, a contradiction. Thus, if $X \cap Y = 0$, $\bar{X} \cap Y = 0$.

For the second part, take $x \neq 0$, x not in C. Since C is closed, there exists a non-zero element x' in $(x|$ such that $(x'| \cap C = 0$. Then $(\overline{x'|} \cap C = 0$ by the first part of this lemma. Setting $C' = (\overline{x'|}$, we have $C \cap C' = 0$.

Theorem 23. *R has D.C.C. for closed left ideals.*

Proof. We first show that for every closed left ideal X, there exists a closed left ideal X' such that $X \cap X' = 0$, $\overline{X + X'} = R$. We may call X' the complement of X. To see this, consider all closed left ideals which meet X in 0 and let X' be a maximal such closed left ideal (by A.C.C.). Then, of course, $X \cap X' = 0$. Now suppose that $\overline{X + X'} \neq R$. Then, by Lemma 43, there exists a non-zero closed left ideal Y such that $\overline{X + X'} \cap Y = 0$. By Lemma 42,

$$(\overline{X + X'}) \cap (\overline{X' + Y}) = \overline{X' + ([X + X'] \cap Y)}.$$

The right-hand side is X'. Now $X \cap (\overline{X' + Y})$ is certainly in X, but it is also in $(\overline{X + X'}) \cap (\overline{X' + Y})$, which is X'. Since $X \cap X' = 0$, we can conclude that $X \cap (\overline{X' + Y}) = 0$. Now $\overline{X' + Y} \supseteq X'$ and equality cannot hold since Y is not in X'. This contradicts the maximality of X' with respect to meeting X only in zero. Thus $\overline{X + X'} = R$. From the lattice point of view we may now say that the lattice of closed left ideals is complemented. Note that the complement of a given closed left ideal X is not necessarily unique. In fact, any closed left ideal which is maximal with respect to meeting X in zero is a complement of X.

Now consider any descending chain $B_1 \supseteq B_2 \supseteq B_3 \supseteq \ldots$ of closed left ideals. Let C_1 be any complement of B_1, that is, C_1 is a closed left ideal such that $B_1 \cap C_1 = 0$, $\overline{B_1 + C_1} = R$. Take C_2, a closed left ideal containing C_1, maximal with respect to meeting B_2 in 0. Then C_2 is a complement of B_2. In this way we obtain an ascending chain $C_1 \subseteq C_2 \subseteq C_3 \subseteq \ldots$ of closed left ideals: we take C_{i+1} containing C_i and maximal with respect to meeting B_{i+1} in 0. If $B_i \supset B_{i+1}$, then we shall show that $C_i \subset C_{i+1}$. We know that $B_i \cap C_i = 0$, $\overline{B_i + C_i} = R$, $B_{i+1} \cap C_{i+1} = 0$, $\overline{B_{i+1} + C_{i+1}} = R$. Clearly, $B_{i+1} \cap C_i = 0$, but if $\overline{B_{i+1} + C_i} = R$, then, by Lemma 42,

$$B_i \cap (\overline{B_{i+1} + C_i}) = \overline{B_{i+1} + (B_i \cap C_i)}.$$

The left-hand side is B_i, while the right-hand side is B_{i+1}. This contradiction proves that $\overline{B_{i+1} + C_i} \neq R$ and therefore $C_i \neq C_{i+1}$. Another way of saying this is that if $C_i = C_{i+1}$, then $B_i = B_{i+1}$. Now by A.C.C. the chain of C_i's must terminate, and therefore the chain of B_i's must terminate. Therefore, R has D.C.C. for closed left ideals.

Another interesting result, though not absolutely necessary for our structure theorems, is the following theorem.

Theorem 24. *The length of any unrefinable chain of closed left ideals joining two fixed closed left ideals is constant.*

Proof. Consider fixed closed left ideals X, Y with $X \subset Y$. By D.C.C. pick a closed left ideal B_1 with $X \subset B_1 \subset Y$ such that there are no closed left ideals between X and B_1. Then select B_2 such that $X \subset B_1 \subset B_2 \subset Y$ and such that there are no closed left ideals between B_1 and B_2. We continue this until, by A.C.C., we arrive at $X \subset B_1 \subset B_2 \subset \ldots \subset B_m \subset Y$, a chain of closed left ideals which cannot be refined and which has no redundancies. This establishes the existence of such a chain and what we must prove is that any other unrefinable and irredundant chain $X \subset C_1 \subset C_2 \subset \ldots \subset C_n \subset Y$ of closed left ideals joining X and Y has the same length, that is, $n = m$.

We prove this by induction on m. First we take $m = 1$. This means that $X \subset B_1 \subset Y$, with no closed left ideals between X and B_1 or between B_1 and Y. Then, if we have $X \subset C_1 \subset C_2 \subset Y$, consider $B_1 \cap C_2$. This contains X and is contained in B_1 and thus, being closed, it must be equal either to X or to B_1. If $B_1 \cap C_2 = B_1$, then $B_1 \subseteq C_2$, but then C_1 cannot exist. Thus $B_1 \cap C_2 = X$. Next consider $\overline{B_1 + C_2}$. This is between B_1 and Y and therefore must equal B_1 or Y. If it equals B_1, then $C_2 \subseteq B_1$ and *again* C_1 cannot exist. Therefore, $\overline{B_1 + C_2} = Y$. Similarly, $B_1 \cap C_1 = X$ and $\overline{B_1 + C_1} = Y$, for $X \subseteq B_1 \cap C_1 \subseteq B_1 \cap C_2 = X$ and if $\overline{B_1 + C_1} = B_1$, then $C_1 \subseteq B_1$. Then $C_1 = B_1$ and C_2 cannot exist. Therefore, $\overline{B_1 + C_1} = Y$. Now we apply Lemma 42 and obtain

$$C_2 \cap \overline{(C_1 + B_1)} = \overline{C_1 + (C_2 \cap B_1)}.$$

The left-hand side is C_2, while the right-hand side is C_1, a contradiction. Therefore, if $X \subset B_1 \subset Y$, unrefinable, there can be only one C_i between X and Y. Thus, the theorem is true for $m = 1$.

Now assume that the theorem is true for $m - 1$. That is, if there is an unrefinable irredundant chain of closed left ideals of length $m - 1$ joining any two closed left ideals, then any other unrefinable irredundant chain joining these same two closed left ideals also has length $m - 1$.

Then consider $X \subset B_1 \subset \ldots \subset B_m \subset Y$ and $X \subset C_1 \subset \ldots \subset C_n \subset Y$. Let $U = \overline{B_1 + C_1}$. The chain joining B_1 to Y via $B_2 \subset \ldots \subset B_m$ has length $m - 1$ and therefore any similar chain joining B_1 to Y has the same length. In particular, any unrefinable irredundant chain joining B_1 to U to Y must have length $m - 1$.

To continue, we must show that there are no closed left ideals between B_1 and U or between C_1 and U. Suppose then, that $B_1 \subset V \subset U$. Then $\overline{B_1 + C_1} = U$ and $B_1 \cap C_1 = X$ (if $B_1 \cap C_1 = B_1$, then $B_1 = C_1$, and in this case it is clear that any chain joining C_1 to Y must have length $m - 1$ and thus $n = m$).

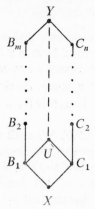

Also $\overline{V + C_1} = U$ and also $V \cap C_1 = X$, for if $V \cap C_1 = C_1$, then $C_1 \subseteq V$, in which case, since $B_1 \subseteq V$, $U = V$, a contradiction. Then, by Lemma 42,

$$V \cap \overline{(B_1 + C_1)} = B_1 + (V \cap C_1).$$

The left-hand side is V and the right-hand side is B_1, a contradiction. Therefore, no such V can exist. Similarly, there are no closed left ideals between C_1 and U.

Since the chain joining B_1 to U to Y has length $m - 1$, the chain joining U to Y has length $m - 2$. Therefore, this same chain gives us a chain from C_1 to U to Y of length $m - 1$. Thus, any chain between C_1 and Y has length $m - 1$ and, in particular, $C_1 \subset C_2 \subset \ldots \subset C_n \subset Y$ is of length $m - 1$ and $X \subset C_1 \subset C_2 \subset \ldots \subset C_n \subset Y$ is of length m. Therefore, $n = m$ and the induction is complete. Therefore, the theorem is established.

In particular, then, the length of any unrefinable irredundant chain of closed left ideals joining 0 to R is finite and fixed.

To obtain a quotient ring for R we must first show that R has some regular elements. To do this, we first study the relationship between the elements which are not left zero-divisors and the elements which are not right zero divisors. Let $G' = $ the set of all elements of R which are not left zero divisors, $D' = $ the set of all elements of R which are not right zero divisors, and $E = $ the set of all elements a of R such that $\overline{(a|} = R$. It is clear that E is also equal to $\{a \in R:$ for every non-zero $x \in R$, $(a| \cap (x| \neq 0\}$, for if $\overline{(a|} = R$, then $(a|$ must meet every non-zero left ideal in a non-zero intersection. If $(a| \cap (x| = 0$, then $\overline{(a|} \cap (x| = (x| = 0$. Conversely if $(a| \cap (x| \neq 0$ for every non-zero x, then $\overline{(a|} = R$, by Lemma 41.

The regular elements of R are those that belong to $D' \cap G'$, but we shall now show that $D' \subseteq G'$ and therefore $D' \cap G' = D' = $ the regular elements of R.

Theorem 25. $E = D' \subseteq G'$.

Proof. If $a \in D'$, a is not a right zero divisor and therefore, by Lemma 37, $(a| \cap (x| \neq 0$ for every non-zero x. Thus, $a \in E$ and $D' \subseteq E$.

If y is not in is G', then there exists a non-zero element z such that $yz = 0$. Therefore y is in z_l, and $\overline{(y|} \subseteq z_l$ since z_l is closed (Lemma 40). Since $z \neq 0$, $z_l \neq R$ since R is semi-prime. Therefore $\overline{(y|} \neq R$, and y is not in E. Therefore $E \subseteq G'$.

It remains to prove that $E \subseteq D'$. We shall assume that a is an element of E which is not in D' and show that this leads to a contradiction. Since a is not in D', it is a right zero divisor and therefore $a_l \neq 0$. We shall show that $0 \subset a_l \subset a_l^2 \subset \ldots$ is a chain of left ideals, which contradicts A.C.C. Proceeding by induction we assume that $a_l^n \subset a_l^{n+1}$. Then there exists an element x such that $xa^n \neq 0$, $xa^{n+1} = 0$. By Lemma 39, there exists a non-zero left ideal C such that $C \cap (xa^n)_l = 0$. Take any non-zero element c in C; then $cxa^n \neq 0$. Since a is in E, $(a| \cap (cx| \neq 0$. Take a non-zero element b in $(a| \cap (cx|$. Then $b = c'x$, where c' is in $(c| \subseteq C$. Now $c'xa^n \neq 0$, for if $c'xa^n = 0$, then c' is in C and in $(xa^n)_l$ and thus $c' = 0$, $b = 0$, a contradiction. Since R is semi-prime, $Rc'xa^n \neq 0$. Take any element v in R such that $vc'xa^n \neq 0$. The element $b = c'x$ is also in $(a|$ and therefore $vb = v'a = vc'x$. Now $v'a^{n+1} = v'aa^n = vc'xa^n \neq 0$. However, $v'a^{n+2} = vc'xa^{n+1} = 0$ since $xa^{n+1} = 0$. Thus $a_l^{n+1} \subset a_l^{n+2}$. This completes the induction, and we obtain a chain of left ideals $0 \subset a_l \subset \ldots \subset a_l^n \subset \ldots$, which contradicts A.C.C. Thus, no such element a can exist and $E \subseteq D'$, which proves the theorem.

We shall call a left ideal U *uniform* if $A \cap B \neq 0$ for any two non-zero left ideals A, B of R which are contained in U.

Lemma 44. *If U is uniform and $ux = 0$ for some non-zero u in U, then $Ux = 0$.*

Proof. If there exists an element u' in U such that $u'x \neq 0$, take a non-zero left ideal C such that $C \cap (u'x)_l = 0$ (Lemma 39). Take a non-zero $c \in C$. Then $cu'x \neq 0$. The element cu' is in U and therefore $(cu'| \cap (u| \neq 0$ since U is uniform. Take a non-zero element y in this intersection. Now y is in $(u|$ and therefore $yx = 0$. On the other hand, $y = c'u'$ with $c' \in (c| \subseteq C$. Then $c'u'x = 0$ and c' is therefore in $(u'x)_l$ as well as in C. Therefore, $c' = 0$ and $y = 0$, which is a contradiction. Thus, no such u' exists and $Ux = 0$.

Lemma 45. $\overline{Rx} = \overline{(x|}$.

Proof. Since $Rx \subseteq (x|$, $\overline{Rx} \subseteq \overline{(x|}$. To get the converse, take $u \in \overline{(x|}$. Then for every non-zero u' in $(u|$, we have $(u'| \cap (x| \neq 0$ (Lemma 41). Take a non-zero element y in this intersection. Now, $Ry \neq 0$ since R is semi-prime. Take v in R such that $vy \neq 0$. Then vy is in $(u'|$ and in Rx. The whole difficulty here is that R may not have a unity element and thus, although y is in $(x|$, $y =$

$(r + i)x$, r in R, i an integer, y may not be in Rx, if $i \neq 0$. However, $vy = v(r + i)x = v'x$ and this *is* in Rx. Thus we have established that for every u in $\overline{(x|}$ there is a non-zero element in $Rx \cap (u' |$for every non-zero u' in $(u|$. Thus u is in $\overline{Rx}$ by Lemma 41. Thus $\overline{(x|} \subseteq \overline{Rx}$, $\overline{(x|} = \overline{Rx}$.

By $(X:a)$ we shall mean the set of all elements y of R such that ya is in X. This is a more general concept than a_l; in fact $a_l = (0:a)$. It is clear that if X is a left ideal, then $(X:a)$ is also a left ideal. We know that $(0:a) = a_l$ is a closed left ideal, but it is not immediately clear when $(X:a)$ is closed.

Lemma 46. *If X is a closed left ideal, then for every a in R, $(X:a)$ is a closed left ideal. If a is in X, then $(X:a) = R$, and if a is not in X, then $(X:a) \neq R$.*

Proof. Take z not in $(X:a)$. Then za is not in X. Since X is closed, there must exist a non-zero element $z'a$ in $(za|$ such that $X \cap (z'a| = 0$. The element z' is in $(z|$. By Lemma 39, take a non-zero left ideal C such that $C \cap (z'a)_l = 0$. Take a non-zero c in C. Then $cz'a \neq 0$.

Consider $(X:a) \cap (cz'|$. Take any y in this intersection. Then $y = c'z'$ with c' in $(c| \subseteq C$, and ya is in X. Then $c'z'a$ is in X. But $c'z'a$ is also in $(z'a|$ and therefore $c'z'a = 0$. Then c' is in $(z'a)_l$ and in C and thus $c' = 0$, $y = 0$. Therefore, $(X:a) \cap (cz'| = 0$.

We then have, for any z not in $(X:a)$, a non-zero element cz' in $(z|$ such that $(X:a) \cap (cz'| = 0$. Thus, by definition, $(X:a)$ is closed.

For the second part, if a is in X, then clearly $Ra \subseteq X$ and thus $R = (X:a)$. On the other hand, if a is not in X, then Ra cannot be in X, for if $Ra \subseteq X$, then $\overline{Ra} = \overline{(a|}$ (Lemma 45) $\subseteq X$. Then a is in X, a contradiction. Therefore $(X:a) \neq R$.

Lemma 47. *If X is a uniform left ideal, then $\overline{X}$ is a uniform left ideal.*

Proof. Take any two left ideals A, B, non-zero and contained in $\overline{X}$. Take a in A, b in B, both non-zero. By Lemma 41, since a is in $\overline{X}$, $(a| \cap X \neq 0$ and, similarly, $(b| \cap X \neq 0$. Take non-zero elements a', b' with a' in $(a| \cap X$, b' in $(b| \cap X$. Then both a' and b' are non-zero and in X, and thus $(a'| \cap (b'| \neq 0$ since X is uniform. Then $(a| \cap (b| \supseteq (a'| \cap (b'| \neq 0$ and thus $A \cap B \supseteq (a| \cap (b| \neq 0$ and $\overline{X}$ is uniform.

We shall say that a non-zero left ideal B is *basic* if it is uniform and no other uniform left ideal properly contains B. We could say that B is basic if it is a maximal uniform left ideal, but when the word maximal is used it usually means $\neq R$ and here it is slightly more convenient to allow B to be equal to R if R is itself uniform. Thus, B is basic if it is equal to R if R is uniform, and otherwise it is a maximal uniform left ideal.

G

Theorem 26. *Minimal closed left ideals coincide with basic left ideals.*

Proof. Let X be any minimal closed left ideal. That is, $0 \subset X$ and there are no closed left ideals between 0 and X. To see that X is uniform, take non-zero elements a, b respectively in A, B, left ideals contained in X. Then $\overline{(a|} = X$ and b is in $\overline{(a|}$. Therefore, $(b| \cap (a| \neq 0$, for if $(b| \cap (a| = 0$, then $(b| \cap \overline{(a|} = 0$ and the non-zero element b is in $(b| \cap \overline{(a|}$. Thus, $A \cap B \supseteq (a| \cap (b| \neq 0$ and X is uniform. If U is any uniform left ideal, $X \subset U$, take z in U, z not in X. Then, since X is closed, there exists a non-zero element z' in $(z|$ such that $(z'| \cap X = 0$. This contradicts the uniformity of U, and thus no such U exists. Therefore, X is basic. Note that this proves that a uniform left ideal cannot properly contain a closed left ideal.

Conversely, if X is basic, then $\bar{X}$ is uniform by Lemma 47. Since $X \subseteq \bar{X}$ and X is basic, we must have $X = \bar{X}$ and therefore X is closed. Since X is uniform, it cannot properly contain a closed left ideal and thus X is a minimal closed left ideal. This proves the theorem.

Corollary. *If X is basic, then for every r in R, either $Xr = 0$ or $\overline{Xr}$ is basic.*

Proof. If $Xr \neq 0$, then $xr \neq 0$ for every non-zero x in X by Lemma 44. Take x_1, x_2, non-zero elements of X. Then $x_1 r \neq 0 \neq x_2 r$. Since X is uniform, $(x_1| \cap (x_2| \neq 0$. Take a non-zero element y in this intersection. Then $yr \neq 0$ and yr is in $(x_1 r| \cap (x_2 r|$. Thus, for any two elements $x_1 r$, $x_2 r$, non-zero, in Xr, we have $(x_1 r| \cap (x_2 r| \neq 0$ and therefore Xr is uniform. By Lemma 47, $\overline{Xr}$ is uniform. It is certainly closed and thus is maximal uniform, by the comment in the proof of Theorem 26. Thus $\overline{Xr}$ is basic.

We are now ready to show that R has some regular elements (i.e. $D' \neq 0$).

Lemma 48. *If X is a left ideal, then all elements of X are right zero divisors if and only if there exists a non-zero left ideal Y such that $X \cap Y = 0$.*

Proof. If $X \cap Y = 0$, then for every x in X and any non-zero y in Y we have $(x| \cap (y| = 0$. Then, by Lemma 37, x is a right zero divisor and thus all elements of X are right zero divisors.

Conversely, suppose that for any non-zero left ideal Y, $X \cap Y \neq 0$. We shall then construct an element in X which is not a right zero divisor and this will prove the lemma.

Let U_1 be any minimal closed left ideal—these exist by D.C.C. (Theorem 23). Then U_1 is basic (Theorem 26) and, in particular, is uniform. There exists an element x_1 in U_1 such that $x_{1,} \cap U_1 = 0$. To see this, suppose that y is in U_1 and $y_l \cap U_1 \neq 0$. Then $uy = 0$ for some $u \neq 0$ in U_1. Then $U_1 y = 0$, by Lemma 44. If this is true for every y in U_1, then we have $U_1 U_1 = 0$, and this is impossible since R is semi-prime.

Let U_2 be a minimal closed left ideal in x_{1_I} (by D.C.C.) and take an element x_2 in U_2 such that $x_{2_I} \cap U_2 = 0$. Then consider the closed left ideal $x_{1_I} \cap x_{2_I}$ and take U_3 to be a minimal closed left ideal in $x_{1_I} \cap x_{2_I}$. In general, take U_i to be a minimal closed left ideal in $x_{1_I} \cap x_{2_I} \cap \ldots \cap x_{i-1_I}$, and take x_i in U_i such that $x_{i_I} \cap U_i = 0$. Continue this process until a stage is reached where $x_{1_I} \cap x_{2_I} \cap \ldots \cap x_{n_I} = 0$. (Note that x_{i_I} is a closed left ideal, for any i, by Lemma 40).

To see that this must happen after a finite number of steps, we first observe that for any i, if $x_{1_I} \cap x_{2_I} \cap \ldots \cap x_{i_I} \neq 0$, then

$$x_{1_I} \cap x_{2_I} \cap \ldots \cap x_{i_I} \cap [U_1 + U_2 + \ldots + U_i] = 0.$$

For if $y = u_1 + \ldots + u_i$, with u_j in U_j, and $yx_j = 0$ for $j = 1, 2, \ldots, i$, then consider $yx_1 = u_1 x_1 + \ldots + u_i x_1 = 0$. Since u_j is in $U_j \subseteq x_{1_I} \cap \ldots \cap x_{j-1_I}$, $u_j x_k = 0$ for every $k < j$. Thus $u_j x_1 = 0$ for $j = 2, 3, \ldots, i$. Then $0 = yx_1 = u_1 x_1$. Then u_1 is in $x_{1_I} \cap U_1 = 0$. Similarly, we show that $u_2 = 0, u_3 = 0$, and, in general, from $yx_j = 0$ we obtain $u_j x_j = 0$, $u_j \in x_{j_I} \cap U_j = 0$. Thus $y = 0$, and therefore

$$x_{1_I} \cap x_{2_I} \cap \ldots \cap x_{i_I} \cap [U_1 + \ldots + U_i] = 0.$$

Consider the ascending chain $U_1 \subseteq U_1 + U_2 \subseteq \ldots \subseteq U_1 + U_2 + \ldots + U_r$ of left ideals. By A.C.C. this must terminate after a finite number of steps, $U_1 + \ldots + U_n = U_1 + \ldots + U_n + U_{n+1}$. However, $U_{n+1} \cap [U_1 + \ldots + U_n] = 0$, since $U_{n+1} \subseteq x_{1_I} \cap \ldots \cap x_{n_I}$. In this case $U_{n+1} = 0$. This can only happen when $x_{1_I} \cap \ldots \cap x_{n_I} = 0$, for otherwise we would have a non-zero minimal closed left ideal, U_{n+1}, in this intersection. Thus, after a finite number of steps we obtain $x_{1_I} \cap \ldots \cap x_{n_I} = 0$. We may assume that n is the smallest integer for which this happens, i.e. $x_{1_I} \cap \ldots \cap x_{n-1_I} \neq 0$, and thus $U_i \neq 0$ for $i = 1, 2, \ldots, n$.

Define $V_i = X \cap U_i$, for $i = 1, 2, \ldots, n$. Since $U_i \neq 0$ and since X meets every non-zero left ideal, $V_i \neq 0$ for $i = 1, \ldots, n$.

If $x_i V_i = 0$, then $U_i V_i = 0$, since U_i is uniform. Then $V_i V_i = 0$, and this is impossible since R is semi-prime. Therefore, $x_i V_i \neq 0$ for every i. Select elements v_i in V_i such that $x_i v_i \neq 0$ for every i.

Now let $d = x_1 v_1 + x_2 v_2 + \ldots + x_n v_n$. Clearly d is in X, and $d \neq 0$. If $d = 0$, $x_n v_n$ is in $V_n \subseteq U_n$ and is also in $V_1 + \ldots + V_{n-1} \subseteq U_1 + \ldots + U_{n-1}$. Then $x_n v_n = 0$, a contradiction.

This element d is the one we have been looking for because it is not a right zero divisor. To see this, suppose that $zd = 0$. Then

$$zx_1 v_1 + zx_2 v_2 + \ldots + zx_n v_n = 0.$$

Then $zx_n v_n$ is in U_n and since it equals $-zx_1 v_1 - \ldots - zx_{n-1} v_{n-1}$, it is also in $U_1 + \ldots + U_{n-1}$. Since $U_n \cap [U_1 + \ldots + U_{n-1}] = 0$, we have $zx_n v_n = 0$. Then, working down one at a time, we obtain

$$0 = zx_n v_n = zx_{n-1} v_{n-1} = \ldots = zx_2 v_2 = zx_1 v_1.$$

If $zx_i \neq 0$, then from $zx_i . v_i = 0$ we conclude that $U_i v_i = 0$ since zx_i is in U_i and U_i is uniform (Lemma 44). However, x_i is in U_i and $x_i v_i \neq 0$. Therefore, $zx_i = 0$ for every i. Therefore z is in $x_{1_i} \cap x_{2_i} \cap \ldots \cap x_{n_i} = 0$. Thus $z = 0$, and d is not a right zero divisor. This finally proves the lemma.

Corollary. *R has at least one element in D', and thus R has some regular elements.*

Proof. Since $R \cap Y \neq 0$ for every non-zero left ideal Y, R has a non right zero divisor. Thus $D' \neq 0$. Since D' consists of the regular elements of R (Theorem 25), R has some regular elements.

Lemma 49. *X is a closed left ideal if and only if ab in X, a not a right zero divisor, implies b in X.*

Proof. If b is not in X, a closed left ideal, then $(X:b) \neq R$ by Lemma 46. If a is in D', then a is in E (Theorem 25). But a is in $(X:b)$ and $(X:b)$ is a closed left ideal (Lemma 46). Therefore $\overline{(a|} \subseteq (X:b) \neq R$. Thus, a is not in E, a contradiction. Therefore b is in X.

Conversely, assume that X is not closed. Take b in $\bar{X}$ but b not in X. Consider $(X:b)$. If $(X:b) = R$, then there exists a regular element y in $(X:b)$ by the corollary to Lemma 48. Then yb is in X, with y in D', and b is not in X. In this case, then, the converse is established. If, however, $(X:b) \neq R$, or rather if $(X:b)$ does not contain an element of D', then all its elements are right zero divisors and, by Lemma 48, there exists a non-zero left ideal Y such that $(X:b) \cap Y = 0$. Take $y \neq 0$ in Y. Then yb is not in X and, in particular, $yb \neq 0$. But $X \cap (yb| \neq 0$ since b is in $\bar{X}$ (Lemma 41). Take $y'b \neq 0$ in this intersection, y' in $(y|$. Then $y'b$ is in X and thus y' is in $(X:b)$. Then y' is in $(X:b) \cap Y = 0$. Thus $y'b = 0$, a contradiction. Thus, $(X:b)$ must contain an element of D' and, as above, we establish the converse and the lemma is proved.

Theorem 27. *For every regular element b of R (i.e. b in D') and every arbitrary element a of R, there exist elements a', b' with b' in D' such that $b'a = a'b$.*

Proof. First we prove that for every non-zero left ideal Y, we have $Y \cap ((b|:a) \neq 0$. If $Ya = 0$, then of course $Ya \subseteq (b|$ and therefore $Y \subseteq ((b|:a)$ and $Y = Y \cap ((b|:a) \neq 0$. On the other hand, if $Ya \neq 0$, then $(b| \cap Ya \neq 0$ since b is in $D' = E$ (Theorem 25). Take a non-zero element $t = ya$ in $(b|$, where y is in Y. Then y is in $((b|:a)$ and in Y and again $Y \cap ((b|:a) \neq 0$.

Therefore, by Lemma 48, $((b|:a)$ must contain an element b'' in D'. Then $b''a$ is in $(b|$ and thus $b''a = (r + i)b$, where r is in R and i is an integer. If $i = 0$ we are through, but if $i \neq 0$ and R has no unity element we merely left-multiply by any element p of D'. Then $pb''. a = p(r + i).b$. Let $b' = pb''$ and $a' = p(r + i)$. Since both b'' and p are in D', they are both regular and therefore their product b' is also regular.

Corollary. *R has a left quotient ring Q.*

Proof. This follows immediately from Theorems 22 and 27.

Lemma 50. *There is a one-to-one correspondence between the left ideals of Q and the closed left ideals of R, preserving order by inclusion, and thus Q has D.C.C. on left ideals.*

Proof. Let Y be any left ideal of Q. Consider $X = Y \cap R$. Clearly X is a left ideal of R. To see that X is closed we shall use Lemma 49. Thus, suppose that ab is in X, where both a, b are in R and a is in D'. We must show that b is in X. Now ab is in X, and thus in Y. Since a is in D', a^{-1} exists in Q. Then $a^{-1}.ab = b$ is in Y because Y is a left ideal of Q. Then b is in $Y \cap R = X$ and therefore X is a closed left ideal.

We shall then map the class of left ideals of Q into the class of closed left ideals of R by $Y \to X = Y \cap R$.

This is a one-to-one mapping, for if $Y_1 \cap R = Y_2 \cap R$, take any y_1 in $Y_1 \subseteq Q$. Then $y_1 = b^{-1}a$ for some a, b in R with b in D'. Then $a = b.b^{-1}a$ is in Y_1 and thus in $Y_1 \cap R$, in $Y_2 \cap R$, and therefore in Y_2. Thus, $Y_1 \subseteq Y_2$. Similarly, $Y_2 \subseteq Y_1$, $Y_2 = Y_1$, and the map is one-to-one. At this point we can conclude that Q has D.C.C. on left ideals, but we go on to show that the mapping is actually onto the class of closed left ideals of R.

Thus, let X be any closed left ideal of R and define $Y = \{b^{-1}x$ with b in D' and x in $X\}$. To show that Y is a left ideal of Q we first show that Y is closed under subtraction. Take $b_1^{-1}x_1$ and $b_2^{-1}x_2$ in Y. There exist elements c, d in R such that $cb_1 = db_2$, by Theorem 27, and they can be chosen so that both c and d are regular, since both b_1 and b_2 are regular (proof of Theorem 22). Then $b_1^{-1}c^{-1} = b_2^{-1}d^{-1}$ and thus $b_1^{-1} = b_2^{-1}d^{-1}c$, while $b_2^{-1} = b_2^{-1}d^{-1}d$. Therefore

$$b_1^{-1}x_1 - b_2^{-1}x_2 = b_2^{-1}d^{-1}cx_1 - b_2^{-1}d^{-1}dx_2 = b_2^{-1}d^{-1}(cx_1 - dx_2)$$

$$= (db_2)^{-1}(cx_1 - dx_2).$$

Now db_2 is in D' since both d and b_2 are in D', while $cx_1 - dx_2$ is in X since X is a left ideal of R, x_1, x_2 are in X and c, d are in R. Therefore, $b_1^{-1}x_1 - b_2^{-1}x_2$ is in Y and Y is closed under subtraction. Secondly, if $b^{-1}x$ is in Y and $f^{-1}g$ is any element of Q, where f, g are in R with f in D', then consider $f^{-1}g.b^{-1}x$.

There exist elements r, s in R such that $rg = sb$, with r in D', by Theorem 27. Then $gb^{-1} = r^{-1}s$ and therefore $f^{-1}gb^{-1}x = f^{-1}r^{-1}sx = (rf)^{-1}.sx$. Since both r and f are in D', rf is in D' and since x is in X, sx is in X. Therefore, $f^{-1}gb^{-1}x$ is in Y and Y is a left ideal of Q.

Finally, we must show that $X = Y \cap R$. First, take any element $b^{-1}x$ which is in R and in Y. Then $b.b^{-1}x = x$ is in X. Since X is a closed left ideal and since b is in D', we can conclude that $b^{-1}x$ must be in X by Lemma 49. Therefore $Y \cap R \subseteq X$. Conversely, take any x in X. Take any b in D'. Then $x = b^{-1}.bx$. Since bx is in X, $b^{-1}.bx = x$ is in Y. Therefore, $X \subseteq Y \cap R$ and $X = Y \cap R$. This proves that the mapping is onto and, in particular, the lemma is established.

Theorem 28. *Q is a semi-simple ring with D.C.C. on left ideals and thus Q is isomorphic to a finite direct sum of matrix rings over division rings.*

Proof. First we show that Q is semi-prime. If $qQq = 0$, with $q = b^{-1}a$, where a, b are in R, and b is in D', then $b^{-1}aQb^{-1}a = 0$. Since $Rb \subseteq Q$, we have $b^{-1}aRbb^{-1}a = 0$, and thus $aRa = 0$. Since R is semi-prime, $a = 0$. Therefore $q = 0$ and Q is semi-prime.

Therefore, Q has no non-zero nilpotent ideals. Since Q has D.C.C. on left ideals and thus Q is semi-simple with respect to the classical radical, Q is a finite direct sum of simple non-trivial rings (Theorem 10) and each of these simple components is a set of square matrices with elements in a division ring.

Summarizing the results of this section, we have:

Theorem 29. *Every semi-prime ring with A.C.C. on left ideals has a left quotient ring Q which is isomorphic to a finite direct sum of matrix rings over division rings.*

Combining this with Theorem 20, we have the following fundamental theorem.

Theorem 30. *If R is any ring with A.C.C. on left ideals, and B is its Baer lower radical, then R/B has a left quotient ring Q which is isomorphic to a finite direct sum of matrix rings over division rings.*

Since a prime ring is semi-prime, all of these theorems hold for prime rings with A.C.C. on left ideals. However, in that case we can prove more.

Theorem 31. *Every prime ring with A.C.C. on left ideals has a left quotient ring Q which is the set of $n \times n$ matrices over a division ring, for some finite n.*

Proof. From Theorem 28 it is clear that a prime ring R with A.C.C. on left ideals has a left quotient ring Q and Q is semi-simple with respect to the classical radical, and in particular Q is semi-prime. But here we can show that

Q is prime. Suppose that $q_1 Q q_2 = 0$, with $q_1 = b_1^{-1} a_1$, $q_2 = b_2^{-1} a_2$, where a_1, a_2, b_1, b_2 are in R and b_1, b_2 are in D'. Then $b_1^{-1} a_1 Q b_2^{-1} a_2 = 0$. Since $R b_2 \subseteq Q$, we have $b_1^{-1} a_1 R b_2 b_2^{-1} a_2 = 0$. Therefore, $a_1 R a_2 = 0$. Since R is prime, either $a_1 = 0$ or $a_2 = 0$. Therefore, either $q_1 = 0$ or $q_2 = 0$, and thus Q is prime.

Finally, we show that Q is simple. We know that Q is semi-simple with respect to the classical radical and therefore is a finite direct sum of simple non-trivial rings S_i. These simple components of Q are ideals whose products satisfy $S_i S_j = 0$ if $i \neq j$. Since Q is prime, two different ideals like this cannot exist. Thus, there can only be one simple ring in this direct sum and, consequently, Q itself must be a simple non-trivial ring with D.C.C. on left ideals. Then Theorem 11 tells us that Q is the set of $n \times n$ matrices with elements in a division ring.

Before Theorem 30 was known, Theorem 31 was used together with Theorem 20 to obtain:

Theorem 32. *If R is any ring with A.C.C. on left ideals, and B is its Baer lower radical, then R/B is isomorphic to a subdirect sum of prime rings A_i, each of which has a left quotient ring Q_i which is a matrix ring over a division ring.*

It is important for the student to compare Theorems 30 and 32. In Theorem 30, one is able to say that R/B has a well-known quotient ring. In Theorem 32, the quotient rings involved are even better known for they are simple rather than semi-simple, but they are quotient rings of components in a subdirect sum. Thus, we have exchanged the direct-sum part of Theorem 30 for a sub-direct sum (at a different place) in Theorem 32. Clearly Theorem 30 is better, sharper, and more useful than Theorem 32.

Nevertheless, Theorem 32 has an historical appeal, in connection with classical D.C.C. Theorems 10 and 11 (see the end of Section 2.8). Instead of D.C.C. we have the weaker A.C.C. Instead of the nil radical, we have the Baer lower radical; instead of a direct sum, we have a subdirect sum; and instead of the components being simple, the components have quotient rings that are simple. Everything fits together beautifully and it is almost presumptuous to expect any more. The difficulty, of course, is with the use of a subdirect sum. Let us use it if we have to, but if there is any finite possibility that is to be preferred.*

Theorem 30 is a highly successful generalization of Theorems 10 and 11. The only loss is the distance between R/B and its quotient ring and this is a very small price to pay for the switch from D.C.C. to A.C.C.

---

*In this connection the reader is referred to a recent paper by Lawrence Levy, "Unique subdirect sums of prime rings," *Trans. Am. Math. Soc.*, **106**, 64–76 (1963), in which the author attempts to improve Theorem 32.

Remark. Of course, one need not assume that R itself has A.C.C. but merely that R/B has A.C.C. In fact, the full A.C.C. condition can be weakened by assuming it not for all left ideals but only for certain special left ideals. Those who insist on the very sharpest results are referred to Goldie's papers [24, 25].

In fact, the converse of Theorem 29 is false as it stands, primarily because it assumes A.C.C. on *all* left ideals. If this is weakened to A.C.C. on left annihilator ideals only and on direct sums of left ideals, then the theorem becomes an "if and only if" theorem.

Remark. In this situation we do not have A.C.C. on right ideals when we have A.C.C. on left ideals, even when the ring is semi-prime (see Example 9). Thus, the analogy with the D.C.C. case for semi-simple rings breaks down. Therefore, a semi-prime ring R with A.C.C. on left ideals having a left quotient ring may not have a right quotient ring. Of course, if we assume that the ring also has A.C.C. on right ideals, then everything goes through on the right and then the ring will have a right quotient ring.

CHAPTER FOUR

THE JACOBSON RADICAL

4.1. Quasi-regularity. Radical properties based on the notion of nilpotence do not seem to yield fruitful results for rings without chain conditions. It was not until Perlis [43] introduced the notion of quasi-regularity and Jacobson [30] used it, in 1945, that significant "chainless" results were obtained.

Let R be a ring, with no assumptions about D.C.C. or A.C.C. We shall say that an element x of R is *right quasi-regular* if there exists an element y in R such that $x + y + xy = 0$.

This generalizes the idea of a nilpotent element, for if x is nilpotent, with $x^n = 0$, let $y = -x + x^2 - x^3 + \ldots \pm x^{n-1}$. Then

$$x + y + xy = x - x + x^2 - x^3 \ldots \pm x^{n-1} - x^2 + x^3 - \ldots$$

$$\mp x^{n-1} \pm x^n = \pm x^n = 0.$$

Thus, every nilpotent element is right quasi-regular. However, we shall soon see that there are many right quasi-regular elements that are not nilpotent.

Another way of looking at right quasi-regularity is to consider a ring with unity element 1. If $1 + x$ has a right inverse, express this right inverse in the form $1 + y$. Then $(1 + x)(1 + y) = 1$, and this is precisely $x + y + xy = 0$. In a ring without a unity element we may, of course, still consider this condition $x + y + xy = 0$. The left-hand side of this, $x + y + xy$, is often abbreviated as $x \circ y$. The element y, in the case when $x \circ y = 0$, is referred to as a right quasi-inverse for x.

Still another point of view is the one associated with right ideals. For any element x, consider $\{r + xr\}$, the set of all elements $r + xr$ as r varies over the ring R. This $\{r + xr\}$ is clearly a right ideal of R. It turns out that x is right quasi-regular if and only if $\{r + xr\} = R$. To see this, suppose that $\{r + xr\} = R$. Then $x = r + xr$ for some r in R and thus $x + (-r) + x(-r) = 0$. Conversely, if x is right quasi-regular, then $x + y + xy = 0$ for some y. Then $x = -y + x(-y)$ is in $\{r + xr\}$. Then xr is in $\{r + xr\}$ and therefore r is in $\{r + xr\}$ for every r. Therefore $\{r + xr\} = R$.

Problems. 1. Prove that:

  (i) $(x \circ y) \circ z = x \circ (y \circ z)$;

  (ii) $x \circ (a + b) = x \circ a + x \circ b - x$;

  (iii) $x \circ 0 = 0 \circ x = x$;

  (iv) $0 = x \circ y = z \circ x \rightarrow y = z$.

2. Prove that if $x \circ y = 0$ and y is unique as a right quasi-inverse for x, then $y \circ x = 0$.

3. [Kaplansky] If every element in a ring R except one is right quasi-regular, then R is a division ring.

We want to establish that right quasi-regularity is a radical property. We shall say that a ring is *right quasi-regular* if every element in it is right quasi-regular. If I is a right ideal (or a left ideal or a two-sided ideal) of a ring R (R is a general ring, not necessarily right quasi-regular), and if every element in I is right quasi-regular, then we shall call I a *right quasi-regular right ideal* (or a right quasi-regular left ideal or a right quasi-regular two-sided ideal in the case when I is a left or two-sided ideal).

A right ideal's right quasi-regularity is in some sense independent of the ring which contains it, for if x is in the right ideal I, and $x + y + xy = 0$, then $y = -x - xy$ is also in I.

The first step in establishing right quasi-regularity as a radical property is to show that every ring has a maximal right quasi-regular two-sided ideal. To do this we begin with:

Lemma 51. *If x is right quasi-regular and if y belongs to a right quasi-regular right ideal I, then $x + y$ is right quasi-regular.*

Proof. Since x is right quasi-regular, we have $x + x' + xx' = 0$ for some x'. Then consider the element $y + yx'$. It is in I and thus is right quasi-regular. Let z be its right quasi-inverse: $y + yx' + z + (y + yx')z = 0$. Now we can show that $x' + z + x'z$ is a right quasi-inverse for $x + y$:

$$x + y + (x' + z + x'z) + (x + y)(x' + z + x'z)$$

$$= x + x' + xx' + y + yx' + z + yz + yx'z + x'z + xz + xx'z$$

$$= 0 + 0 + (x + x' + xx')\, z$$

$$= 0.$$

Corollary. *The union of two right quasi-regular right ideals is a right quasi-regular right ideal.*

Let J be the union of all the right quasi-regular right ideals of a ring R. Since any element in J is a *finite* sum of elements from right quasi-regular right ideals, it is clear that each such element in J is right quasi-regular. Thus, J is a right quasi-regular right ideal, and J contains every right quasi-regular right ideal of R.

Lemma 52. *J is a two-sided ideal of R.*

Proof. Let x be any element in J and r any element of R. It will be sufficient to show that rx is in J. We know that xr is in J, and thus there exists an element w such that $xr + w + xrw = 0$. Then

$$rx + (-rx - rwx) + rx(-rx - rwx) = -r(w + xr + xrw)x = 0.$$

Therefore, rx is right quasi-regular. Next, consider the right ideal generated by rx. This is the set of all $rxi + rxs$, where i is an integer and s is in R. The element $xi + xs$ is in J and, as above, $r(xi + xs)$ is right quasi-regular. Therefore, $\{rxi + rxs\}$ is a right quasi-regular right ideal. It is thus in J and then, in particular, rx is in J.

This proves property (B) of radical properties. Property (A) is immediate, for if R' is a homomorphic image of the right quasi-regular ring R, then every element of R' is right quasi-regular. If $x \to x'$ and $x + y + xy = 0$ in R, then $y \to y'$ and $x' + y' + x'y' = 0$ in R'.

We must finally establish (C), i.e. that R/J is semi-simple with respect to right quasi-regularity. To see this, suppose that R/J has a right quasi-regular right ideal T/J, and take $x + J$ to be an element of T/J. Then there exists a coset $x' + J$ such that

$$x + J + x' + J + (x + J)(x' + J) = 0$$

in R/J. This means that $x + x' + xx'$ is in J. Then there must exist an element u in R such that

$$0 = (x + x' + xx') + u + (x + x' + xx')u$$
$$= x + (x' + u + x'u) + x(x' + u + x'u).$$

Therefore, x is right quasi-regular as an element of R. Consequently, every element in the coset $x + J$ is right quasi-regular, by Lemma 51. Thus, every element of T is right quasi-regular. Since T is a right ideal of R and since J contains all right quasi-regular right ideals of R, $T \subseteq J$ and thus $T/J = 0$ in R/J. Therefore, R/J is semi-simple with respect to right quasi-regularity.

This establishes property (C) and we have the following

Theorem 33. *Right quasi-regularity is a radical property.*

The two main questions that arise are: Where does J, the Jacobson radical, fit into the general radical scheme of things? And, even more important, what structure theory can we get for J-semi-simple rings?

First we shall show that $\mathcal{N} \leqslant J \leqslant \mathcal{T}$.

It is clear that every nil right ideal of a ring is in J because every element in such a right ideal is right quasi-regular and, therefore, the right ideal is quasi-regular. Thus, every two-sided nil ideal is in J, $\mathcal{N} \leqslant J$. However, J also contains every nil left ideal.

To see this, we observe that the entire construction of the Jacobson radical could have been developed using left quasi-regularity, i.e. $x + y + yx = 0$, and left quasi-regular left ideals. Everything goes through as on the right and thus every ring has a two-sided ideal J' which is the union of all the left quasi-regular left ideals of the ring R. Every element in J' is left quasi-regular.

We wish to show that every element in J' is also right quasi-regular. For this, we require:

Lemma 53. *If an element z is both right quasi-regular, $z + w + zw = 0$, and left quasi-regular, $z + t + tz = 0$, then $t = w$, $wz = zw$, and w is unique.*

Proof.
$$t = t + (z + w + zw) + t(z + w + zw)$$
$$= w + (z + t + tz) + (z + t + tz)w$$
$$= w.$$

Clearly, $wz = zw$. Finally, if $z + z' + zz' = 0$, then, as above, $z' = t = w$.

The element w is called the quasi-inverse of z.

Returning to J', let x be any element of J'. Then there exists an element y such that $x + y + yx = 0$, for x is left quasi-regular. Furthermore, $y = - x - yx$ is in J' since J' is an ideal. Thus y is left quasi-regular, $y + r + ry = 0$ for some r. But $y + x + yx = 0$, y is right quasi-regular, and, by Lemma 53, $r = x$. Thus $xy = yx$ and, in particular, $x + y + xy = 0$. Consequently, every element in J' is right quasi-regular, J' is a right quasi-regular ideal, a right ideal, and thus $J' \subseteq J$.

Symmetrically, we can prove that $J \subseteq J'$ and thus $J = J'$.

Since every nil left ideal is a left quasi-regular left ideal, every nil left ideal is contained in J.

We have established that $\mathcal{N} \leqslant J$. To see that $J \leqslant \mathcal{T}$, we must show that any matrix ring over a division ring is Jacobson semi-simple (Lemma 4). However, any ring with a unity element cannot be Jacobson radical for the element -1 is not quasi-regular. If $-1 + x + (-1)x = 0$, then $-1 = 0$, an impossibility. In particular, then, any matrix ring over a division ring, having a unity element, is not Jacobson radical. Since it is simple, it must be semi-simple in the sense of Jacobson and thus $J \leqslant \mathcal{T}$. By Lemma 27 we can conclude that for rings with D.C.C., $J = \mathcal{N}$. Thus, J coincides with the classical radical, for rings with D.C.C.

Before we delve further into J's relationship to the other radical properties (e.g. to show that $\mathcal{N} < J < \mathcal{T}$, and to discuss the partition of the simple rings associated with J) we should first see how useful J can be.

4.2. Semi-simple rings. Our first step will be the study of semi-simple rings (from here on, to the end of the section, semi-simple will mean Jacobson semi-simple). First we must obtain a different representation of J.

If R is not a radical ring (in this chapter, radical will mean Jacobson radical), then R contains an element x which is not right quasi-regular, i.e. $\{xr + r\}$ $\neq R$. Now $\{xr + r\}$ is a right ideal of R which does not contain x. If it did, it would be all of R. If a right ideal contained both $\{xr + r\}$ and the element x, then it would have to be all of R. By considering all right ideals which contain $\{xr + r\}$ and which do not contain x, by ordering these right ideals by inclusion, and by using Zorn's Lemma (see Section 3.5), we obtain a right ideal, maximal with respect to the exclusion of x and with respect to the inclusion of $\{xr + r\}$. However, such a right ideal is a maximal right ideal of R, for if any right ideal properly contains it, it must also contain x and thus be all of R. Consequently, every ring which is not a radical ring possesses maximal right (and left) ideals (unless, of course, it has no non-zero proper right ideals, in which case 0 is a maximal right ideal).

We shall say that a right ideal V is *regular* if there exists an element e in R such that $er - r$ is in V for every r in R. Such an element e is called a left unit of V.

Lemma 54. *The Jacobson radical of any ring R is equal to (α), the intersection of all the regular maximal right ideals of R, to (β), the intersection of all the regular maximal left ideals of R, to (γ) $\{x : xr$ is right quasi-regular, for every r in $R\}$, to (δ) $\{x : rx$ is left quasi-regular, for every r in $R\}$.*

Proof. If x is in J, then xr is in J for every r in R, and xr is right quasi-regular. Thus, $J \subseteq (\gamma)$.

Now take any element x in (α). This means that x is in every regular maximal right ideal of R. Either x is right quasi-regular, or if it is not, then $\{r + xr\} \neq R$. Let M be a maximal right ideal containing $\{r + xr\}$ but not containing x. Then M is regular, for $-xr - r = x(-r) + (-r)$ is in M for every r in R. In this case $x \in M$ and therefore $M = R$. This is a contradiction and, consequently, every x in (α) is right quasi-regular. Since (α) is also a right ideal, it is a right quasi-regular right ideal. Thus $(\alpha) \subseteq J$.

Now take x to be any element of (γ). Thus xr is right quasi-regular for every r in R. Now either $x \in (\alpha)$ or, if not, there exists a regular maximal right ideal M such that x is not in M. Since M is maximal, the right ideal generated by M and x is all of R. Thus, $R = \{m + x(r + i)\}$, where i is an integer. Let e be the left unit of M, i.e. $er - r$ is in M for every r of R. Then there exists an m in M, r in R, i an integer, such that

$$-e = m + x(r + i).$$

Then $-e^2 = me + x(r + i)e$. Now $x(r + i)e$ is right quasi-regular and thus there exists an element z such that $x(r + i)e + z + x(r + i)ez = 0$. Then $mez + x(r + i)ez = -e^2z$. Thus,

$$mez - x(r + i)e - z + eez = 0.$$

Now $et - t$ is in M for every t. Thus $ee - e$ is in M, $eez - ez$ is in M, $ez - z$ is in M, and therefore $eez - z$ is in M. Also mez is in M since M is a right ideal. Therefore, $x(r + i)e$ is in M. Therefore, $-e^2 = me + x(r + i)e$ is in M. Since $e^2 - e$ is in M, e is in M. Then er and $er - r$ are both in M, $-r$ and r are in M for every r, and $M = R$. This is impossible. Therefore, x is in (α). Thus $(\gamma) \subseteq (\alpha) \subseteq J \subseteq (\gamma)$ and $J = (\alpha) = (\gamma)$.

Similarly, $J = (\beta) = (\delta)$, and the lemma is established.

Observe that if R has a unity element, then every one-sided ideal is regular (modular) and thus J is the intersection of all the maximal right ideals (or left ideals).

Now let M be a regular maximal right ideal.

Definition. $(M:R) \equiv \{r \in R : Rr \subseteq M\}$.

It is clear that $(M:R)$ is a two-sided ideal of R.

Lemma 55. *If M is a regular right ideal (not necessarily maximal), then $(M:R) \subseteq M$ and it is the largest two-sided ideal of R that is contained in M.*

Proof. Let e be the left unit of M, i.e. $er - r$ is in M for every $r \in R$. If x is in $(M:R)$, then $Rx \subseteq M$. Then ex is in M, and since $ex - x$ is in M, x is in M. Thus $(M:R) \subseteq M$.

Furthermore, if Q is any two-sided ideal of R, $Q \subseteq M$, then $RQ \subseteq M$ and thus $Q \subseteq (M:R)$.

We wish to show that J is the intersection of a certain set of *two*-sided ideals.

Definition. R is *right primitive* if R contains a maximal right ideal M such that $(M:R) = 0$.

Definition. An *ideal (two-sided)* P of R is a *right primitive* ideal if R/P is right primitive.

We note that $(M:R)$ is a right primitive ideal of R if M is a maximal regular right ideal of R. To see this, consider $R/(M:R)$. If $(M:R) = M$, then M is a two-sided ideal of R, and $R/M = R/(M:R)$ has no proper non-zero ideals (i.e. it is simple) because M is maximal. In fact, R/M has no proper non-zero right ideals, for if T/M is a right ideal of R/M, then T is a right ideal of R and T contains M. Then $\{0\}$ is a maximal right ideal of R/M such that $(\{0\} : R/M) = \bar{0}$. For if $R/M . \bar{x} = \bar{0}$, then $Rx \subseteq M$. Then x is in $(M:R) = M$ and thus $\bar{x} = \bar{0}$. Consequently, $(M:R)$ is a right primitive ideal of R when $(M:R) = M$.

On the other hand, if $(M:R) \neq M$, then by Lemma 55, $(M:R) \subset M$. Then in $R/(M:R)$ consider the right ideal $M/(M:R)$. Clearly, $M/(M:R)$ is a maximal right ideal in $R/(M:R)$. Also $(M/(M:R) : R/(M:R)) = 0$, for if $R/(M:R) . \bar{x} \subseteq M/(M:R)$, then $Rx \subseteq M$. Consequently, x is in $(M:R)$ and

$\bar{x} = \bar{0}$. Therefore, $R/(M:R)$ is a right primitive ring and thus $(M:R)$ is a right primitive ideal.

Theorem 34. *The radical J = the intersection of all the right primitive (two-sided) ideals of R.*

Proof. Every regular maximal right ideal M of R contains a right primitive ideal, namely $(M:R)$. Therefore, J, which is the intersection of the regular maximal right ideals, contains the intersection of the right primitive ideals of R.

Conversely, we shall show that J is contained in every right primitive ideal of R and this will end the proof.

Let P be a right primitive ideal of R. Then R/P contains a maximal right ideal M/P such that $(M/P:R/P) = \bar{0}$, or $(M:R) \subseteq P$.

If M is regular, then $J \subseteq M$. Also $J \subseteq (M:R)$, for $(M:R)$ is the largest ideal of R contained in M (Lemma 55). Then $J \subseteq (M:R) \subseteq P$. However, we do not know whether M is regular.

Since $P \subseteq M$, $(M:R) \subseteq M$, and we can at least conclude that $(M:R)$ is the largest ideal of R contained in M. For if Q is an ideal of R, and $Q \subseteq M$, then $RQ \subseteq Q \subseteq M$. Therefore, $Q \subseteq (M:R)$. In particular, then, $P = (M:R)$. Now if the radical J is not contained in P, then it cannot be contained in $(M:R)$ and therefore it cannot be contained in M. We shall therefore assume that $J \nsubseteq M$ and attempt to reach a contradiction. If we do this, we shall then be able to conclude that $J \subseteq P$.

First, we observe that $\{x : xR \subseteq M\} = M$. The left-hand side of this equation is a right ideal, which clearly contains M. Since M is maximal, it is either M or R. If $\{x : xR \subseteq M\} = R$, then $RR \subseteq M$. Then $(M : R)$ and thus $M = R$, a contradiction.

Now assume that $J \nsubseteq M$ and take x in J, $x \notin M$. Then Rx is not in M, for otherwise x would be in $(M:R) \subseteq M$. Take an element z in R such that $zx \notin M$. Then $zxR \nsubseteq M$ since $\{w : wR \subseteq M\} = M$. Since M is maximal, $M + zxR = R$, and thus there exists an $m \in M$ and v in R such that $m + zxv = -z$. Then $z + zxv$ is in M.

Since x is in J, xv is right quasi-regular and therefore there exists an element w such that $xv + w + xvw = 0$. Then

$$z = z + z(xv + w + xvw)$$
$$= (z + zxv) + (z + zxv)w.$$

Thus, z itself is in M, but this contradicts the fact that $zx \notin M$. Therefore, $J \subseteq M$, and thus $J \subseteq P$ and the theorem is proved.

The same sort of proof establishes that the intersection of the regular maximal left ideals is equal to the intersection of all the left primitive (two-sided) ideals of R. (We, of course, define an ideal Q of R to be a left primitive ideal if R/Q is left primitive; and a ring R to be left primitive if R contains a maximal left ideal L such that $(L:R) = 0$, where $(L:R) = \{r \in R : rR \subseteq L\}$.) With Lemma 54, we then have:

Corollary. *The radical* $J = $ *the intersection of all the left primitive (two-sided) ideals.*

Now that we have J represented as an intersection of two-sided ideals, we are in a position to make a potentially powerful statement about semi-simple (with respect to the Jacobson radical, of course) rings.

Theorem 35. *Every (Jacobson) semi-simple ring is isomorphic to a sub-direct sum of right primitive rings.*

Proof. If $J = 0$, then the intersection of the right primitive ideals P_i is 0. Then, by Theorem 19, R is isomorphic to a subdirect sum of rings R_i, where each $R_i \cong R/P_i$. But each of these is, by definition, a right primitive ring.

This generalizes, as we shall see, Theorems 10 and 20. But its utility rests on the hope that we can say something important about the structure of a right primitive ring. Just as we studied simple rings with D.C.C. and prime rings with A.C.C., we must now study right primitive rings (without any chain conditions).

4.3. Right primitive rings. Let R be right primitive, i.e. R contains a maximal right ideal M such that $(M:R) = \{r \in R : Rr \subseteq M\} = 0$. To obtain models with which to represent such rings we are again faced with our meagre stockpile. We have used division rings and matrices of finite size. Now we shall consider matrices of infinite size and large subrings of the set of all infinite matrices.

Since M is only a right ideal, R/M is not a ring. However, it is at least an additive group. Let E be the set of all endomorphisms (i.e. group homomorphisms from R/M to R/M) of R/M. This set E is a ring with a unity element. Now we shall show that R is isomorphic to a subring of E.

Take any element x in R and consider the mapping

$$x':r + M \to rx + M.$$

Then x' is an endomorphism of R/M, for it preserves sums. Then we can send R into E by means of the mapping $x \to x'$. Let R' be the set of all such x' in E. Then R is mapped onto R' and this is a ring homomorphism. To see this, let $y \to y'$, where y' is the endomorphism of M/R given by $r + M \to ry + M$. Then

$$(x + y)':r + M \to r(x + y) + M = rx + M + ry + M$$

and therefore $(x + y)' = x' + y'$. Furthermore,

$$(xy)':r + M \to r.xy + M = rx.y + M$$

and thus $(xy)' = x'y'$, for $x'y':r + M \to rx.y + M$.

This homomorphism of R onto R' is an isomorphism, for if x' is the zero endomorphism, then $rx + M = M$ for every $r \in R$. Then $Rx \subseteq M$. However, in that case, x is in $(M:R) = 0$ and thus $x = 0$. Therefore, R is isomorphic to R'.

We wish to show that R' is in some sense large in E and that E is the set of all linear transformations of a vector space over a division ring. We begin by proving:

Lemma 56. *Let* $D = \{\alpha \in E: \alpha x' = x'\alpha$, *for every* x' *in* $R'\}$. *Then* D *is a division ring.*

Proof. It is clear that D is a ring and that it contains the unity element of E. Let α be any non-zero element of D. Consider $\{r\alpha + M\}$, the image of R/M under α.* Since $\alpha \neq 0$, $\{r\alpha + M\} \neq M$. We wish to show that $\{r\alpha + M\} = R/M$. There exists an $r \in R$ such that $r\alpha \notin M$. Since M is a maximal right ideal, the right ideal generated by M and $r\alpha$ must be all of R. Thus, for any y in R there exists an m in M, a in R, and an integer i such that

$$y = m + r\alpha.a + r\alpha.i.$$

Since α is in D, $ra.\alpha = r\alpha.a$ and, of course, $r\alpha.i = ri.\alpha$. Thus,

$$y = m + (ra + ri)\alpha.$$

Then $y + M = (ra + ri)\alpha + M$ and therefore $y + M$ is in $\{r\alpha + M\}$, for any y in R. Therefore, α sends R/M onto R/M.

We, therefore, know that α is an onto homomorphism. To show that it is an isomorphism, consider any coset $r + M$ which α sends into M, i.e. $r\alpha + M = M$. Then, $r\alpha$ is in M. If $r \notin M$, then, since M is a maximal right ideal, every y in R can be written as

$$y = m + ra + ri,$$

for some $m \in M$, $a \in R$, and integer i. Then

$$y\alpha = m\alpha + ra.\alpha + ri.\alpha = m\alpha + r\alpha.a + r\alpha.i.$$

Since $r\alpha$ is in M and $m\alpha$ must also be in M, $y\alpha$ is in M, for every y of R. Then α sends all of R/M onto the zero coset M. Since $\alpha \neq 0$, this is impossible, and therefore r itself must be in M and thus α is an isomorphism.

Then α has an inverse α^{-1} in E. But α^{-1} must then be in D itself, for $\alpha x' = x'\alpha$

*The notation $r\alpha$ is somewhat slipshod. Since α sends $r + M$ into some coset, say $s + M$, we may define $r\alpha$ to be s. This is not unique, but it is well defined modulo M.

H

implies that $x'\alpha^{-1} = \alpha^{-1}x'$. Therefore D is a division ring.

Notice that this lemma is true even if $(M:R) \neq 0$.

Lemma 57. *R/M is a right vector space over the division ring D.*

Proof. Let v be any element of R/M, $v = r + M$. Take α in D. Then $v\alpha = r\alpha + M$ is again an element of R/M, i.e. $v\alpha \in R/M$. Clearly $v.1 = v$, $v(\alpha_1 + \alpha_2) = v\alpha_1 + v\alpha_2$, $v.\alpha_1\alpha_2 = v\alpha_1.\alpha_2$, and $(v_1 + v_2)\alpha = v_1\alpha + v_2\alpha$. This is all there is to prove!

In general, R/M will not be finite-dimensional over D. In general then, E, the set of all linear transformations on R/M, can be represented as the set of all infinite row-finite matrices with elements in D. We shall not do anything with this type of representation. We observe, however, that if R/M happens to be finite-dimensional, say n, over D, then E is the set of all $n \times n$ matrices over D and thus E is a simple non-trivial ring with D.C.C.

We wish, finally, to show that R' is large in E.

We shall say that W is a *dense* ring of linear transformations on a vector space V over a division ring D if for any finite linearly independent set x_1, $x_2, \ldots, x_n$ in V and any finite arbitrary set $y_1, y_2, \ldots, y_n$ in V, there exists an element w in W such that $w : x_i \to y_i$, for $i = 1, 2, \ldots, n$.

In particular, if V is finite-dimensional, then a dense ring W must be the ring of all linear transformations of V.

We shall show that R' is dense with respect to R/M over D. But first we require:

Lemma 58. *If G is a finite-dimensional subspace of R/M and v is in R/M but not in G, then there exists an element in R' which annihilates G but not v.*

Proof. We shall proceed by induction on the dimension of G. Assume then that the lemma is true for all spaces of dimension $n - 1$ and assume that G has a basis $b_1, b_2, \ldots, b_{n-1}, b_n$. Take v outside of G, in R/M, and suppose that every r' in R' which annihilates G also annihilates v. Let S' be the subset of R' that annihilates the vector space generated by $b_1, \ldots, b_{n-1}$. Then S' is a right ideal of R'. Consider $b_n.S'$. This is not zero, by induction, for there must exist an element of R' which annihilates $b_1, \ldots, b_{n-1}$ (and is therefore in S') but which does not annihilate b_n.

Now $R/M = b_n.S'$, for S' is the isomorphic image of a right ideal S of R, while $b_n = b_n{}^* + M$ and $M + b_n{}^*S = R$ since $b_n{}^*S$ is not in M and $M + b_n{}^*S$ is a right ideal of R which properly contains the maximal right ideal M. Thus, every element in R/M can be represented as $b_n s'$ with s' in S'.

Now consider the mapping $b_n s' \to v s'$. First we make sure that this is well defined. If $b_n s' = b_n s''$, then $b_n(s' - s'') = 0$. Thus $s' - s''$ annihilates b_n, but it is certainly in S' and therefore annihilates $b_1, \ldots, b_{n-1}$. Therefore it annihilates G and, therefore, by our assumption $v(s' - s'') = 0$, or $vs' = vs''$. Consequently, $b_n s' \to vs'$ is well defined, for if $b_n s' = b_n s''$, then $vs' = vs''$.

This is a mapping on all of R/M and we wish to show that it is in D. To see this, take any h' in R' and observe that $b_n s' . h = b_n . s' h \to v . s' h$, since $s' h$ is in S'. And $v . s' h = vs' . h$. Thus the mapping $b_n s' \to vs'$ commutes with every h' in R' and therefore it is in D. Therefore, there exists an α in D such that $b_n s' . \alpha = vs'$, for every s' in S'. And $b_n s' . \alpha = b_n \alpha . s'$. Thus, $(b_n \alpha - v)s' = 0$ for every s' in S'. If $b_n \alpha - v$ is not in the subspace generated by $b_1, \ldots, b_{n-1}$, then, by induction, there would exist an element in S' which does not annihilate $b_n \alpha - v$. Since all of S' does annihilate $b_n \alpha - v$, we can conclude that $b_n \alpha - v$ must be in the space generated by $b_1, \ldots, b_{n-1}$. Then v must be in G. This is a contradiction, and therefore if the lemma holds for subspaces of dimension $n - 1$, then it holds for subspaces of dimension n.

To get the induction started, we must simply take $n = 1$. Precisely the same proof goes through as above, and thus the lemma is established.

Theorem 36. *Every right primitive ring is isomorphic to a dense ring of linear transformations on a right vector space over a division ring.*

Proof. We must merely show that R' is a dense ring of linear transformations on R/M.

Let $x_1, x_2, \ldots, x_n$ be any finite, linearly independent set in R/M. Let G be the finite-dimensional subspace of R/M generated by $x_2, \ldots, x_n$. By Lemma 58 there exists an element t_1 in R' which annihilates G and does not annihilate x_1. Suppose that $x_1 t_1 = z_1 \neq 0$. Similarly, we can find t_i in R' such that $x_i t_i = z_i \neq 0$ and $x_j t_i = 0$ for $j \neq i, j = 1, \ldots, n$.

For any $z_i \neq 0$, $z_i R' \neq 0$, for Lemma 58 tells us that R' contains an element that does not annihilate z_i. As in the proof of Lemma 58, we can get the fact that $R/M = z_i R'$, for any $i = 1, \ldots, n$. Therefore, for any y_i in R/M there exists u_i in R' such that $z_i u_i = y_i$. Then $x_i t_i u_i = y_i$. Let $\beta = t_1 u_1 + t_2 u_2 + \ldots + t_n u_n$. Then β is in R' and

$$x_i \beta = x_i(t_1 u_1 + \ldots + t_n u_n)$$

$$= x_i t_i u_i$$

$$= y_i, \quad \text{for every } i = 1, \ldots, n.$$

Therefore R' is dense, and the theorem is proved.

Corollary. *If R is a ring of linear transformations on a right vector space V over a division ring Δ and if for any $v \neq 0$ in V, and any other $w \in V$, R contains an element x such that $vx = w$, then R is right primitive. In particular, if R is a dense ring of linear transformations on V, then R is right primitive.*

Proof. First, we observe that the condition assumed in this corollary, i.e. that for every $v \neq 0$, w in V, there exists an x in R such that $vx = w$, is weaker than denseness. It is called "one-transitiveness" and density is n-transitiveness for any finite n.

Take any $v \neq 0$ in V. Then we note that $v.R = V$. Now let $M = \{r \in R: vr = 0\}$. Clearly, M is a right ideal of R and $M \neq R$, for $vR = V \neq 0$. Now $(M:R) = \{r \in R : Rr \subseteq M\} = 0$, for if $Rr \subseteq M$, then $v.Rr = 0$. Since $vR = V$, this means that $Vr = 0$. But the only linear transformation on V which sends all of V into 0 is the 0 transformation. Therefore $r = 0$, $(M:R) = 0$.

Finally, to show that M is a maximal right ideal of R, suppose that $M \subset N$, where N is a right ideal of R. Then there exists an x in N which is not in M. Then $vx \neq 0$. Then $vx.R = V$. Since $xR \subseteq N$, we must have $v.N = V$. Now take any $r \in R$, and let $v_1 = vr$. There exists n in N such that $vn = v_1$, $vn = vr$, $v(n - r) = 0$. Therefore, $n - r = m$, for some m in M. Then $r = n - m$ and this is in N since $M \subseteq N$. Thus $R \subseteq N$, $N = R$.

Therefore, R contains a maximal right ideal M such that $(M:R) = 0$ and, thus, R is right primitive, by definition.

Remark. This does not prove that R is dense on V over Δ, or that one-transitiveness is equivalent to density. In using Lemma 56 on the primitive ring R, we would, in general, obtain a larger division ring D than Δ. Then R would be dense on V over D but not on V over Δ.

For example, suppose V is the complex numbers thought of as a vector space over the reals. Let R be the complex numbers, and think of R as a ring of linear transformations on V over the reals. Then $vR = V$ for every non-zero v in V and thus R is one-transitive on V over the reals. Then R is right primitive. Then, using Lemma 56, we find that $D = V$ itself and therefore R is dense on V over V. That is, when V is thought of as a vector space over itself, R is dense. However, R is not dense on V over the reals. Take 1 and i in V. They are linearly independent over the reals (but *not* over the complex numbers). Can we find an element in R which sends 1 into 1 and i into 1? No, for if $1(a + bi) = 1$, then $a = 1$, $b = 0$. Then $i(a + bi) = i(1) = i \neq 1$.

Remark. A difficult question that is still open is the following: If R is a right primitive ring, is it also a left primitive ring? [As we go to press an example of a ring which is right primitive but not left primitive has been found—see the June 1964 issue of the *Proceedings of the American Mathematical Society.*]

Putting Theorems 35 and 36 together, we have the following fundamental theorems.

Theorem 37. *Every Jacobson semi-simple ring is isomorphic to a subdirect* *sum of dense rings of linear transformations on right vector spaces over division rings.*

Theorem 38. *If J is the Jacobson radical of an arbitrary ring R, then R/J is isomorphic to a subdirect sum of dense rings of linear transformations on right vector spaces over division rings.*

These generalize the classical D.C.C. result (Theorems 10 and 11) quite nicely. Instead of the nil radical we throw away the larger Jacobson radical. We get a subdirect sum instead of a direct sum, and the components are dense subrings of linear transformations on infinite-dimensional vector spaces instead of full rings of linear transformations on finite-dimensional vector spaces. This is a really deep and remarkable result, which holds without any chain conditions whatsoever. It is doubly impressive because, even with A.C.C., the best we were able to prove until very recently also involved subdirect sums and a large subring of the set of linear transformations (Theorem 32).

However, Theorem 30 points the way for future work and makes us less satisfied with Theorems 37 and 38. We wish, in short, to relieve ourselves of any connection with subdirect sums. What is required is some theorem which tells us that a Jacobson semi-simple ring can be embedded in a tightly fitting over-ring whose structure is relatively well known to us. But this is for future mathematicians to solve.

Problem. Prove that if R is right primitive, then R is prime.

4.4. The Jacobson radical and general radical theory. Now that the Jacobson radical has proved its usefulness, let us examine how it fits into the scheme of things. First, we need an example of a ring which is Jacobson radical but which is nil semi-simple.

Example 10. Let W be the set of all rational numbers of the form $2x/(2y + 1)$, where x and y are integers, and the greatest common divisor of $2x$ and $2y + 1$ is 1. This set is a commutative ring under the usual operations of addition and multiplication, and it contains the ring of even integers. There are, of course, no nilpotent elements in W and therefore W is nil semi-simple. The surprise about W is that every element in it is quasi-regular! For any element $2x/(2y + 1)$ we simply take $2(-x)/[2(x + y) + 1]$ and compute:

$$\frac{2x}{2y + 1} + \frac{-2x}{2(x + y) + 1} + \frac{2x}{2y + 1}\left(\frac{-2x}{2(x + y) + 1}\right)$$

$$= \frac{2x[2x + 2y + 1] - 2x[2y + 1] - 4x^2}{(2y + 1)(2x + 2y + 1)} = 0.$$

Therefore, W is a Jacobson radical ring.

This is the promised example mentioned just before Theorem 14 (p. 44) and before Lemma 28 (p. 41). It proves that $\mathcal{N} < J$.

Although the Jacobson radical J of a ring R is, in general, not nil, very little restriction on R forces it to be nil. We already know that if R has D.C.C., J must coincide with the classical radical and then J is not only nil but is nilpotent. However, D.C.C. is a rather heavy restriction. We can get some surprising results with much less. These results are for algebras rather than for rings, and as we pointed out in the discussion of Example 5 (p. 37), there is a distinction between algebra ideals and ring ideals. However, we can prove [26]:

Lemma 59. *The Jacobson radical of an algebra R is the same as the Jacobson radical of R, thought of as a ring.*

Proof. The distinction, if any, lies in the fact that some ring ideals are not necessarily algebra ideals. We shall show that every regular maximal right ideal M of the ring R is also an algebra ideal. Then, by Lemma 54, the lemma will be established.

For M to be an algebra right ideal it must merely be closed under right multiplication by elements in the base field F of the algebra R. Thus, if α is in F, we must show that $M\alpha \subseteq M$. Suppose that $M\alpha \nsubseteq M$. Now, $M\alpha$ is a right ideal of the ring R because $m\alpha . x = mx . \alpha \in M . \alpha$. Since M is a maximal right ideal of the ring R, $M + M\alpha = R$. Then

$$R^2 = M^2 + M\alpha M + MM\alpha + M\alpha M\alpha \subseteq M + MR = M.$$

Since M is regular, there exists an element e in R such that $er - r$ is in M for every r in R. Now, er is in $R^2 \subseteq M$ and therefore $-r$ is in M for every r, $M = R$. This is a contradiction, and therefore $M\alpha \subseteq M$. This proves the lemma.

This result can be extended to all radical properties, and it holds not only for algebras but also for general rings with operators [22].

If R is a ring and φ is an arbitrary set, we say that φ is a set of operators for R if for any α in φ and any x in R, the composition αx is defined and is an element of R, and if this composition satisfies:

$$\alpha(x + y) = \alpha x + \alpha y,$$
$$\alpha(xy) \quad = (\alpha x)y = x(\alpha y),$$

for any α in φ and any x, y in R.

Then we have the following theorem.

Theorem 39. *If R is any ring with operator domain φ and S is a radical property, then the S-radical of R, thought of as a ring with operators, exists, and is equal to the S-radical of R, thought of merely as a ring.*

Proof. Let I be an S-ideal of R, i.e. just a ring ideal which is an S-ring. For any α in φ define $I_\alpha \equiv I + \alpha I$. Clearly, I_α is an ideal of R, for if x is in R and y is in I, then $x.\alpha y = \alpha.xy$. Since xy is in I, $\alpha.xy$ is in αI, and therefore $R.\alpha I \subseteq \alpha I$. Similarly, $\alpha I.R \subseteq \alpha.IR \subseteq \alpha I$.

Furthermore, I_α is an S-ring. To see this, consider the natural homomorphism h from I_α to I_α/I. Then let g be a mapping from I to I_α/I defined as follows:

$$g(y) \equiv h(\alpha y)$$

for any y in I. To see that g is a homomorphism consider

$$g(y_1 + y_2) = h(\alpha[y_1 + y_2]) = h(\alpha y_1 + \alpha y_2) = h(\alpha y_1) + h(\alpha y_2)$$
$$= g(y_1) + g(y_2),$$

and

$$g(y_1 y_2) = h(\alpha(y_1 y_2)) = h(\alpha y_1 . y_2) = 0 \text{ in } I_\alpha/I$$

because $\alpha y_1 . y_2$ is in I and h maps I into the 0 coset of I_α/I.

However, $g(y_1).g(y_2) = h(\alpha y_1).h(\alpha y_2) = h(\alpha y_1.\alpha y_2) = h(y_1.\alpha(\alpha y_2)) = 0$ in I_α/I because $y_1.\alpha(\alpha y_2)$ is in I.

Therefore, $g(y_1 y_2) = g(y_1).g(y_2)$, and g is a homomorphism.

Now, g is a homomorphism from I onto I_α/I, for if $y_1 + \alpha y_2 + I = \alpha y_2 + I$ is an arbitrary element in I_α/I, then $g(y_2) = h(\alpha y_2) = \alpha y_2 + I$. Since I is an S-ring, so is I_α/I by (A) of Section 1.1. But then I_α itself must be an S-ring, for if I_α is not an S-ring, let V be its S-radical. Since I is an S-ring and an ideal of I_α, $I \subseteq V$. Then $I_\alpha/V \cong (I_\alpha/I)/(V/I)$ is both S-semi-simple and S-radical (for the right-hand side is a homomorphic image of the S-ring I_α/I). This is impossible unless $V = I_\alpha$, and thus I_α is itself an S-ring.

Let S be the S-radical of R, thought of merely as a ring. If $S_\alpha = S$, then $\alpha S \subseteq S$ and S is also the S-radical of R, thought of as a ring with operators. However, S_α is an S-ring and an ideal of R and therefore $S_\alpha \subseteq S$, by (B) of Section 1.1. Therefore $S_\alpha = S$ and the theorem is established.

Returning to the Jacobson theory, we now let R be an algebra over a field F. An element r is said to be *algebraic* if it satisfies some monic polynomial over F, or if it generates a finite-dimensional algebra over F. The algebra R is said to *algebraic* over F if every element of R is algebraic over F.

Theorem 40. *If R is an algebraic algebra over F, then J, its Jacobson radical, is nil.*

Proof. Let X be the algebra generated over F by any element x of J. Now, X is a finite-dimensional algebra over F and if x is not nilpotent, then X must contain an idempotent e (by Theorem 8 as applied to algebras). Now $X \subseteq J$ and therefore $e \in J$. However, J can never have any idempotents, for if $-e$ is right quasi-regular, then $-e + g - eg = 0$. Multiplying on the left by e, we get $-e + eg - eg = -e = 0$, and thus $e = 0$. This is a contradiction and, therefore, every x in J is nilpotent and J is nil.

But even more surprising is the following beautiful result due to Amitsur [5].

Theorem 41. *If R is an algebra over a field F and if the cardinality of F exceeds the dimension of R over F, then the Jacobson radical J of R is nil.*

Proof. We must first prove the following lemma.

Lemma 60. *If R is an algebra over F, if R has a unity element, and if x is in J, the Jacobson radical of R, then either x is algebraic over F or if it is not, then for any finite set $\alpha_1, \alpha_2, \ldots, \alpha_n$ of distinct non-zero elements of F, the elements $(x - \alpha_1)^{-1}, (x - \alpha_2)^{-1}, \ldots, (x - \alpha_n)^{-1}$ are linearly independent over F.*

Proof. First we note that since x is in J, so is $-\alpha^{-1}x$. Thus, there exists a y in R such that $-\alpha^{-1}x + y - \alpha^{-1}xy = 0$. Then

$$(x - \alpha)(-\alpha^{-1}y - \alpha^{-1}) = -\alpha^{-1}x + y - \alpha^{-1}xy + 1 = 1.$$

Thus, $x - \alpha$ has an inverse for any non-zero α in F.

Now, if $(x - \alpha_1)^{-1}, \ldots, (x - \alpha_n)^{-1}$ are linearly dependent, there exist elements $\beta_1, \ldots, \beta_n$, in F, not all zero, such that

$$\beta_1(x - \alpha_1)^{-1} + \beta_2(x - \alpha_2)^{-1} + \ldots + \beta_n(x - \alpha_n)^{-1} = 0.$$

Multiplying by $\prod_{i=1}^{n} (x - \alpha_1)$, we have

$$\sum_{i=1}^{n} \beta_i(x - \alpha_1)(x - \alpha_2)\ldots(x - \alpha_{i-1})(x - \alpha_{i+1})\ldots(x - \alpha_n) = 0.$$

Now consider the polynomial

$$f(z) = \sum_{i=1}^{n} \beta_i(z - \alpha_1)(z - \alpha_2)\ldots(z - \alpha_{i-1}) \cdot (z - \alpha_{i+1})\ldots(z - \alpha_n).$$

This $f(z)$ is not identically 0, for if it is, then $f(\alpha_j) = 0$ for every $j = 1, \ldots, n$. Then

$$(\alpha_j) = \beta_j(\alpha_j - \alpha_1)(\alpha_j - \alpha_2)\ldots(\alpha_j - \alpha_{j-1}) \cdot (\alpha_j - \alpha_{j+1})\ldots(\alpha_j - \alpha_n) = 0.$$

Since the α_i are all distinct, we must have $\beta_j = 0$ for every j. This is a contradiction and therefore $f(z)$ is not identically 0. However, $f(x) = 0$. Thus, x is algebraic over F.

This proves that if x is not algebraic, then the elements $(x - \alpha_1)^{-1}, \ldots,$ $(x - \alpha_n)^{-1}$ are linearly independent, and thus the lemma is established.

Now suppose that R has a unity element. Take x in J. Then, for every $\alpha \neq 0$ $(x - \alpha)^{-1}$ exists in R. Since the cardinality of F is bigger than the dimension of

R over F, the set of all $(x - \alpha)^{-1}$ cannot be linearly independent. Therefore, the set of all $(x - \alpha)^{-1}$ is a linearly dependent set and this means that there exists a *finite* set $\alpha_1, \ldots, \alpha_n$ of distinct elements (non-zero) in F such that $(x - \alpha_1)^{-1}, \ldots, (x - \alpha_n)^{-1}$ form a linearly dependent set over F. Then, by Lemma 60, x must be algebraic over F.

Therefore, J is algebraic over F. Then by Theorem 40, J is nil.

Finally to prove Theorem 41, we must consider the case when R does not have a unity element. We require several interesting lemmas.

Lemma 61. (Andrunakievic [8]). *Let A be an ideal of a ring R and let B be an ideal of A. Let B^* be the ideal of R generated by B. Then $B^{*3} \subseteq B$.*

Proof. $B^{*3} \subseteq AB^*A = A(B + RB + BR + RBR)A \subseteq ABA \subseteq B$.

Lemma 62. *If J is the Jacobson radical of R and T is an ideal of R, then thinking of T as a ring, the Jacobson radical of $T = J \cap T$. In particular, if R is semi-simple, then so is T.*

Proof. Let A be the Jacobson radical of T and let A^* be the ideal of R generated by A. By Lemma 61, $A^{*3} \subseteq A$. Now A^{*3} is an ideal of R and since it is in A, it is right quasi-regular.

If R is semi-simple, then $A^{*3} = 0$, A^* is a nilpotent ideal of R, $A^* = 0$, and therefore $A = 0$, T is semi-simple.

If R is not semi-simple, then $(T + J)/J$ is an ideal of the semi-simple ring R/J. Thus, $(T + J)/J$ is semi-simple. But $(T + J)/J \cong T/(T \cap J)$. Thus $T/(T \cap J)$ is semi-simple. Now, $T \cap J$ is an ideal of T and it is right quasi-regular. Therefore $T \cap J \subseteq A$. If $T \cap J \neq A$, then $A/(T \cap J)$ is a non-zero right quasi-regular ideal of $T/(T \cap J)$. This is impossible. Therefore $T \cap J = A$.

Remark. The property of Lemma 62 holds for certain radical properties, including of course the Jacobson radical, but it does not hold for all radical properties. A study of conditions required in order for it to hold has been made. See Andrunakievic [8], Amitsur [3], Sulinski [47], and Section 5.3.

Lemma 62 tells us that every ideal of a Jacobson radical ring is itself Jacobson radical. To see that this is not true in general, consider the partition of the simple rings for which all simple rings are in the upper class and no simple rings are in the lower class. Let U be the upper radical property of this partition. Then a ring is U-radical if and only if it cannot be mapped homomorphically onto a simple ring. See the discussion preceding Example 1. Then Example 1, the zero ring on p^∞, is a U-radical ring. However, each of its ideals has only a finite number of elements and therefore each of them can be mapped homomorphically on a simple ring because each has a maximal ideal. Thus, none of the ideals of the zero ring on p^∞ is U-radical. In particular, then, Lemma 62 does not hold for this radical property U.

Lemma 63. *Any ring R can be embedded in a ring S with unity such that the Jacobson radical of R equals the Jacobson radical of S.*

Proof. If R has a unity, then we merely take $S = R$. If R does not have a unity, then we adjoin one in the standard way by taking ordered pairs of elements of R and integers. Call this larger ring S. Then R is an ideal of S and $S/R \cong$ integers. Since S/R is semi-simple, R must contain J_S, the Jacobson radical of S. On the other hand, by Lemma 62, J_R, the Jacobson radical of R, is equal to $J_S \cap R$. Since $J_S \subseteq R$, we have $J_S = J_R$.

At last we can prove Theorem 41. Let R be any algebra without a unity. Embed it in an algebra with a unity. By Lemma 63 for algebras, the Jacobson radical is undisturbed. Consequently, by the case where R had a unity, we can conclude that the Jacobson radical is nil.

Remark. Lemma 62 tells us that every ideal of a radical ring must be radical (for the Jacobson radical). The question arises as to whether every subring of a radical ring must be radical. This was raised as a problem in the *American Mathematical Monthly*, and the solution appears on page 350, volume 63 (1956).

The answer is "No." Our Example 10 is a radical ring; it contains the ring of even integers, but this subring is not radical, for 2 cannot be right quasi-regular in it: the equation $2 + x + 2x = 0$, i.e. $2 + 3x = 0$, has no solution among the even integers.

Let us now return to the relationship of the Jacobson radical to the other radicals. We have shown that $\mathcal{N} < J$.

To show that $J < \mathcal{T}$, the upper radical determined by all simple rings which are isomorphic to matrix rings over division rings, we must inquire a little more carefully into $\mathcal{T}$, but first we shall consider linear transformations on vector spaces which are not finite-dimensional.

Let V be a right vector space over a division D. This means that V is a commutative group, written additively, such that $VD \subseteq V$, and such that for every x and y in V and every α and β in D, we have:

$$(x + y)\alpha = x\alpha + y\alpha; \quad x(\alpha + \beta) = x\alpha + x\beta; \quad x.\alpha\beta = x\alpha.\beta; \quad x.1 = x,$$

where 1 is the multiplicative unity element of D.

A set $\{x_1, x_2, x_3, \ldots\}$ (not necessarily countable) of elements of V is linearly independent if for any finite sum $\sum x_i \alpha_i = 0$, we must have $\alpha_i = 0$ for every i. A basis of V is a linearly independent set with the property that any element of V is a *finite* linear combination of elements from the set.

Using the Schroeder–Bernstein Theorem [16] one can prove that any two bases of V have the same cardinal number. We shall assume that V has a countable basis.

Example 11. Let W be the set of all linear transformations of V into V. It is well known that W is a ring, and, of course, if V is finite-dimensional over D then W is isomorphic to the set of all $n \times n$ matrices over D. However, if V is of infinite dimension over D, then W is associated with infinite matrices. Since we are assuming that V is of countable dimension over D, let us take a basis of V, and order the basal elements as: $x_1, x_2, \ldots$. Each T in W is completely determined by its action on the x_i. Since $x_i{}^T$ is a finite sum: $x_i{}^T = \sum a_{ij} x_j$, T can be represented by an infinite matrix in which each row has only a finite number of non-zero entries. For, if x_i is represented by the vector with 1 in the ith place and zeros elsewhere, then the ith row of the matrix which will represent T will have a_{ij} in the jth column, for a finite number of j's, and zeros in the rest of the ith row. Similarly, every row of this matrix will have only a finite number of non-zero entries. Thus, W is isomorphic to the set of all row-finite matrices.

Although $W \cong M_n \times D$ is simple when V is finite-dimensional over D, W, or the set of all row-finite matrices, is not simple when V is infinite-dimensional. To prove this fact we must consider the so-called finite-valued or finite-rank transformations of W.

We shall say that a linear transformation T of W is *finite-valued* if the range of T is finite-dimensional over D, i.e. $\{x^T,$ for x in $V\}$ is a finite-dimensional subspace of V.

Let Z be the set of all finite-valued elements of W. Then Z is an ideal of W. To see this, take T_1 and T_2 in Z. Then the range of $T_1 - T_2$ is $\{x^{T_1} - x^{T_2},$ for all x in $V\}$ and this is finite-dimensional because both $\{x^{T_1},$ for x in $V\}$ and $\{x^{T_2},$ for x in $V\}$ are finite-dimensional. If T is a general element of W, then the range of TT_1 is contained in the range of T_1 and is therefore finite-dimensional. And the range of $T_1 T$ is the range of T_1 acted upon by T. Since any T in W sends a finite-dimensional subspace of V onto a finite-dimensional subspace of V, the range of $T_1 T$ is finite-dimensional. Thus, both TT_1 and $T_1 T$ are in Z and therefore Z is an ideal of W.

It is interesting to observe that the set F of all matrices with only a finite number of non-zero entries is not an ideal of W. The set F is contained in Z, of course, and it is a right ideal of W, but not a left ideal. To see this, let T be the matrix with 1's in every position of the first column, and zeros elsewhere. Then T is not in F, but it is in Z, for its range is finite, in fact of dimension one. Let U be the matrix with 1 in the top left-hand corner, and zeros elsewhere. Then U is in F, but $TU = T$ is not in F and thus F is not a left ideal of W, or of Z.

The ideal Z is certainly not the zero ideal. It is also not all of W because the identity matrix has all of V for its range and is therefore not in Z. Thus, Z is a proper non-trivial ideal of W.

One can show that if V is of countable dimension, then Z is the only proper non-trivial ideal of W. For higher cardinals we get one more ideal at each cardinal step.

If W is represented by the set of all row-finite matrices, and Z properly contains the set of all matrices with only a finite number of non-zero entries, what set of matrices represents Z?

Suppose first that T_i is finite-valued and that its range is one-dimensional, say the space generated by x_i. Then T_i is represented by a matrix with non-zero entries only in the ith column. It is more than row-finite, for each row has at most one non-zero entry and this must be in the ith column. Now, every finite-valued T has a range which has a basis: $x_{i_1}, \ldots, x_{i_n}$. Then $T = T_{i_1} + \ldots + T_{i_n}$ is represented by a matrix with non-zero entries only in the $i_1, i_2, \ldots, i_n$ columns. Thus, every T in Z is represented as a matrix which not only is row-finite, but also has only a finite number of columns with non-zero entries.

We shall now prove that Z is simple, is Jacobson semi-simple, but is radical with respect to the radical property $\mathcal{T}$. And this will prove that $J < \mathcal{T}$.

To see that Z is simple, let I be a non-zero ideal of Z. If T is any element of Z, $T = T_{i_1} + \ldots + T_{i_n}$, where the T_i have one-dimensional ranges. It is thus sufficient to show that I contains all T's which have one-dimensional ranges. Let T be in Z and let the range of T have $\{x\}$ as a basis. Then T maps all of V onto the multiples of x. In particular, there will exist an element y in V such that $y^T = x$.

Since I is non-zero, let G be a non-zero element of I. Since it does something in a non-zero way, it must send some non-zero r into a non-zero s, both r and s in V. Let A be the transformation which sends y into r and everything that T sends into zero, into zero. Then A has finite range and, therefore, A is in Z. Similarly, let B be the transformation which sends s into x and everything independent of s into zero, and observe that B is in Z. Then AGB sends y via r and s into x, and everything that T sends into zero, into zero. Thus $AGB = T$. Consequently, T is in I, since G is in I and I is an ideal of Z. Therefore $I = Z$, and Z is simple. Then Z is either a Jacobson radical ring or is Jacobson semi-simple. Consider the matrix C with -1 in the top left-hand corner and zeros elsewhere. Then C represents an element in Z, and C is not right quasi-regular. For if $C + D + CD = 0$, consider the matrix which represents D and let x be the element in the top left-hand corner of D. Then the top left-hand corner of $C + D + CD$ is $-1 + x + -x = -1$, and this is not zero. Thus, $C + D + CD$ cannot be 0, C is not right quasi-regular, and therefore Z is semi-simple with respect to the Jacobson radical. Since Z is simple, it must be right primitive (Theorem 35) and, in fact, it is clear that Z is a dense ring of linear transformations on a right vector space over a division ring (Theorem 36), for Z contains all the finite-valued transformations and thus for any finite set $y_1, \ldots, y_n$ and any finite linearly independent set $z_1, \ldots, z_n$ of elements of V, Z will contain an element which sends z_i into y_i.

We note that Z does not contain a unity element.

Before we establish that Z is radical with respect to $\mathcal{T}$, we must be a bit more careful about our definition of $\mathcal{T}$. We had defined it as the upper radical determined by all simple rings which are isomorphic to matrix rings over division rings. But are these all finite-dimensional? If we consider the set of all row-finite infinite matrices, then this set is not simple, for it has Z as a non-zero proper ideal. If we wish to consider all infinite matrices, then if M is the infinite matrix with 1's everywhere, MM is meaningless. Therefore, if a simple ring is isomorphic to a matrix ring over a division ring, the matrices must be finite. The ring Z is therefore $\mathcal{T}$-radical, for it cannot be mapped isomorphically on an $M \times D$ since Z is simple and has no unity element, whereas any finite $M \times D$ does have a unity. This finally establishes the fact that $J < \mathcal{T}$.

It would be pleasant to identify the Jacobson radical as the upper or lower radical property associated with some class of rings. This is an extremely difficult task. First, let us consider the partition of the simple rings that is determined by the Jacobson radical.

Lemma 64. *A simple non-trivial ring R is Jacobson semi-simple if and only if R has some maximal right ideals.*

Proof. If R is simple, non-trivial (i.e. $R^2 \neq 0$), and not Jacobson radical, then there exists an element x in R which is not right quasi-regular. Then, as was shown at the beginning of Section 4.2, R contains maximal right ideals.

Conversely, if R is simple, non-trivial, and contains a maximal right ideal M, take x in R, x not in M. Consider xR. Since M is maximal, xR cannot be in M. To see this, consider $\{y : yR \subseteq M\}$. This set is clearly a right ideal of R, and it certainly contains M. However, it cannot be all of R because RR is a non-zero ideal of R and must be equal to R because R is simple. Thus $RR \nsubseteq M$. Consequently, $\{y : yR \subseteq M\}$ must be equal to M. Then if $xR \subseteq M$, x is in M. Since we selected x not in M, xR is not in M.

Then R equals the right ideal generated by M and xR. In particular, there must exist m in M and x' in R such that $x = m + xx'$. Let $R_x = \{a : xa \in M\}$. This is a right ideal. Observe that $\{c - x'c\}$ is contained in R_x, for $x(c - x'c) = (x - xx')c = mc$ is in M. Now if R is Jacobson radical, then $-x'$ is right quasi-regular and there exists an element z such that $-x' + z - x'z = 0$. Then $x' = z - x'z$, and this is in R_x. Therefore $-x'c$ is in R_x, for every c. Then c is in R_x for every c, $R_x = R$. However, in that case $xR \subseteq M$, a contradiction. Therefore, $-x'$ cannot be right quasi-regular, R is not Jacobson radical, and therefore R is Jacobson semi-simple.

If a simple ring is trivial, then it is nilpotent and therefore Jacobson radical. Thus, the simple rings that are semi-simple with respect to Jacobson are the non-trivial ones with maximal right ideals, or from the point of view of Theorem 35, the non-trivial ones that are primitive.

For many years mathematicians wondered whether there were any simple non-trivial rings without maximal right ideals, and only recently has such an example been constructed. This was done by Sasiada, and his work is to appear in *Fundamenta Mathematica*. We have a brief summary of his construction, which we give as the following example.

Example 12. Let x and y be two non-commutative indeterminates. Let A be the set of all formal power series in x and y, with coefficients in the integers modulo 2. Thus A is the set of all power series, either finite or infinite, with coefficients that are either 0 or 1, and A has characteristic 2. Let S be the subset of A of all elements of A with a zero constant term. We propose to show that S is the Jacobson radical of A. Clearly, S is an ideal of A. Furthermore, every element in S is a non-unit of A. That is, if β is in S, then $\beta\alpha \neq 1$, no matter what α in A is chosen, for the degree of $\beta\alpha$ is at least 1. However, every element not in S *is* a unit. If γ is not in S, then

$$\gamma = 1 + a_1 x + a_2 y + a_3 xy + a_4 yx + a_5 x^2 + a_6 y^2 + \ldots.$$

Now let

$$\delta = 1 + a_1 x + a_2 y + xy(a_3 + a_1 a_2)$$
$$+ yx(a_4 + a_2 a_1) + x^2(a_5 + a_1{}^2) + y^2(a_6 + a_2{}^2) + \ldots,$$

where the rest of δ is chosen in such a way as to cancel everything out in $\gamma\delta$ except 1. Thus $\gamma\delta = 1$. Therefore γ is a unit.

Now let β be any element in S. It is not a unit. However, $1 + \beta$ is a unit (and it is not in S). Then there exists an element of the form $1 + \alpha$, with α in S, such that

$$(1 + \beta)(1 + \alpha) = 1.$$

Then $\beta + \alpha + \beta\alpha = 0$, and β is right quasi-regular. Thus, every element in S is right quasi-regular, and therefore S is a Jacobson radical ring. It is also the Jacobson radical of A, for any element not in S is a unit and therefore cannot be in the Jacobson radical. For, if α is a unit and is in the radical, then $\beta\alpha = 1$ is in the radical, -1 is in the radical, but $-1 + \tau + -1(\tau) = -1 \neq 0$.

We state that x is not contained in the ideal of S generated by $x + yx^2y$. This seems somewhat obvious intuitively, but its proof probably requires a lot of calculation. By Zorn's Lemma, select an ideal M maximal with respect to the exclusion of x and the inclusion of $x + yx^2y$. Although M may not be a maximal ideal of S, at least S/M is subdirectly irreducible, for every ideal in S/M contains the coset $x + M$. Let J be the heart of S/M, that is, the minimal ideal of S/M. Now we shall show that J is a simple non-trivial radical ring!

Since S is radical, S/M is radical because S/M is a homomorphic image of S. Since J is an ideal of the radical ring S/M, by Lemma 62, J is itself a radical ring.

To see that J is simple, let I be any non-zero ideal of J. The ideal of S/M generated by I must be J itself because J is the minimal ideal of S/M. By Lemma 61, $J^3 \subseteq I$. To finish the example, we must merely show that $J^2 = J$, for then $J^3 = J \subseteq I \subseteq J$ and thus J would be simple, and non-trivial ($J^2 \neq 0$).

Now J contains the non-zero coset $x + M$. Therefore, it also contains the cosets $xy + M$ and $yx + M$, and thus J^2 contains the coset $(yx + M) \cdot (xy + M) = yx^2y + M$. However, $x + yx^2y = m$, for some $m \in M$. Therefore, $yx^2y = x + m$ (characteristic $= 2$). Thus $yx^2y + M = x + m + M = x + M$, and this is a non-zero coset. Therefore $J^2 \neq 0$, $J^2 = J$, and the example is established.

J is a simple non-trivial Jacobson radical ring.

Now we know which simple rings are in the upper class of the partition associated with the Jacobson radical and we know that the lower class contains more than just the trivial simple rings. In particular, we know that the Jacobson radical corresponds to a different partition of the simple rings than the classical nil radical, for Example 12 is in the lower class for J but in the upper class for N.

The next question (raised by Kurosh in 1953) is whether the Jacobson radical coincides with the upper radical property determined by all the simple primitive rings. In 1962, Sasiada and Sulinski [45] gave a negative answer to this question with the following example.

Example 13. This is a slightly more complicated version of Example 8. Let F be a field of characteristic 0 and let S be an automorphism of F such that no integral power of S is the identity automorphism. For example, F might be the field generated by the real numbers and an infinite number of independent variables labelled $\ldots x_{-2}, x_{-1}, x_0, x_1, x_2, \ldots$. Then S could be the automorphism which leaves the real numbers alone and which sends x_i into x_{i+1} for every i. Clearly, $S^n \neq I$ for any integral n.

Then let R be the set of all polynomials in an indeterminate z, $a_0 + za_1 + \ldots + z^n a_n$, where the coefficients a_i belong to F. Addition of such polynomials is defined in the usual way and multiplication is defined in the standard way except that z does not commute with the coefficients a. We define $az = za^S$, where a^S is the image of a under the automorphism S. Then $az^m = za^{S^m}$. This definition, together with the distributive law, makes R into a ring. We may refer to R as $F[z, S]$.

As in Example 8, we may speak about the degree of a polynomial in R, and we observe that R has no zero divisors, for the degree of a product of polynomials is the sum of their separate degrees. Thus, R is an integral domain and the only units of R are the non-zero elements of F. Also as in Example 8, we may divide one polynomial into another. Let

$$f(z) = a_0 + za_1 + \ldots + z^m a_m \text{ and } g(z) = b_0 + zb_1 + \ldots + z^r b_r.$$

Assuming $m \geqslant r$,

$$f(z) - g(z)z^{m-r}(b_r^{-1})^{S^{m-r}} . a_m$$

is a polynomial of degree less than m. Carrying on in this way, we obtain $f(z) = g(z) q(z) + r(z)$ with the degree of $r(z) <$ the degree of $g(z)$, or $r(z) \equiv 0$. Similarly, we can divide $f(z)$ on the left and get $f(z) = q_1(z) g(z) + r_1(z)$ with the degree of $r_1(z) <$ the degree of $g(z)$, or $r_1(z) \equiv 0$.

As in Example 8, we can then show that every right ideal of R is of the form $f(z).R$ and every left ideal is of the form $R.f(z)$, or to put it another way, R is a principal ideal domain.

In Example 8 the ring turned out to be simple, but our R here has many two-sided ideals.

Let I be a two-sided ideal of R. Then $I = f(z)R = Rg(z)$. Then $f(z) = h(z) \cdot g(z)$ and $g(z) = f(z) k(z)$. Then $g(z) = h(z) g(z) k(z)$, and both $h(z)$ and $k(z)$ must be of degree 0, i.e. elements of F. Then $g(z) = f(z).k$ and $Rg(z) = Rf(z).k$. But $f(z) = h.f(z).k$ and therefore $f(z).k = h^{-1}.f(z)$. Thus $R.g(z) = Rf(z).k = R.h^{-1}.f(z)$. Since h^{-1} is a unit, $Rh^{-1} = R$ and thus $Rg(z) = Rf(z)$ and $I = f(z)R = Rf(z)$.

A polynomial $f(z)$ must be somewhat special to have the property that $f(z)R = Rf(z)$. In fact, we shall show that the only polynomials with this property are monomials, that is $f(z) = z^k a$.

To prove this, suppose that $f(z) = z^n + z^{n-1}a_{n-1} + \ldots + za_1 + a_0$ with $a_0 \neq 0$. Then, for any b in F, $f(z).b$ is in $R.f(z)$. Thus, there exists an element, clearly of degree 0, i.e. an element of F, say c, such that $f(z)b = c.f(z)$. Then

$$z^n b + z^{n-1}a_{n-1} b + \ldots + za_1 b + a_0 b = z^n c^{S^n} + z^{n-1}a_{n-1} c^{S^{n-1}} + \ldots + za_1 c^S + a_0 c.$$

Then $a_0 b = a_0 c$ and since $a_0 \neq 0$, $b = c$. Thus, from $b = c^{S^n} = b^{S^n}$, we have that $S^n = I$ on F. But we have chosen S so that $S^n \neq I$ for any integral n. Thus, $f(z)$ cannot have a non-zero constant if it has any z's in it.

Then suppose that $f(z) = z^n + z^{n-1}a_{n-1} + \ldots + z^k a_k$, with $a_k \neq 0$. Then $f(z) = z^k g(z)$, where $g(z) = z^{n-k} + z^{n-k-1}a_{n-1} + \ldots + a_k$. We know that $Rz^k g(z) = z^k g(z)R$, and we also know that $Rz^k = z^k R$, because

$$(z^r d_r + \ldots + zd_1 + d_0)z^k = z^k(z^r d_r^{S^k} + \ldots + zd_1^{S^k} + d_0^{S^k}).$$

Thus, we have $z^k.Rg(z) = z^k.g(z)R$. Since R is an integral domain, $Rg(z)$

must $= g(z)R$. But this is impossible because $g(z)$ has a non-zero constant *and* some z's. The only way out of this contradiction is to have $g(z) = a$ constant, and in that case $f(z) = z^k \cdot a$. Then the only ideals of R are those of the form $z^k \cdot aR$, and these are equal to $z^k R$ since a is a unit.

Next we would like to show that R is a right primitive ring. Let $M = (z - 1)R$. Clearly M is a right ideal, but not a two-sided ideal. Thus $M \neq R$. However, M is maximal, for if $M \subseteq I$, then $I = f(z) \cdot R$ for some $f(z)$. However, $f(z)$ if of minimal degree in I and since M contains polynomials of degree $1, f(z)$ must be of degree 1, or less. But if $f(z)$ is of degree $0, f(z)$ is in F and then $I = R$. Thus, let $f(z) = za_1 + a_0$. Then $f(z) = (z - 1)a_1 + (a_0 + a_1)$. Then $a_0 + a_1 = f(z) - (z - 1)a_1$ is in I and if $a_0 + a_1 \neq 0$, then $I = R$. Consequently, $a_0 = -a_1$ and $f(z) = (z - 1)a_1$. Then $I = M$. Since R has a unit element, every right ideal, and in particular M, is regular.

Now consider $(M:R) = \{r \in R : Rr \subseteq M\}$. This is a two-sided ideal of R and it is $\subseteq M$ (Lemma 55). Since it is an ideal, it is equal to $z^k R = Rz^k$. Thus z^k is in M. But this is impossible, for if

$$z^k = (z - 1)g(z) = (z - 1)(z^{k-1}d_{k-1} + \ldots + d_0),$$

then $z^k = z^k d_{k-1} + z^{k-1}(d_{k-2} - d_{k-1}) + \ldots + z^1(d_0 - d_1) - d_0$.

Then $0 = d_0 = d_1 = \ldots = d_{k-1}$. But $d_{k-1} = 1$. Therefore, $(M:R)$ must be the zero ideal and, therefore, R is right primitive.

Finally, let $T = zR$. We shall show that T is not a Jacobson radical ring, but that T is radical with respect to the upper radical property determined by the simple primitive rings. This will prove that the Jacobson radical does *not* coincide with this upper radical.

The ring T is not simple, for it contains many two-sided ideals, namely $z^k R$ for $k = 2, 3, 4, \ldots$. To show that it is radical with respect to the upper radical determined by the simple primitive rings, we shall show that every homomorphic image of T with non-zero kernel is a nilpotent ring. This will prove that T cannot be mapped onto a simple primitive ring, and thus T will be radical with respect to this upper radical. Thus, let A be any non-zero ideal of T and A^* be the ideal of R generated by A. Then $A^* = z^k R$ for some $k \geq 1$. Now $A^{*3} = z^{3^k} R$ and $T/A^{*3} = zR/z^{3^k} R$ is a nilpotent ring. By Lemma 60, $A^{*3} \subseteq A$ and therefore T/A is a homomorphic image of T/A^{*3} and thus T/A is nilpotent. Finally, by Lemma 62, T is Jacobson semi-simple since R is.

I

CHAPTER FIVE

THE BROWN–McCOY RADICAL

5.1. G-regularity. The Jacobson radical is a good generalization of the classical nil radical. Nevertheless, dense rings of linear transformations do not have quite the same appeal as simple rings, and it is quite natural to attempt to find a slightly larger radical in order to obtain simple rings in the subdirect sum representation of a semi-simple ring. Brown and McCoy succeeded in doing this [17, 18, 19] by generalizing the notion of quasi-regularity.

For right quasi-regularity, we considered the right ideal $\{ar + r\}$ associated with the element a, and it turned out that a was right quasi-regular if and only if this right ideal was the entire ring R. Now we consider the two-sided ideal generated by this right ideal, and ask when this two-sided ideal is all of R. Thus, all right quasi-regular elements will have this property, but there will be other elements which are not right quasi-regular, i.e. for which $\{ar + r\} \neq R$, but for which the two-sided ideal generated by $\{ar + r\}$ *is* all of R.

To be more specific, for each element a of a ring R, we associate the ideal

$$G(a) = \{ar + r + \sum(x_i a y_i + x_i y_i)\},$$

where r, x_i, y_i range over R, and the summation is finite. We shall say that a is *G-regular* if a is in $G(a)$. Then $G(a) = R$, for if a is in $G(a)$, so is ar, and since $ar + r$ is in $G(a)$, then r is in $G(a)$ for every r. And, of course, if $G(a) = R$ for some a, then a is in $G(a)$ and a is G-regular.

We shall say that an ideal I is *G-regular* if every element in I is G-regular.

We repeat that if an element is right quasi-regular, then it is G-regular.

To show that G-regularity is a radical property we first show that every ring has a maximal G-regular ideal which contains all other G-regular ideals of the ring. To do this, we begin with:

Lemma 65. *The union of two G-regular ideals is also a G-regular ideal.*

Proof. Let I_1 and I_2 be two G-regular ideals and take a in I_1 and b in I_2. Then a is in $G(a)$ and thus there exist elements r, x_i, and y_i such that

$$a = ar + r + \sum(x_i a y_i + x_i y_i).$$

With these elements r, x_i, y_i, let us consider the element

$$c = (a + b)r + r + \sum(x_i(a + b)y_i + x_i y_i).$$

Now

$$a + b - c = b + ar + r + \sum (x_i a y_i + x_i y_i) - br - ar - r$$
$$- \sum (x_i(a + b)y_i + x_i y_i)$$
$$= b - br - \sum x_i b y_i.$$

Since b is in the ideal I_2, so is $b - br + \sum x_i b y_i$, and therefore $a + b - c$ is G-regular. We also note that c is in the ideal $G(a + b)$. Since $a + b - c$ is G-regular, there exist elements w, u_i, and v_i such that

$$a + b - c = (a + b - c)w + w + \sum (u_i[a + b - c]v_i + u_i v_i).$$

Then

(1) $\quad a + b = (a + b)w + w + \sum (u_i[a + b]v_i + u_i v_i) + c - cw - \sum u_i c v_i.$

Since c is in $G(a + b)$, so is $c - cw - \sum u_i c v_i$. Furthermore,

$$(a + b)w + w + \sum (u_i[a + b]v_i + u_i v_i)$$

is in $G(a + b)$, and therefore the right-hand side of (1) is in $G(a + b)$. Thus, $a + b$ is in $G(a + b)$ and $a + b$ is G-regular. This establishes the lemma.

Remark. Actually the element a need not belong to a G-regular ideal. All that is required is that a be G-regular, and that b belong to a G-regular ideal, exactly as in Lemma 51.

Let G be the union of all the G-regular ideals of a ring R. Since every element in G is a finite sum of elements from G-regular ideals, it is clear that each such element is G-regular. Thus, G is a G-regular ideal and it contains every G-regular ideal of R.

This proves property (B) of radical properties. Property (A) is immediate, for if R' is a homomorphic image of the G-regular ring R, then every element of R' is G-regular. For if

$$a - ar - r - \sum (x_i a y_i + x_i y_i) = 0 \text{ in } R,$$

then $\qquad a' - a'r' - r' - \sum (x'_i a' y'_i + x'_i y'_i) = 0 \text{ in } R'.$

We must finally establish property (C), i.e. that R/G is semi-simple with respect to G-regularity. To see this, suppose that R/G has a G-regular ideal T/G. Take $t + G$ in T/G. Then there exist elements r, x_i, y_i in R such that

$$t - tr - r - \sum (x_i t y_i + x_i y_i)$$

is in G. Let us put

$$tr + r + \sum (x_i t y_i + x_i y_i) = c.$$

Then $t - c$ is in G and, thus, is G-regular. Then there exist elements w, u_i, v_i in R such that

$$t - c = (t - c)w + w + \sum (u_i[t - c]v_i + u_i v_i).$$

Then

$$t = tw + w + \sum (u_i tv_i + u_i v_i) + c - cw - \sum u_i cv_i.$$

Now, c is in $G(t)$ and therefore $c - cw - \sum u_i cv_i$ is also in $G(t)$. Furthermore, $tw + w + \sum(u_i tv_i + u_i v_i)$ is in $G(t)$. Therefore, the right-hand side is in $G(t)$. Therefore, t is in $G(t)$ and t is G-regular. This holds for all t in T, and thus T is a G-regular ideal of R. Then $T \subseteq G$ and T/G is the zero coset. Therefore, R/G is semi-simple with respect to G-regularity. This establishes (C) and we have:

Theorem 42. *G-regularity is a radical property.*

Since all right quasi-regular ideals are also G-regular, it is clear that the Jacobson radical property $J \leqslant \mathscr{G}$, the Brown–McCoy or G-regular radical property. It is also clear that in a commutative ring $J = \mathscr{G}$, for the essential difference between them is two-sided ideals versus one-sided ideals. However, in general, they are different and we shall establish that $J < \mathscr{G} < \mathscr{T}$.

To see that $\mathscr{G} < \mathscr{T}$, we must show that any matrix ring over a division ring is G-semi-simple (Lemma 4). However, any ring with a unity element cannot be G-radical for the element -1 is not G-regular. If $-1 = (-1)r + r + \sum(x_i(-1)y_i + x_i y_i)$, then $-1 = 0$, an impossibility. In particular, then, any matrix ring over a division ring, having a unity element, is not G-radical. Since it is simple, it must be G-semi-simple and thus $\mathscr{G} < \mathscr{T}$. Therefore, $J \leqslant \mathscr{G} < \mathscr{T}$ and in the classical D.C.C. situation, $\mathscr{G}$ coincides with the classical radical.

Before we delve into the partition of the simple rings associated with $\mathscr{G}$, and into examples establishing that $J < \mathscr{G} < \mathscr{T}$, we shall first examine the usefulness of $\mathscr{G}$.

5.2. G-semi-simple rings. If R is not G-radical, then R contains an element x which is not G-regular, i.e. $I \equiv \{xr + r + \sum(u_i xv_i + u_i v_i)\} \neq R$. By considering all ideals which contain I but which do not contain x, by ordering these ideals by inclusion, and by using Zorn's Lemma (Section 3.5), we obtain an ideal, maximal with respect to the exclusion of x and to the inclusion of I. However, such an ideal is a maximal ideal of R, for if any ideal properly contains it, it must also contain x and thus be all of R. Consequently, every ring which is not G-radical possesses maximal ideals (unless, of course, R is simple, in which case 0 is a maximal ideal).

Lemma 66. *The G-radical of any ring R is equal to the intersection of all ideals M of R such that R/M is simple and is G-semi-simple.*

Proof. If x is not in G, the G-radical of R, then the ideal which x generates is not G-regular. Let y be an element in the ideal generated by x such that $y \notin G(y)$, i.e. y is not G-regular. Then, as above, there exists a maximal ideal

M_y which does not contain y. Then R/M_y is simple. However, $G(y) \subseteq M_y$ and thus $G(y + M_y) = 0$ in the factor ring R/M_y. Thus, $y + M_y$ is not G-regular in R/M_y and therefore R/M_y is G-semi-simple. Now $y \notin M_y$ and thus $y \notin \cap M$. Then $x \notin \cap M$, for if $x \in \cap M$, the ideal generated by x would be $\subseteq \cap M$ and, in particular, y would then be in $\cap M$. Thus, if $x \notin G$, then $x \notin \cap M$ and therefore $\cap M \subseteq G$.

Conversely, if x is in G and M is any ideal of R such that R/M is simple and G-semi-simple, then $(G + M)/M$ is a G-regular ideal of R/M. Then $(G + M)/M$ is 0 in R/M, G is in M, $x \in M$, and thus $G \subseteq \cap M$.

Therefore, $G = \cap M$ and the lemma is established.

Lemma 67. *A simple, G-semi-simple ring R has a unity element.*

Proof. Since R is G-semi-simple, there exists an x in R such that x is not G-regular. Then $x \notin G(x)$, $G(x) \neq R$, and therefore $G(x) = 0$. Then $xr + r = 0$ for every r in R and therefore $-x$ is a left unity element for R.

Let $I = \{rx + r\}$. Then $IR = 0$ and $RI \subseteq I$. Therefore I is an ideal of R. If $I = R$, then there exists an element t such that $tx + t = x$. Multiplying on the right by t, we get $0 = xt = -t$. Thus, $t = 0$, $x = 0$, a contradiction. Therefore $I = 0$ and thus $rx + r = 0$ for every r, $-x$ is also a right unity element, and therefore $-x$ is a unity element.

Putting Lemmas 66 and 67 together, we have:

Theorem 43. *The G-radical of any ring R is equal to the intersection of all ideals M of R such that R/M is a simple ring with unity element.*

We then have:

Theorem 44. *For any ring R, with G-radical G, R/G is isomorphic to a subdirect sum of simple rings with unity.*

Proof. The G-radical of R/G is 0 (property (C)) and thus by Theorem 19, R/G is isomorphic to a subdirect sum of rings R_i, where $R_i \cong (R/G)/(M/G) \cong R/M$ and R_i is simple with unity by Theorem 43.

This parallels Theorems 35 and 38. We have discarded a bit more than the Jacobson radical and the gain is that instead of dense rings of linear transformations we have simple rings with units, in the subdirect sum. Thus the gain does not improve the weakest part, i.e. the subdirect sum, but it does give us slightly nicer components. It thus generalizes Theorems 10 and 11 somewhat more elegantly, for there also we had simple rings with unities.

Every simple ring with unity is both left and right primitive. For, we may take a right ideal, I, maximal with respect to the exclusion of 1, by Zorn's Lemma. This right ideal I is then truly maximal, for if any right ideal properly contains I, it also contains 1 and is therefore the whole ring. Now $(I : R) = 0$ because $(I : R)$ is a two-sided ideal of R, and if it is equal to R, then $RR \subseteq I$.

But $RR = R$. Thus, $(I:R) = 0$ and R is right primitive. Similarly, R is left primitive.

However, there exist rings which are both left and right primitive but which are not simple. Example 11 furnishes us with such an example, namely W, the set of all row-finite matrices. W is not simple, but it is certainly a dense ring of linear transformations, on both the right and the left. Therefore, by the corollary to Theorem 36, W is both right and left primitive.

5.3. The Brown–McCoy radical and the general theory.

We know that $J \leqslant \mathscr{G} \leqslant \mathscr{T}$ and now we require two examples to show that, in general, $J < \mathscr{G} < \mathscr{T}$.

In Example 11 we showed that Z, the set of finite-valued linear transformations, was Jacobson semi-simple, simple, but radical with respect to $\mathscr{T}$. And Z did not contain a unity element. Since it is simple, it is either G-radical or G-semi-simple. But it cannot be G-semi-simple, for then, by Lemma 67, it would have to have a unity element. Thus, Z is G-radical. This proves that $J < \mathscr{G}$.

For the other part we consider Example 8. It is a simple ring with unity, and therefore it is G-semi-simple, because -1 is not G-regular. However, we have established that this ring is not of the form $\mathscr{M}D$, i.e. finite matrices over a division ring. Since it is simple, all of its non-zero homomorphic images are isomorphic to itself. Consequently, none of them can be of the form $\mathscr{M}D$. Therefore, this ring cannot be mapped homomorphically on an $\mathscr{M}D$ ring and, therefore, by definition, it is $\mathscr{T}$ radical. This proves that $\mathscr{G} < \mathscr{T}$.

It is clear that $\mathscr{G}$ corresponds to the partition of the simple rings in which the upper class consists of all simple rings with unity and the lower class consists of all simple rings without a unity. This is, in fact, a different partition than the partition associated with J, the Jacobson radical, for Z of Example 11 is in the upper class for J but in the lower class for $\mathscr{G}$.

We were not able to identify J with the upper radical property determined by the simple primitive rings (i.e. the simple rings in the upper class of its partition), but we *can* do this for $\mathscr{G}$.

Theorem 45. $\mathscr{G}$, *the Brown–McCoy radical property, is the upper radical property U determined by the class of all simple rings with unity.*

Proof. Since all simple rings with unity are G-semi-simple, we know that $\mathscr{G} \leqslant U$ (Lemma 4) or that every G-radical ring is U-radical. To show that $\mathscr{G} = U$ it will be sufficient to show that every U-radical ring is G-radical. Or, equivalently, to show that if a ring is not G-radical, then it is not U-radical.

Thus, let R be a ring which is not G-radical. Then R/G is G-semi-simple and it is a non-zero homomorphic image of R. Then R/G is isomorphic to a subdirect sum of simple rings with unity (Theorem 44). Then R/G can be mapped homomorphically onto one of the non-zero components in this subdirect sum. Thus, R can be mapped, homomorphically, onto a simple ring with unity. Therefore, by the definition of the upper radical property, R is not U-radical. This ends the proof.

Remark. The reason that the Jacobson radical does not coincide with the upper radical property of its partition is that the components in its subdirect sum representation, although they are right primitive, are not necessarily simple.

Semi-simple rings, in general, are somewhat delicate. For example, the ring of integers I is nil semi-simple (it is also Jacobson and Brown–McCoy semi-simple), but its homomorphic image $I/(4)$ is not nil semi-simple for it contains the nil (nilpotent!) ideal $(2)/(4)$.

Thus, it is not immediately obvious that a subdirect sum of simple semi-simple rings is semi-simple.

However, it is not difficult to show that for any radical property P a subdirect sum of simple P-semi-simple rings is again P-semi-simple. Let $R =$ the subdirect sum of the simple rings A_i, where each A_i is P-semi-simple. Then R contains a set of ideals C_i such that $R/C_i \cong A_i$ and $\cap C_i = 0$. Let P be the P-radical of R. If $P \neq 0$, then it cannot be contained in every C_i. Take C_i such that $P \nsubseteq C_i$. Since C_i is a maximal ideal of R (because R/C_i is simple), $C_i + P = R$. Then $A_i \cong R/C_i = (C_i + P)/C_i \cong P/(C_i \cap P)$. The right-hand side is a homomorphic image of the P-radical ring P and thus is P-radical. Therefore, A_i is P-radical. This is impossible, and thus $P = 0$ and R is P-semi-simple.

However, there exist radical properties for which some semi-simple rings cannot be represented as a subdirect sum of simple semi-simple rings. The question arises: For which radical properties can *every* semi-simple ring be so represented?

Sulinski [47] has shown that the Brown–McCoy radical property is essentially the smallest radical property for which every semi-simple ring is isomorphic to a subdirect sum of simple semi-simple rings, which proves that Brown and McCoy chose very wisely!

Theorem 46. *Let U be the upper radical property of a partition of the simple rings. Then the upper class of the partition contains only simple rings with unities if and only if* (1) *every U-semi-simple ring is isomorphic to a subdirect sum of simple rings from this upper class, and* (2) *every ideal of a U-radical ring is also U-radical.*

Proof. Suppose that the upper class of the partition contains only simple rings with unity, and let R be a non-zero semi-simple ring. Consider all ideals M_i of R such that R/M_i is a simple ring in the upper class of the partition. If R

is simple itself, it is in the upper class and (1) holds. However, if R is not simple, then it contains some maximal ideals M_i such that R/M_i is in the upper class, because it can be mapped homomorphically onto an upper-class simple ring (otherwise R would be U-radical).

Now let S be the intersection of all these maximal ideals. If $S = 0$, then we have (1). If S is not zero, then as an ideal of a U-semi-simple ring it can be mapped homomorphically on an upper-class simple ring T. By assumption, T has a unity element. Let e be an element in S which maps onto the unity in this homomorphism $h : S \to T$.

We now define a homomorphism $k\colon R \to T$ by

$$k(x) = h(exe).$$

This is a homomorphism, for

$$k(x + y) = h(e[x + y]e) = h(exe) + h(eye) = k(x) + k(y)$$

and

$$k(xy) = h(exye) = h(ex)h(ye) = h(ex)h(e)h(e)h(ye)$$

$$= h(exe)h(eye) = k(x)k(y).$$

Thus, k is a homomorphism from R to T and it coincides with h on the ideal S. Therefore, $k(e)$ must also be the unity element of T.

In particular, e is not in the kernel of k. However, the kernel of k is precisely one of the M_i and $e \in S = \cap M_i$; thus, e must be in M_i. This is a contradiction and therefore $S = 0$ and we have (1).

To establish (2), let R be a U-radical ring, i.e. R cannot be mapped homomorphically onto an upper-class simple ring. Let M be an ideal of R and suppose that M is not U-radical, i.e. M can be mapped homomorphically onto an upper-class simple ring T. Then T has a unity element, M has an element which maps into this unity, and, as above, we can extend the homomorphism to go from R to T. This would contradict the fact that R cannot be so mapped onto an upper-class simple ring, and therefore M must be U-radical and we have (2).

Conversely, suppose that we have conditions (1) and (2) for an upper radical property U. Let R be any simple U-semi-simple ring and suppose that R does not contain a unity element. Then we embed R in the usual way, in a ring R' with unity. Since we must do some careful analysis now, it may be best to remind ourselves what this "usual way" is.

Let R' be the set of all pairs (i, r), where i is in the set of integers I and where r is in R. Addition and multiplication are defined as:

$$(i, r_1) + (j, r_2) = (i + j, r_1 + r_2),$$

$$(i, r_1) \cdot (j, r_2) = (ij, ir_2 + jr_1 + r_1 r_2).$$

Then R' is a ring with unity element $(1, 0)$ and the set of all pairs $(0, r)$ is isomorphic to R. We shall identify R with this isomorphic ring of all pairs $(0, r)$. Furthermore, R'/R is isomorphic to the ring I of integers, R is an ideal of R', and since R is simple, R is a minimal ideal of R'.

For any ideal M of R', we may consider the set of all integers i that appear in pairs belonging to M. Call this set M_I. Thus, the integer i is in M_I if there exists an r in R such that (i, r) is in M. It is not difficult to show that M_I is an ideal of I. For if i is in M_I, (i, r) is in M, and then for any j in I, $(i, r) . (j, 0) = (ij, jr)$ is in M and ij is in M_I.

Now we wish to show that R is contained in every maximal ideal of R'. Let M be a maximal ideal of R', and suppose that $M \cap R = 0$. For a maximal ideal M, M_I must equal all of I, for if $M_I \neq I$, then let $Q = \{(m, r)\}$, with m just in M_I and r ranging over all of R. Then Q is a proper ideal of R' and Q contains R. But Q also contains M. Since M is maximal and Q is proper, $M = Q$. However, $Q \cap R = R$ and this contradicts the assumption that $M \cap R = 0$. Thus $M_I = I$. Now M must contain a pair $(1, k)$ with $k \neq 0$, for if $(1, 0)$ is in M, then so is $(1, 0).(0, r) = (0, r)$ for any r and then $M \cap R \neq 0$. Since $M_I = I$, 1 must appear in some pair in M.

Then $(1, k)(0, r) = (0, r + kr)$ and $(0, r)(1, k) = (0, r + rk)$ are both in M and since $M \cap R = 0$, we must have $r + kr = 0 = r + rk$ for every r. Then $-k$ is a unity element for R. However, this contradicts our assumption that R has no unity. Therefore, $M \cap R \neq 0$. Since R is a minimal ideal, $M \cap R = R$, and thus R is contained in every maximal ideal of R'.

Then, the intersection of all the maximal ideals of R' contains R and is not zero. Then R' can never be represented as a subdirect sum of simple rings and thus, by (1), R' cannot be U-semi-simple.

Let U be the U-radical of R', $U \neq 0$. Now, R'/U is U-semi-simple and, by (1), it can be represented as a subdirect sum of upper-class simple rings. Thus, R'/U must contain a set of maximal ideals whose intersection is zero. Thus, there exists a set of maximal ideals of R' whose intersection is in U. Since R is in every maximal ideal of R', R must be in U. Now U is U-radical and it contains the ideal R which is U-semi-simple. This contradicts condition (2).

Therefore, R must have had a unity element to start with and the theorem is established.

The second condition of Theorem 46 is intimately connected with the property stated in Lemma 62. First we prove:

Lemma 68. *For any radical property R the following two conditions are equivalent:*

(a) Every ideal of an R-radical ring is itself an R-radical ring.

(a') For any ring A and any ideal I of A, we have $R(I) \supseteq I \cap R(A)$.

Proof. If (a') holds, let A be an R-radical ring, $R(A) = A$. Let I be an ideal of A. Then $R(I) \supseteq I \cap R(A) = I \cap A = I$. However, $R(I) \subseteq I$ and thus $R(I) = I$, and I is itself an R-radical ring.

Conversely, suppose that (a) holds. Again let I be an ideal of a ring A, and consider $I \cap R(A)$. This is an ideal contained in the R-radical ring $R(A)$. Thus, by (a), $I \cap R(A)$ is an R-radical ring. It is contained in I and therefore must be contained in $R(I)$, i.e. $R(I) \supseteq I \cap R(A)$.

We may also prove:

Lemma 69. *For any radical property* R *the following two conditions are equivalent:*

(b) *Every ideal of an R-semi-simple ring is itself R-semi-simple.*

(b') *For any ring A and any ideal I of A, we have* $R(I) \subseteq I \cap R(A)$.

Proof. If (b') holds, let A be an R-semi-simple ring, $R(A) = 0$. Let I be an ideal of A. Then $R(I) \subseteq I \cap R(A) = I \cap 0 = 0$. Thus, I is itself R-semi-simple.

Conversely, suppose that (b) holds. Again let I be an ideal of a ring A, and consider the R-semi-simple ring $A/R(A)$. The ideal $[I + R(A)]/R(A)$, of $A/R(A)$, must be R-semi-simple. However,

$$\frac{[I + R(A)]}{R(A)} \cong \frac{I}{[I \cap R(A)]}.$$

Therefore $I/[I \cap R(A)]$ is R-semi-simple. Consequently, $R(I) \subseteq I \cap R(A)$, for if not,

$$\frac{R(I) + [I \cap R(A)]}{I \cap R(A)} \cong \frac{R(I)}{R(I) \cap [I \cap R(A)]}$$

would be an R-radical ideal (since it is a homomorphic image of the R-radical ring $R(I)$) of the R-semi-simple ring $I/[I \cap R(A)]$ and this is impossible.

There was a study made of the relationship between conditions (a) and (b) and, surprisingly enough, it was discovered that condition (a) implied condition (b). However, this, as well as Lemma 69, lost some of its point when the following result was proved (by Divinsky and Sulinski):

Theorem 47. *If R is any radical property, then for any ring A and any ideal I of A, $R(I)$ is an ideal of A.*

Proof. If $R(I)$ is not an ideal of A, then there exists an element x of A such that either $x.R(I)$ or $R(I).x$ is not contained in $R(I)$. Assume first that $x.R(I) \nsubseteq R(I)$. Then $xR(I) + R(I)$ properly contains $R(I)$. It is contained in I for I is an ideal of A and $R(I) \subseteq I$. Furthermore, $xR(I) + R(I)$ is an ideal of I, because $R(I)$ is an ideal of I and $I.xR(I) = Ix.R(I) \subseteq I.R(I) \subseteq R(I)$.

Since $I/R(I)$ is R-semi-simple, the ideal $[xR(I) + R(I)]/R(I)$ cannot be an

R-ring. We will, however, show that this ideal is a homomorphic image of the R-ring $R(I)$ and is therefore an R-ring. This contradiction will prove that $xR(I) \subseteq R(I)$ for every x in A. Similarly, $R(I).x \subseteq R(I)$ and $R(I)$ is an ideal of A.

To set up the homomorphism, let y be any element in $R(I)$ and define

$$\theta(y) \equiv xy + R(I).$$

Thus, θ is a mapping from $R(I)$ to $[xR(I) + R(I)]/R(I)$. Clearly, θ is an onto mapping, and θ preserves addition. To see that $\theta(y_1 y_2) = \theta(y_1).\theta(y_2)$ we shall show that both of these are the zero coset.

First, $\theta(y_1 y_2) = xy_1 y_2 + R(I)$. Since y_1 is in $R(I) \subseteq I$, $xy_1 \in I$ and thus $xy_1 y_2 \in I.R(I) \subseteq R(I)$. Thus, $\theta(y_1 y_2) = 0 + R(I)$.

On the other hand

$$\theta(y_1).\theta(y_2) = [xy_1 + R(I)][xy_2 + R(I)] = xy_1 xy_2 + R(I).$$

However, $xy_1 x$ is in I and $xy_1 xy_2$ is in $I.R(I) \subseteq R(I)$. Thus, $\theta(y_1).\theta(y_2) = 0 + R(I) = \theta(y_1 y_2)$. This proves that θ is a homomorphism, that $[xR(I) + R(I)]/R(I)$ is an R-radical ring, and that $xR(I) \subseteq R(I)$. The theorem is thus established.

Corollary 1. *If R is any radical property, then for any ring A with ideal I, we have $R(I) \subseteq I \cap R(A)$.*

Proof. Since $R(I)$ is an ideal of A, it must be $\subseteq R(A)$ because it is an R-radical ring. It is, of course, in I and thus $R(I) \subseteq I \cap R(A)$.

Corollary 2. *For any radical property R, every ideal of an R-semi-simple is itself R-semi-simple.*

Thus, the conditions considered in Lemma 69 hold for every radical property R! Consequently, whenever $R(I) \supseteq I \cap R(A)$ we can conclude that $R(I) = I \cap R(A)$. Thus, Lemma 68 can be rewritten as:

Theorem 48. *For any radical property R, the following conditions are equivalent:*

(a) Every ideal of an R-radical ring is itself an R-radical ring.

(c) For any ring A and any ideal I of A, we have $R(I) = I \cap R(A)$.

We shall say that a radical property R is *hereditary* if conditions (a) and (c) hold for it.

The discussion following Lemma 62 shows that there exist radical properties which are not hereditary. And Lemma 62 proves that the Jacobson radical is hereditary.

Problem. Prove that the Brown-McCoy radical is hereditary.

CHAPTER SIX

THE LEVITZKI RADICAL

6.1. Local nilpotency. In Chapter II we briefly mentioned the idea of local nilpotence, and now to round out our study of various radical properties we shall consider it more carefully.

A ring is *locally nilpotent* if any finite set of elements generates a subring which is nilpotent. Thus, every nilpotent ring is locally nilpotent and every locally nilpotent ring is nil. The question whether every nil ring is locally nilpotent, which was an open question when we wrote Chapter 2, is no longer an open question! (See footnote on page 21.)

We wish to show that local nilpotence is a radical property and, for this, we require a few lemmas. We say that an ideal I of a ring R is *locally nilpotent* if, thought of as a ring, I is locally nilpotent.

Lemma 70. *If an ideal I of a ring R is locally nilpotent and if R/I is locally nilpotent, then R itself is locally nilpotent. Furthermore, if R is locally nilpotent, then so is every subring and every homomorphic image of R.*

Proof. Let $\{r_1, r_2, \ldots, r_n\}$ be any finite subset of R, and let S be the subring generated by these elements. Then consider R/I and the finite number of cosets $r_1 + I, \ldots, r_n + I$. Since R/I is locally nilpotent, $\bar{S}$, the subring of R/I generated by $r_1 + I, \ldots, r_n + I$, is nilpotent, say $\bar{S}^m = 0$ in R/I. Thus $S^m \subseteq I$. Now S^m is generated by a finite set of elements, namely the set of all products of m of r_i. Since I is locally nilpotent, S^m must be nilpotent, $S^{mt} = 0$. Therefore, S is a nilpotent subring of R and therefore R itself is locally nilpotent.

The fact that every subring and every homomorphic image of a locally nilpotent ring are locally nilpotent is immediate from the definitions.

Thus, local nilpotency has property (A) of radical properties.

Lemma 71. *The sum of two locally nilpotent ideals I_1 and I_2 of a ring R is again a locally nilpotent ideal.*

Proof. Since $(I_1 + I_2)/I_2 \cong I_1/(I_1 \cap I_2)$, and since the right-hand side is a homomorphic image of the locally nilpotent ideal I_1, the right-hand side, and thus the left-hand side, is locally nilpotent, by Lemma 70. Furthermore, since I_2 and $(I_1 + I_2)/I_2$ are both locally nilpotent, so is $I_1 + I_2$, again by Lemma 70.

Corollary. *The sum of any finite number of locally nilpotent ideals is a locally nilpotent ideal.*

Lemma 72. *The union L of all the locally nilpotent ideals of a ring R is a locally nilpotent ideal.*

Proof. Take any finite set of elements $x_1, \ldots, x_n$ in L. Each x_i comes from a finite set of locally nilpotent ideals. Thus, the entire set $x_1, \ldots, x_n$ is contained in a finite set of locally nilpotent ideals. By the corollary to Lemma 71, the union of this finite set of locally nilpotent ideals is a locally nilpotent ideal. Since it contains $x_1, \ldots, x_n$, the set $x_1, \ldots, x_n$ must generate a nilpotent subring. Therefore, L is itself locally nilpotent.

This gives us property (B) of radical properties. Finally, we show that property (C) also holds.

Lemma 73. *R/L has no locally nilpotent non-zero ideals.*

Proof. If W/L is a locally nilpotent ideal of R/L, then, by Lemma 70, W is itself locally nilpotent. Since L contains all the locally nilpotent ideals of R, $W \subseteq L$ and W/L is the 0 ideal in R/L.

Thus, we have:

Theorem 49. *Local nilpotence is a radical property.*

We may say, then, that this radical property is the lower radical property determined by all locally nilpotent rings.

Since Levitzki [39] developed this material, this radical property is referred to as the Levitzki radical.

We know that L, the Levitzki radical of any ring R, contains all the locally nilpotent ideals of R. We can actually prove more.

Theorem 50. *The Levitzki radical contains all the one-sided locally nilpotent ideals.*

Proof. Let A be a locally nilpotent left ideal of R. We consider R/L, which is Levitzki semi-simple. Then $(A + L)/L$ is a locally nilpotent (it is $\cong A/(A \cap L)$ and thus a homomorphic image of the locally nilpotent ring A) left ideal of R/L. Thus, we may as well assume that R itself is Levitzki semi-simple.

Consider AR. It is a two-sided ideal of R, and it is locally nilpotent. To see this, take any finite set $x_1, \ldots, x_n$ in AR. Then each $x_i = \sum_j a_{ij} r_{ij}$, a finite sum, with a_{ij} in A and r_{ij} in R. Now consider the finite set of elements $y_{ijkm} = r_{ij} a_{km}$. These are all in A, since A is a left ideal. Since A is locally nilpotent, the set of all y_{ijkm} generates a nilpotent subring. Thus, there exists an integer N such that the product of any N of the y_{ijkm} is 0. Now consider the product of any $N + 1$ elements x_i. Such a product begins with some a_{ij}, then N elements of the form $r_{ij}a_{km} = y_{ijkm}$ follow, and at the end there is some r_{pq}. Therefore, such a product is also 0. Thus, the x_i generate a nilpotent subring and therefore AR is locally nilpotent. We are assuming, however, that R has no non-zero locally nilpotent ideals. Therefore, $AR = 0$. Then, in particular, $A^2 = 0$ and thus $A = 0$. Thus, a Levitzki semi-simple ring has no one-sided locally nilpotent ideals (the proof for right ideals is exactly the same except we consider RA instead of AR), and therefore the Levitzki radical contains all the one-sided locally nilpotent ideals.

Levitzki introduced this radical for two reasons. In the first place, for general rings, ordinary nilpotence is not a radical property. On the other hand, the nil radical may not contain all the one-sided nil ideals (this also is still an open question). Local nilpotence is a radical property and the L-radical does contain all the one-sided locally nilpotent ideals. Thus, he solved both difficulties simultaneously. Of course, with D.C.C. or A.C.C. the three properties (nil, local nilpotence, and nilpotence) coincide.

We now know that not every nil ring is locally nilpotent, and we also know that there exist rings that are locally nilpotent but that are not nilpotent (e.g. Example 3). Such rings must exist because local nilpotence is a radical property and nilpotence is not. Example 7 is another ring that is locally nilpotent but not nilpotent.

The Baer lower radical β (see Chapter 3) is the lower radical property determined by all nilpotent rings. Thus, it is clear that $\beta \leqslant L \leqslant \mathcal{N}$. Example 7 is locally nilpotent and therefore L-radical, but it is β-semi-simple. Then $\beta < L$. Regarding the relation $L \leqslant \mathcal{N}$, we now know that L and N are different.

Theorem 18 tells us that the Baer radical β is the intersection of *all* the prime ideals of a ring. Recently Babic [12] proved a similar theorem about the Levitzki radical.

Theorem 51. *The Levitzki radical L of a ring R is the intersection of all the prime ideals P of R for which R/P is Levitzki semi-simple.*

Remark. This fits in very well with Theorem 18. We know that the Levitzki radical is, in general, larger than the Baer radical. This theorem tells us that instead of being the intersection of *all* the prime ideals, it is the intersection of just those prime ideals whose factor rings are Levitzki semi-simple.

Proof. First we observe that for any element x that is not in L, the ideal generated by x, is not locally nilpotent. This means that there must exist a subring $T \subseteq X$ such that T is generated by a finite number of elements, and such that T is not nilpotent. Furthermore, since T^m, for any positive integer m, is also generated by only a finite number of elements (see the proof of Lemma 70), no positive integral power of T can be in L. For if T^m is in L, it would have to be nilpotent; then T would be nilpotent, which is a contradiction.

Now let us consider the set of all prime ideals P_α of R such that R/P_α is an L-semi-simple and, of course, prime ring. Let $P = \cap P_\alpha$. Since R/P_α is L-semi-simple, $L \subseteq P_\alpha$ for every α and thus $L \subseteq P$.

To prove that $P \subseteq L$, we assume that there exists an element x in P, where x is not in L. Then, as above, there must exist a subring $T \subseteq P$ such that $T^m \nsubseteq L$, for any $m = 1, 2, \ldots$. Let us consider all ideals Q_β of R such that $L \subseteq Q_\beta$ and $T^m \nsubseteq Q_\beta$, for any $m = 1, 2, \ldots$. Such ideals exist, for L is one. We order the Q_β by inclusion and we wish to apply Zorn's Lemma in order to select a maximal ideal Q among these Q_β. The only thing to check is that the union of an infinitely ascending chain of the Q_β is again in the set (i.e. contains L, but does not contain any power of T). However, T^m is finitely generated, for any m, and thus if T^m is in this union, it must be contained in some member Q_β of the ascending sequence. This is not possible, and thus the union contains no power of T. Therefore, by Zorn's Lemma, there exists a maximal Q such that $L \subseteq Q$ and $T^m \nsubseteq Q$, for every $m = 1, 2, \ldots$.

Consider R/Q. First we shall show that R/Q is a prime ring. If $I_1/Q \cdot I_2/Q = 0$, for ideals I_1/Q and I_2/Q of R/Q, then $I_1 I_2 \subseteq Q$. If I_1/Q and I_2/Q are both not zero, then I_1 and I_2 are ideals of R which properly contain Q. Since Q is maximal with respect to excluding powers of T, both I_1 and I_2 must contain some powers of T. Suppose that $T^{n_1} \subseteq I_1$ and $T^{n_2} \subseteq I_2$. Then $T^{n_1 + n_2} \subseteq I_1 I_2 \subseteq Q$. However, this is impossible, for Q does not contain any power of T. Therefore, R/Q is a prime ring.

Next we want to show that R/Q is L-semi-simple. Suppose then that W/Q is a locally finite ideal of R/Q. If $W/Q \neq 0$, then W properly contains Q and again, by the maximality of Q, W must contain some power of T, say $T^s \subseteq W$. Since T^s is finitely generated in R, $(T^s + Q)/Q$ is finitely generated in R/Q. Since it is in W/Q and W/Q is locally finite, $(T^s + Q)/Q$ must be nilpotent, $[(T^s + Q)/Q]^t = 0$, or $T^{st} \subseteq Q$. However, this is impossible because Q does not contain any powers of T. Therefore, R/Q is L-semi-simple.

Therefore, Q is a prime ideal belonging to the set of P_α. Thus $P = \cap P_\alpha \subseteq Q$. However, $T \subseteq P$, and this would mean that $T \subseteq Q$, a contradiction.

Thus, there cannot exist an element x in P, $x \notin L$, and thus $P \subseteq L$ and therefore $P = L$.

Then we can extend Theorem 20.

Theorem 52. *Every L-semi-simple ring R is isomorphic to a subdirect sum of prime, L-semi-simple rings.*

6.2. Applications. We shall not study prime L-semi-simple rings, for in the D.C.C. or A.C.C. case they coincide with the Baer and nil results, and in the chainless case we use the Jacobson or Brown–McCoy results.

Nevertheless, the Levitzki radical has some further interesting features.

Theorem 53. *If there exists a fixed positive integer n such that $x^n = 0$ for every x in a ring R, then R is locally nilpotent.*

Remark. Of course, R is nil, but the condition of this theorem does not mean that the product of any n elements in R is 0. Does a ring exist which satisfies the conditions of the theorem but which is not nilpotent?

Proof. If $n = 2$, then $x^2 = 0$ for every x in R. Take any two elements x, y in R. Then $x^2 = 0$, $y^2 = 0$, and $(x + y)^2 = 0 = x^2 + y^2 + xy + yx$. Thus $yx = -xy$. Then if T is the subring generated by the finite number of elements $a_1, a_2, \ldots, a_m$, $T^{m+1} = 0$. Given any monomial in T^{m+1}, it is the product of $m + 1$ of the a_i. Since there are only m distinct a_i, two of them in such a product must be the same. We can then move them together, using $yx = -xy$, and since $a_i^2 = 0$ for each a_i, such a monomial is 0. Thus, T is nilpotent and R is locally nilpotent.

We shall proceed by induction and assume that the theorem is true for all $m < n$.

Let R be a ring such that $x^n = 0$ for every x in R. Let L be its Levitzki radical and consider R/L. We wish to show that $R/L = 0$, that $R \subseteq L$, and that R is locally nilpotent. However, suppose that $R/L \neq 0$. Then $\bar{x}^n = 0$ for every $\bar{x}$ in R/L. Thus, we might just as well assume that R itself is Levitzki semi-simple, that $x^n = 0$ for every x in R, and show that a contradiction must then follow.

Since we are assuming that R is Levitzki semi-simple, R has no non-zero locally nilpotent one-sided ideals (Theorem 50).

Take any element $r \neq 0$ in R such that $r^2 = 0$, and consider rR. For any x in R,

$$(rx + r)^2 = (rx)^2 + rxr, \qquad (rx + r)^3 = (rx)^3 + (rx)^2 r,$$

$$\ldots, (rx + r)^n = (rx)^n + (rx)^{n-1} r.$$

Since $(rx + r)^n = 0 = (rx)^n$, we have $(rx)^{n-1} r = 0$. Now let $S = \{y \in rR : yr = 0\}$. Then S is an ideal of the ring rR, for S is obviously a left ideal and $S . rR = 0$. Also $S^2 \subseteq S . rR = 0$. Furthermore, since $(rx)^{n-1} . r = 0$, $(rx)^{n-1}$ is in S for any element rx of rR. Now consider rR/S. Since the $(n - 1)st$ power of every element in this factor ring is zero, i.e. is in S, we may apply our inductive hypothesis to conclude that rR/S is a locally nilpotent ring. Since S itself is nilpotent, we can conclude (Lemma 70) that rR is locally nilpotent. Since R is Levitzki semi-simple, and since rR is a right ideal of R, we have $rR = 0$. Then the right ideal generated by r is $\{ir\}$, with i an integer. Since $r^2 = 0$, this is a nilpotent right ideal and therefore it must be zero. Therefore, r itself must be 0.

Thus, we have shown that if $r^2 = 0$, then $r = 0$. Now take any x in R, $x^n = 0$. Let m be the smallest positive integer such that $x^m = 0$. If $m \neq 1$, $(x^{m-1})^2 = 0$ and thus $x^{m-1} = 0$. This contradicts the minimality of m, unless $m = 1$. Thus, $x^1 = 0$ for every x, and $R = 0$.

Thus, in the general case, R must be contained in its Levitzki radical, and R is locally nilpotent. This concludes the induction, and the theorem is established.

As Herstein [26] points out, this result was used to prove the following theorem, which was needed to classify simple alternative rings.

Theorem 54. *If there exists a fixed positive integer n such that $(xy - yx)^n = 0$ for every x, y of a ring, then the set of all nilpotent elements of R is an ideal.*

Remark. We observe that many rings have nilpotent elements lying about loosely, so to speak. For example, the simple ring of two-by-two matrices over the reals has nilpotent elements. In fact, it is rare for the set of *all* nilpotent elements to form an ideal. There is, of course, the maximal nil ideal but it rarely contains all the nilpotent elements.

Proof. The Levitzki radical L of R is, of course, nil and thus all elements in L are nilpotent. We plan to show that there are no nilpotent elements outside of L, and thus L will coincide with the set of all nilpotent elements. Since L is an ideal, this will prove the theorem.

As in Theorem 53, we shall work with R/L and try to show that it has no non-zero nilpotent elements. Thus, we shall assume that R is Levitzki semi-simple. Let x be any nilpotent element of R. Let m be the smallest positive integer such that $x^m = 0$. If $m \neq 1$, then $x^{m-1} \neq 0$ and $(x^{m-1})^2 = 0$. Let $a = x^{m-1}$. For any r in R, $(ra - ar)^n = 0$. Multiplying on the left by a, and recalling that $a^2 = 0$, we find that $a(ra)^n = 0$. Thus, $(ra)^{n+1} = 0$, for any r. Thus, the ring Ra satisfies the condition of Theorem 53 and we may conclude that Ra is locally nilpotent. Since Ra is a left ideal, Ra must be in the Levitzki radical of R and since we are assuming that R is L-semi-simple, $Ra = 0$. Then the left ideal generated by a consists just of the integral multiples of a and this is nilpotent. Thus, it must be zero and $a = 0$. Thus $x^1 = 0$ for every nilpotent x, and R has no non-zero nilpotent elements.

Thus, in the general case, there are no nilpotent elements outside of L and the theorem is established.

Remark. This theorem proves that, in this case, the Levitzki radical is equal to the nil radical. Superficially it might seem to be easier to show that all the nilpotent elements are in the nil radical, because, in general, the nil radical may be larger than L. However, we know that L contains the one-sided locally nilpotent ideals, but we do not know whether the nil radical contains the one-sided nil ideals.

к

Herstein conjectures that if $xy - yx$ is nilpotent for every x and y in the ring R, without the index of nilpotency being fixed, then the set of all nilpotent elements still form an ideal.

Theorems 53 and 54 are studies of rings that satisfy a polynomial identity. In the first case, the polynomial $x^n = 0$ is satisfied by every element in the ring and, in the second, $(xy - yx)^n = 0$. These have been studied by Kaplansky [33] and Amitsur [4], among others.

A polynomial identity can be thought of as a generalization of commutativity $(xy - yx = 0)$ or, simply, as a restriction on the ring, perhaps an extremely mild type of chain condition. In any case many difficult results which are unsettled in the general case can be established for polynomial identity rings. For example, one can prove that every nil algebra is locally nilpotent, if it satisfies a polynomial identity [33].

Example 12 is a simple non-trivial Jacobson radical ring. We do not know whether or not there exists a simple non-trivial nil ring. We can show that there does not exist a simple non-trivial nilpotent ring. For if R is simple and non-trivial, $R^2 \neq 0$. Since R^2 is an ideal, $R^2 = R$. Thus, $R^n = R$ for every $n = 1, 2, 3, \ldots$. Therefore, R is not nilpotent. We close our discussion of local nilpotence with the following theorem.

Theorem 55. *A simple non-trivial locally nilpotent ring does not exist.*

Proof. There exists an element x in a simple non-trivial ring for which $RxR \neq 0$. Otherwise $R^3 = 0$. Since RxR is an ideal, $RxR = R$. Therefore, there exist elements r_i and s_i such that

$$x = \sum_{i=1}^{m} r_i x s_i.$$

Let W be the subring generated by the r_i and s_i. If R is locally nilpotent, then W is nilpotent, $W^v = 0$.

Now
$$x = \sum r_i x s_i = \sum r_i (\sum r_i x s_i) s_i$$
$$= \sum r'_i x s'_i$$

with r'_i, s'_i all in W^2. Now replace x again in the sum by $\sum r_i x s_i$ and get $x = \sum r''_i x s''_i$ with r''_i and s''_i all in W^3. Continuing in this way, we obtain $x = \sum r_i x s_i$ with r_i, s_i all in $W^v = 0$. Thus $x = 0$, a contradiction. Thus, R cannot be locally nilpotent.

CHAPTER SEVEN

THE EIGHT RADICALS AND RECENT RESULTS

7.1. The partitions of the simple rings. The eight radicals that we have discussed can be summarized as follows:

$\mathcal{S}$: lower radical determined by the class of all zero simple rings.

$\mathcal{D}$: lower radical determined by the class of all nilpotent rings which are nil radicals of rings with D.C.C.

β: [Baer Lower] lower radical determined by the class of all nilpotent rings.

$\mathcal{L}$: [Levitzki] lower radical determined by the class of all locally nilpotent rings.

$\mathcal{N}$: [Baer Upper, Koethe] lower radical determined by the class of all nil rings.

J: [Jacobson] quasi-regularity.

$\mathcal{G}$: [Brown–McCoy] upper radical determined by the class of all simple rings with unity.

$\mathcal{T}$: upper radical determined by the class of all matrix rings over division rings.

In general, $\mathcal{S} < \mathcal{D} < \beta < \mathcal{L} < \mathcal{N} < J < \mathcal{G} < \mathcal{T}$, all inclusions being sharp. For rings with D.C.C. all eight are equal, the top seven in the strong sense and $\mathcal{S}$ equals the others in the weak sense. For rings with A.C.C., $\beta = \mathcal{L} = \mathcal{N}$, and these were used successfully in Chapter III. For general rings, J and $\mathcal{G}$ are the really useful ones (Chapters IV and V).

The smaller four radicals all correspond to the same partition of the simple rings, whereas J, $\mathcal{G}$, and $\mathcal{T}$ correspond to different partitions. The various partitions are perhaps best illustrated by a diagram (see next page).

7.2. Subdirectly irreducible rings and special radicals. There is certainly nothing sacred about these radicals and there are many properties that we wish radicals to have that these may not have. For example, it would be useful to know whether a radical property is hereditary, or when a semi-simple ring can be expressed as a subdirect sum of semi-simple rings from some special class. Furthermore, each of these radicals was created more or less on its own and we would like to know more about the inner relationships between them. Finally, we may try to find a radical which will provide a more useful structure theory.

The Class of All Simple Rings

Without unity elements	Without maximal right ideals	Trivial rings $A^2 = 0$	Partition for $\mathscr{S}$, $\mathscr{D}$, β, $\mathscr{L}$	With $A^2 = A$
		Non-trivial, $A^2 = A$. But without maximal right ideals, i.e. J-radical	Partition for J	
		Non-trivial and with maximal right ideals, but without unity elements, i.e. J-semi-simple but Brown–McCoy radical	Partition for $\mathscr{G}$ — With maximal right ideals	With maximal right ideals
		Non-trivial, with maximal right ideals, with unity elements, but not matrix rings over division rings, i.e. Brown–McCoy semi-simple but $\mathscr{T}$-radical	Partition for $\mathscr{T}$ — With unity elements	
		Matrix rings over division rings, i.e. $\mathscr{T}$-semi-simple		

Consequently, it is quite reasonable to seek new radicals and, in particular, to seek new methods for constructing radical properties. It is, of course, advisable to try to keep the radical between $\mathscr{D}$ and $\mathscr{T}$ for it should coincide with $\mathscr{N}$ on rings with D.C.C. Nevertheless, we should be prepared to study wierd creations if they might lead us to more familiar radicals between $\mathscr{D}$ and $\mathscr{T}$.

Recently, Andrunakievic [7, 8, 9] has delved into these matters and we shall follow his work here.

We begin with two observations. First, subdirectly irreducible rings are in some ways similar to simple rings and may be partitioned by a given radical property if the radical property is carefully selected. Secondly, there are many classes with property (E) besides classes of simple rings. These classes may be easy to find and handle and will yield upper radical properties.

To make these observations more precise we prove:

Lemma 74. *Let R be any radical property which is hereditary (see Theorem 48), and let K be any subdirectly irreducible ring with heart H. Then H is either R-radical or R-semi-simple. Furthermore, K is R-semi-simple if and only if H is R-semi-simple.*

Proof. Since R is hereditary, $R(H) = H \cap R(K)$. This is an ideal of K contained in H and, since H is minimal, $R(H)$ either equals H or equals 0. Thus H is either R-radical or R-semi-simple.

To prove the second part, if K is R-semi-simple, then H is R-semi-simple by Theorem 47, Corollary 2. Conversely, if $R(H) = 0$, then $H \cap R(K) = 0$. However, if $R(K) \neq 0$, then $H \subseteq R(K)$ and thus $H \cap R(K) = H = 0$, a contradiction. Thus, $R(K)$ must be equal to 0 and K is R-semi-simple.

Thus, every hereditary radical splits the class of all subdirectly irreducible rings into two parts—those with R-radical hearts and those with R-semi-simple hearts. For example, Lemma 62 tells us that J, the Jacobson radical, is hereditary. What sort of split does it give, of the subdirectly irreducible rings? What does a subdirectly irreducible ring with a Jacobson semi-simple heart look like?

Suppose that H is the heart of some subdirectly irreducible ring K. Then H^2 is an ideal of K, $H^2 \subseteq H$, and thus $H^2 = H$ or $H^2 = 0$. Suppose further that $H^2 = H$. Then H is a simple non-trivial ring! For if $I \neq 0$ is an ideal of H, and I^* is the ideal of K generated by I, then by Lemma 61, $I^{*3} \subseteq I$. However, $I^* \subseteq H$ and thus $I^* = H$. Consequently, $I^{*3} = H^3 = H$ and thus $H \subseteq I$. Therefore $I = H$ and H is simple. Thus, we have:

Lemma 75. *The heart of a subdirectly irreducible ring is either a simple non-trivial ring or it is a zero ring.*

Corollary. *If I is any minimal ideal of an arbitrary ring K, then either I is a simple non-trivial ring or $I^2 = 0$.*

The proof of this is the same as the proof of the lemma, since we used only the minimality of the heart.

Thus, if a heart is J-semi-simple, it must be a simple J-semi-simple ring. The Jacobson radical thus splits the class of all subdirectly irreducible rings into a lower class—the class of all subdirectly irreducible rings with nilpotent hearts or with simple non-trivial J-radical hearts (e.g. Sasiada's Example 12)—and an upper class of all subdirectly irreducible rings with hearts which are simple rings with maximal right ideals.

Similarly, the nil radical (which is obviously hereditary) splits the subdirectly irreducible rings into a lower class of rings with nilpotent hearts and simple nil but non-nilpotent hearts if any exist, and an upper class of rings with idempotent non-nil hearts (i.e. $H^2 = H$).

Since the class of subdirectly irreducible rings contains the class of simple rings, the splitting of the subdirectly irreducible rings is in some sense an extension of the splitting of the simple rings. One must remember, however, that when the simple rings are split, all members of the upper class are semi-simple and all members of the lower class are radical. However, for the subdirectly irreducible split the upper-class rings are all semi-simple but the lower-class rings are not necessarily radical. They are not semi-simple, but this does not mean that they are radical. It simply means that their radical is not zero. Thus, in working with this split we can work successfully only with the upper class, and thus we shall concentrate on upper radicals.

Since we wish to gain more insight into rings without any chain conditions, we shall concern ourselves with radicals that contain β, the Baer lower radical, for it seems likely that we shall have to discard at least β, and perhaps more, to obtain useful structure theorems. We shall call a radical property *supernilpotent* if it is hereditary and if it contains all nilpotent ideals, i.e. if it is $\geqslant \beta$. We shall show later that β itself is hereditary.

Let M be a subset of the set of all subdirectly irreducible rings with idempotent hearts such that any subdirectly irreducible ring with a heart that is isomorphic to a heart of a ring of M is itself in M. Or take a partition of all the subdirectly irreducible rings such that all those with nilpotent hearts are in the lower class, and let M be the upper class of this partition, with the same proviso that any subdirectly irreducible ring with a heart which is isomorphic to a heart of a ring in M is also in M. It may be easier to think of M as a class of subdirectly irreducible rings with idempotent hearts such that each heart has property φ, where φ is some arbitrary but fixed algebraic (i.e. preserved under ring isomorphisms) property. Let us, therefore, call this class M_φ. We may also construct M_φ by taking a partition of the simple rings for which the zero simple rings are all in the lower class, and by letting M_φ be the class of all subdirectly irreducible rings which have hearts isomorphic to a simple ring of the upper class.

Lemma 76. *Every non-zero ideal of a subdirectly irreducible ring with idempotent heart is itself subdirectly irreducible with the same heart.*

Proof. Let $B \neq 0$ be an ideal of the subdirectly irreducible ring K. Let $C = C^2$ be the heart of K. Let A be any non-zero ideal of B. Then $BA \neq 0$, for if $BA = 0$, then $BA' = 0$ where A' is the ideal of K generated by A. But $C \subseteq B$ and $C \subseteq A'$ and thus $C^2 \subseteq BA' = 0$. However, $C^2 = C \neq 0$ and thus $BA \neq 0$. Similarly, $BA.B \neq 0$. Now BAB is an ideal of K and thus $C \subseteq BAB$. But $BAB \subseteq A$. Therefore $C \subseteq A$ and B is subdirectly irreducible with heart C.

Corollary. *Every non-zero ideal of a ring of M_φ is itself a ring of M_φ.*

Thus, the class M_φ has condition (E) and (see Section 1.2) therefore determines an upper radical property R_φ, for which all the rings in M_φ are R_φ-semisimple. An R_φ-radical ring is one which cannot be mapped homomorphically onto a ring of M_φ. If W is a nilpotent ring, then each of its ideals is nilpotent and therefore W cannot be mapped homomorphically onto a subdirectly irreducible ring with idempotent heart; in particular, W cannot be mapped onto a ring of M_φ and, thus, W is R_φ-radical. Consequently, R_φ contains all nilpotent ideals. We shall show that R_φ is supernilpotent by showing that it is hereditary.

Lemma 77. *If $B \neq 0$ is a subdirectly irreducible ring with idempotent heart C, and B is an ideal of K, then K/B^* is subdirectly irreducible with heart $\cong$ heart of B, where $B^* = \{x \in K : xB = Bx = 0\}$.*

Proof. Since $C^2 = C$, C must also be an ideal of K, for

$$CK = CCK \subseteq C.B \subseteq C \text{ and } KC = KCC \subseteq BC \subseteq C.$$

Thus, C is a minimal ideal of K. Furthermore, $C \cap B^* = 0$, for if $C \cap B^* \neq 0$, then it is an ideal contained in C and since C is minimal, $C = C \cap B^*$. Then $C \subseteq B^*$. Now $C^2 \subseteq B.B^* = 0$. But $C^2 = C \neq 0$. Thus $C \cap B^* = 0$. Then

$$\frac{C + B^*}{B^*} \cong \frac{C}{C \cap B^*} \cong C.$$

We plan to show that K/B^* is subdirectly irreducible and that its heart is $(C + B^*)/B^*$.

This will then prove the lemma.

First we shall show that K/B^* is a prime ring, or that B^* is a prime ideal of K. Thus, suppose that $U.V \subseteq B^*$ for ideals U and V of K. Then

$$BU.VB \subseteq B B^* B = 0.$$

However, BU and VB are ideals of B, and therefore they must each contain C if they are not zero, and thus $C = C^2 \subseteq BU.VB = 0$. Since $C \neq 0$, we can conclude that either BU or VB is zero. Suppose that $BU = 0$. Then $UB.UB = 0$. If UB is not zero, it must contain C and, as before, we obtain $C = 0$, a contradiction. Thus $UB = 0$. Therefore $U \subseteq B^*$. Similarly, if $VB = 0$ we get $BV = 0$ and $V \subseteq B^*$. Therefore, B^* is a prime ideal or K/B^* is a prime ring.

Finally, let T/B^* be any non-zero ideal of K/B^*. Then $(T/B^*).[(C + B^*)/B^*] \neq 0$ since K/B^* is prime. Thus, $TC \nsubseteq B^*$ and, in particular, $TC \neq 0$. Thus $T \cap C \neq 0$. Since C is minimal and $T \cap C \subseteq C$, we must have $T \cap C = C$ or $C \subseteq T$. Therefore $(C + B^*)/B^* \subseteq T/B^*$. Thus, K/B^* is subdirectly irreducible with heart $(C + B^*)/B^* \cong C$.

Lemma 78. R_φ *is a hereditary radical.*

Proof. Let K be an R_φ-radical ring and suppose that $B \neq 0$ is an ideal of K such that B is not an R_φ-radical ring. This means that B can be mapped homomorphically onto a ring in M_φ, i.e. onto a subdirectly irreducible ring with idempotent heart, belonging to M_φ (i.e. the heart has property φ). Thus, there must exist an ideal I of B such that B/I is subdirectly irreducible with idempotent heart C/I.

Then I must be an ideal of K. To see this, observe that $IK \subseteq BK \subseteq B$ and $IK.B \subseteq IB \subseteq I$. If $IK \nsubseteq I$, then $(IK + I)/I$ is a non-zero ideal of B/I and thus must contain C/I. Furthermore, $(IK + I)/I.B/I$ is the zero ideal in B/I for $IKB \subseteq I$. Then $C/I.C/I \subseteq (IK + I)/I.B/I$ = zero. Since $C/I = C/I.C/I$ is not zero, we have a contradiction. Therefore I is a right ideal of K. Similarly, I is a left ideal of K.

We then consider K/I. It contains the ideal B/I, a non-zero subdirectly irreducible ring with idempotent heart C/I. By Lemma 77, $(K/I)/(B/I)^*$ is a subdirectly irreducible ring with a heart isomorphic to C/I. Now $(K/I)/(B/I)^*$ is a non-zero homomorphic image of K and since its heart is isomorphic to C/I, this image is a ring of M_φ. However, we assumed that K was R_φ-radical, i.e. K cannot be mapped homomorphically onto a ring of M_φ. This contradiction proves that every ideal of K must also be R_φ-radical and thus that R_φ is a hereditary radical by Theorem 48.

Corollary. R_φ *is a supernilpotent radical.*

We can make one further observation about all the rings in M_φ, an observation which has grown out of the above proofs.

Lemma 79. *Every subdirectly irreducible ring with idempotent heart is prime.*

Proof. If C is the heart of the subdirectly irreducible ring K, $C = C^2$. Then, if $B.G = 0$ for ideals B and G of K, $C \subseteq B$ and $C \subseteq G$ if neither B nor G is zero. Then $C = C^2 \subseteq BG = 0$, a contradiction. Therefore, either $B = 0$ or $G = 0$ and K is prime.

Corollary. *Every ring in M_φ is a prime ring.*

Since the restriction to classes of subdirectly irreducible rings is somewhat confining, we shall extend our horizons, while attempting to keep the useful property of supernilpotency for the resulting radical. We shall say that a class M of rings is a *special class of rings* if it satisfies the following three conditions:

(x) *Every ring in the class M is a prime ring.*

(y) *Every non-zero ideal of a ring in M is itself a ring in M.*

(z) *If A is a ring in M, and A is an ideal of a ring K, then K/A^* is in M, where A^* is the annihilator of A, i.e. $A^* = \{x \in K : xA = Ax = 0\}$.*

The corollary to Lemma 79, the corollary to Lemma 76, and Lemma 77 then yield the following theorem.

Theorem 56. M_φ *is a special class of rings.*

In general, a special class of rings M will contain rings which are not subdirectly irreducible, and thus this notion generalizes the idea of M_φ. However, the radicals we can get from special classes are almost as useful as those from M_φ.

If M is a special class of rings, then by (y) it has (E) and therefore it defines an upper radical property S_M for which all the rings in M are semi-simple. An S_M-radical ring is one which cannot be mapped homomorphically on a ring of M. Since a nilpotent ring is not prime, and every homomorphic image of a nilpotent ring is again nilpotent, it is clear that all nilpotent rings are S_M-radical.

Lemma 78 goes through for S_M just as it did for R_φ because of (z). For, in the proof, I is an ideal of K because B/I is a prime ring and all rings in M are prime. Thus $(K/I)/(B/I)^*$ is, by (z), a ring in M, which contradicts the fact that K is S_M-radical. Thus, we have:

Theorem 57. *The upper radical property S_M determined by a special class M is supernilpotent.*

An interesting open question is the following: Is every supernilpotent radical an upper radical property determined by some special class?

Let us call an upper radical property determined by a special class a *special radical.*

It is remarkable how useful the notion of a special radical can be and how it connects up with many of the radicals we have studied.

One useful property of special radicals is established in:

Lemma 80. *The special radical S_M of any ring K is equal to the intersection of all ideals T_α of K such that K/T_α is a ring in the special class M. Thus, every S_M-semi-simple ring is a subdirect sum of rings from M.*

Proof. If T_α is an ideal of K such that K/T_α is in M, then K/T_α is an S_m-semi-simple ring, for all rings in M are S_m-semi-simple. Therefore, $S_m \subseteq T_\alpha$. Thus, $S_m \subseteq \cap T_\alpha$.

On the other hand, let T be defined as $\cap T_\alpha$. If T is S_M-radical, then $T \subseteq S_M$ and $S_M = T$. However, if T is not S_M-radical, then T can be mapped homomorphically onto a ring of M. Let I be an ideal of T such that T/I is in M. Then, as in Lemma 78, I is an ideal of K for $(IK + I)/I$. T/I is the zero ideal in T/I. However, T/I, being in M, is a prime ring and thus $IK \subseteq I$. Similarly, $KI \subseteq I$ and I is an ideal of K. Thus, K/I has an ideal T/I which is in M. Thus, $(K/I)/(T/I)^*$ is itself in M, by (z).

Let $Q = \{x \in K : xT \subseteq I \text{ and } Tx \subseteq I\}$. Then $K/Q \cong (K/I)/(T/I)^*$. Clearly $I \subseteq Q$. Furthermore, $(T/I)^*$ is the set of elements of K/I which multiply T/I, on either side, into I/I. Thus, $(T/I)^* \cong V/I$, where $V = \{x \in K : xT \subseteq I \text{ and } Tx \subseteq I\}$. Thus $V = Q$ and $(T/I)^* \cong Q/I$. Then $(K/I)/(T/I)^* \cong (K/I)/(Q/I) \cong K/Q$.

Since K/Q is in M, Q must be equal to one of the T_α's. Thus $T = \cap T_\alpha \subseteq Q$. However, if $T \subseteq Q$, then $TT \subseteq I$ and this means that T/I is a nilpotent ring.

Since T/I is in M, it is a prime ring and therefore this is impossible. Thus, T must be an S_M-radical ring, $T \subseteq S_M$, and the lemma is proved.

7.3. The Baer lower radical and special radicals.

Theorem 58. *The class M of all prime rings is a special class of rings.*

Proof. Clearly M has (x). To see that M has (y), let K be a prime ring, and B a non-zero ideal of K. Suppose that $U.V = 0$ where U and V are non-zero ideals of B. Then $B.U \neq 0$, for if $B_r = \{x \in K : Bx = 0\}$, then B_r is a right ideal of K and $B.B_r = 0$. By Lemma 35, $B_r = 0$. Thus if $BU = 0$, $U \subseteq B_r = 0$. Since $U \neq 0$, $BU \neq 0$. Similarly, $BU.B \neq 0$, for the left annihilator of B in K is 0. Now BUB is a non-zero ideal of K and its right annihilator in K is 0. Thus, $BUBV \neq 0$ since $V \neq 0$. However, $BUBV \subseteq UV = 0$. This contradiction proves that either $U = 0$ or $V = 0$, that B is a prime ring, and that M has (y).

Finally, to establish (z), let A be a prime ring, let A be an ideal of a ring K, let $A^* = \{x \in K : xA = Ax = 0\}$ and consider K/A^*. We wish to show that K/A^* is prime, or that A^* is a prime ideal of K.

Suppose then that $F.G \subseteq A^*$ where F and G are ideals of K. Then $AF.GA \subseteq AA^*A = 0$. Since AF and GA are ideals of A and A is prime, either $AF = 0$ or $GA = 0$. Suppose that $AF = 0$. Then $FA.FA = 0$, and $FA = 0$ since it is a nilpotent ideal of A. Thus, $F \subseteq A^*$. Similarly, if $GA = 0$, then $AG = 0$ and $G \subseteq A^*$. Thus, A^* is a prime ideal, K/A^* is a prime ring, (z) is established, and the theorem is proved.

It is clear that this special class of all prime rings is the largest possible special class of rings. Consequently, the special radical that it determines is the smallest special radical.

What is the special radical determined by the class M of all prime rings? By Lemma 80, it is the intersection of all ideals T_α such that K/T_α is in M, i.e. is a prime ring. Thus, it is the intersection of all the prime ideals of a ring. By Theorem 18 this is precisely the Baer lower radical!

Thus the Baer lower radical is the upper radical property determined by the class of all prime rings. It is also the lower radical property determined by the class of all nilpotent rings.

This clearly points out that the partition of the simple rings is too narrow. For, with respect to the simple rings alone, β corresponds to the partition where the zero simple rings are in the lower class and the idempotent simple rings in the upper class. Thus, β lies between the lower radical property determined by the class of zero simple rings, $\mathscr{S}$, and the upper radical property determined by all idempotent simple rings, which we shall call I. We know that $\mathscr{S} < \beta$ (see Theorem 14) and $\beta < I$, for $\mathscr{N}$, the nil radical, $\leqslant I$ and $\beta < \mathscr{N}$ (Example 7). Thus, β cannot be identified with either $\mathscr{S}$ or I, the end radicals of the partition.

However, if we abandon simple rings and consider all nilpotent rings on the one hand and all prime rings on the other, we can express β both as a lower and as an upper radical.

Let us state this in a theorem.

Theorem 59. *The Baer lower radical is the smallest radical for which all nilpotent rings are radical rings, and it is the largest radical for which all prime rings are semi-simple rings. It is a special radical and it is the smallest special radical.*

Corollary. *The Baer lower radical is hereditary.*

7.4. Jacobson and special radicals. Now let us consider the class M of all primitive rings. (We shall use the word primitive for the more precise term right primitive). Recall that a ring K is primitive if it contains a maximal right ideal I such that $(I:K) = \{x \in K : Kx \subseteq I\} = 0$.

Lemma 81. *Every primitive ring is a prime ring.*

Proof. Suppose that K is primitive and that I is a maximal right ideal such that $(I:K) = 0$. Then 0 is the only two-sided ideal of K contained in I, for if A is an ideal of K, $A \subseteq I$, then $KA \subseteq I$, $A \subseteq (I:K) = 0$. Thus, if $B \cdot C = 0$ for ideals B, C of K and if $B \neq 0$, then $B \nsubseteq I$. Therefore, $K = I + B$, for I is a maximal right ideal. Multiplying on the right by C, we get $KC = IC + BC \subseteq I$. Thus $C \subseteq (I:K) = 0$. Therefore $C = 0$ and K is a prime ring.

Remark. The class of all primitive rings is a proper subset of the class of all prime rings for there exist prime rings which are not primitive. Example 10 is Jacobson radical and therefore not primitive. However, it has no divisors of zero and it is therefore prime. An easier example is the ring of integers. It is prime but not primitive.

The next step in establishing that the class of primitive rings is a special class of rings is to prove:

Lemma 82. *Every non-zero ideal of a primitive ring is itself a primitive ring.*

Proof. Again we take K to be a primitive ring with I a maximal right ideal such that $(I:K) = 0$. However, I is not quite what we want. We shall show that K contains a regular maximal right ideal I_1 such that $(I_1:K) = 0$. Of course, I itself may be regular, in which case this construction is not necessary. But in general I will not be regular.

Take a not in I and let $I_1 = \{x \in K : ax \in I\}$. Then, of course, I_1 is a right ideal of K. However, $I_1 \neq K$ for if $aK \subseteq I$, then we represent $K = I + (a)_r$, where $(a)_r$ is the right ideal generated by a. Since I is maximal and a is not in

I, K can be so represented. Then $KK = IK + (a)_r K \subseteq I$. Then $K \subseteq (I:K) = 0$, a contradiction. Thus $I_1 \neq K$.

Take any b not in I_1, i.e. $ab \notin I$. Then, as above, $abK \nsubseteq I$ for if $abK \subseteq I$ we get $K^2 \subseteq I$ and $K \subseteq (I:K) = 0$. Since I is maximal and abK is a right ideal not contained in I, we have $K = abK + I$. Thus, for any y in K, there exist elements c in K, i in I such that $ay = abc + i$. Thus $a(y - bc)$ is in I. Thus $y - bc$ is in I_1. Therefore every y is in $I_1 + bK$, or $K = I_1 + bK$. This proves that I_1 is a maximal right ideal of K.

To show that I_1 is regular, take $K = aK + I$. This is possible because $aK \nsubseteq I$. Thus there exist elements e in K and i' in I such that $a = ae + i'$. Thus, for any x in K, we have $ax = aex + i'x$, or $a(x - ex)$ is in I. Therefore $x - ex$ is in I_1 and I_1 is a regular maximal right ideal of K.

Finally, to see that $(I_1:K) = 0$, let x be an element in $(I_1:K)$. Then Kx is in I_1 and thus $aKx \subseteq I$. However, $K = aK + I$ and $Kx = aKx + Ix \subseteq I$. Thus x is in $(I:K) = 0$. Therefore $x = 0$ and $(I_1:K) = 0$.

As in Lemma 81, we can conclude that 0 is the only two-sided ideal of K contained in I_1.

Thus, I_1 is precisely the same sort of right ideal as I except that it is regular. We shall, therefore, without loss of generality, assume that I is itself a regular maximal right ideal of K, with $(I:K) = 0$.

Now let A be a non-zero ideal of K. Then $A \nsubseteq I$.

We consider $A \cap I$ and propose to show that it is a regular maximal right ideal of A. Take $a \in A$, $a \notin I$. Then $I + (a)_r = K$, where $(a)_r$ is the right ideal of K generated by a. This is interesting, but we require something a little stronger. We wish to show that $I + (a)_r{}^2 = K$, or that $(a)_r{}^2 \nsubseteq I$. From $K = I + (a)_r$ we know that $e = i + a_1$, where a_1 is in $(a)_r$, $i \in I$, and e is the element such that $x - ex$ is in I for every x of K. Take any b in $(a)_r$, and multiply $e = i + a_1$ on the right to get $eb = ib + a_1 b$. Now $eb = b + i_1$ for some i_1 in I. Then $b = -i_1 + ib + a_1 b$. Now $-i_1 + ib$ is in I and $a_1 b$ is in $(a)_r{}^2$, and b is a general element of $(a)_r$. If $(a)_r{}^2 \subseteq I$, then $b \in I$ for every b in $(a)_r$, or $(a)_r \subseteq I$, a contradiction. Thus $(a)_r{}^2 \nsubseteq I$ and $K = I + (a)_r{}^2$. Let Q be the right ideal of A generated by a. Then $Q \subseteq (a)_r$ and, in fact, $(a)_r = Q + QK$. However,

$$(a)_r{}^2 = (Q + QK)(a)_r = Q \cdot (a)_r + Q \cdot K(a)_r \subseteq Q + QA \subseteq Q.$$

Therefore, $K = I + Q$. Therefore, $A = K \cap A = (I + Q) \cap A = (I \cap A) + Q$, because every x in A is of the form $x = i + q$, where i is in I, q is in Q, and $i + q$ is in A. Since $Q \subseteq A$, q is in A and therefore $i = x - q$ is in A. Thus, i is in $I \cap A$ and $A = (I \cap A) + Q$.

This establishes that $I \cap A$ is a maximal right ideal of A, because for any element a not in $A \cap I$, $A \cap I + Q = A$.

Now let us show that $A \cap I$ is regular in A. Again let e be the element of K

for which $x - ex$ is in I for every x of K. Since $K = I + A$, we know that $e = i + e_1$, where i is in I and e_1 is in A. Since e is not in I (if it were, I would be all of K), the element e_1 cannot be in I. Now take $a - ea$ for any a in A. This element, $a - ea = a - (i + e_1)a = a - e_1a - ia$, must be in I. Thus, $a - e_1a = ia + (a - ea)$ is also in I. However, $a - e_1a$ is certainly in A and therefore in $A \cap I$. Since e_1 is not in I, it is not in $A \cap I$. Therefore, $A \cap I$ is a regular maximal right ideal of A.

Since I does not contain any non-zero ideals of K, $A \cap I$ cannot contain any non-zero ideals of K. We wish to show that $A \cap I$ cannot contain any non-zero ideals of A. Suppose then that (x) is a non-zero ideal of A generated by an element x of A and that $(x) \subseteq A \cap I$. Let $(x)'$ be the ideal of K generated by (x). Then by Lemma 61, $(x)'^3 \subseteq (x)$. Then $(x)'^3 \subseteq A \cap I$ and thus $(x)'^3 = 0$. Since K is primitive, it is prime by Lemma 81. Therefore, $(x)' = 0$, $(x) = 0$. Thus, $A \cap I$ does not contain any non-zero ideals of A. Since $(A \cap I : A)$ is an ideal of A, contained in A (Lemma 55), it must be 0. Thus, the ring A is primitive, for it has a maximal right ideal $A \cap I$ such that $(A \cap I : A) = 0$.

This finally ends the proof of Lemma 82.

Finally we require:

Lemma 83. *If $A \neq 0$ is a primitive ring and A is an ideal of K, then K/A^* is a primitive ring, where $A^* = \{x \in K : xA = Ax = 0\}$.*

Proof. Let I be a maximal right ideal of A such that it contains no non-zero ideals of A, or $(I:A) = 0$. We can, as in Lemma 82, select I so that I is regular and let e be the element of A such that $x - ex$ is in I for every x of A.

Now I is a right ideal of K, for $IK \subseteq AK \subseteq A$. Thus, $(IK)^2 \subseteq IK.A \subseteq IA \subseteq I$. If $IK \nsubseteq I$, then $I + IK = A$ since I is maximal. Thus, $e = i + \alpha$, where α is in IK. Then for any β in IK, $e\beta = i\beta + \alpha\beta$. Now $e\beta = \beta + i_1$ for some i_1 in I and $\alpha\beta$ is in $(IK)^2 \subseteq I$. Therefore, $\beta = -i_1 + i\beta + \alpha\beta$ is in I, $IK \subseteq I$, a contradiction. Thus, $IK \subseteq I$ and I is a right ideal of K.

Define $I_1 \equiv I + \{x - ex\}$, where x ranges over K. Then I_1 is a right ideal of K and it is regular, for $x - ex$ is in I_1 for every x in K. Furthermore, $I_1 \neq K$. In particular e is not in I_1, for if e is in I_1, then

$$eA \subseteq I_1A = (I + \{x - ex\})A \subseteq IA + \{x - ex\}A \subseteq I.$$

Since $a - ea$ is in I for every a in A, we would then have a in I for every a, $A = I$, a contradiction. Therefore, I_1 is a regular right ideal of K, and $\neq K$. By Zorn's Lemma we may select a right ideal of K which is maximal with respect to excluding e and including I_1. Let I_2 be this right ideal. Then I_2 is a maximal right ideal of K, for any right ideal of K which properly contains I_2 must contain e. It also contains I_1, and thus must be all of K. This maximal right ideal I_2 is regular, for $x - ex$ is in $I_1 \subseteq I_2$ for every x of K.

Now $I_2 \cap A \supseteq I$, for $I \subseteq I_1 \subseteq I_2$ and $I \subseteq A$. On the other hand, the element

e is not in I_2 and therefore not in $I_2 \cap A$. However, e is in A. Then $A \supset I_2 \cap A \supseteq I$. Since I is a maximal right ideal of A, we must have $I_2 \cap A = I$.

Now let us bring A^* into the picture. If $A^* \nsubseteq I_2$, then $K = A^* + I_2$, since I_2 is maximal. Multiplying on the right by A, we get $KA = A^*A + I_2 A = I_2 A$. But $I_2 A \subseteq I_2 \cap A = I$. Thus $KA \subseteq I$ and, in particular, $AA \subseteq I$. Thus, $A \subseteq (I{:}A) = 0$, a contradiction. Therefore $A^* \subseteq I_2$.

We wish to show that K/A^* is primitive and to do this we shall show that I_2/A^* is a maximal right ideal of K/A^* such that I_2/A^* does not contain any non-zero two-sided ideals of K/A^*. It is clear that I_2/A^* is a maximal right ideal of K/A^* because I_2 is a maximal right ideal of K. To show that 0 is the largest two-sided ideal of K/A^* contained in I_2/A^*, it is sufficient to show that there are no two-sided ideals of K between I_2 and A^*. Thus, let B be any ideal of K which is contained in I_2. Then $BA \subseteq I_2 A \subseteq I$. Now BA is an ideal of A and it is in I. Since I does not contain any non-zero ideals of A, $BA = 0$. Then $(AB)^2 = AB.AB = 0$. Since A is primitive, it is prime, and thus $AB = 0$. Therefore $BA = AB = 0$, and $B \subseteq A^*$. Thus, there are no ideals of K that are contained in I_2 and that properly contain A^* and therefore K/A^* is primitive.

Putting these last three lemmas together, we have:

Theorem 60. *The class of all primitive rings is a special class of rings.*

What is the special radical determined by the class M of all primitive rings? By Lemma 80 it is the intersection of all ideals T_α such that K/T_α is a primitive ring. By Theorem 34, this is precisely the Jacobson radical! Thus we have:

Theorem 61. *The Jacobson radical is the largest radical for which all primitive rings are semi-simple.*

We have thus shown that the Jacobson radical is an upper radical property determined by some class of rings, i.e. the primitive ones. Example 13 convinced us that J was definitely smaller than the upper radical determined by the class of all simple primitive rings, but now the picture is much clearer. By extending our sights to this class of all primitive rings, we have established J as an upper radical.

In particular, we know that J is hereditary (Theorem 57) and thus we have established Lemma 62 in another way.

7.5. $\mathscr{S}$, $\mathscr{D}$, $\mathscr{L}$, $\mathscr{N}$, $\mathscr{G}$, $\mathscr{T}$, and special radicals.

Theorem 62. *The class M of all simple rings with unity is a special class of rings.*

Proof. Clearly every ring in M is prime and every non-zero ideal (*ha!*) is also a simple ring with unity. The only thing that really requires proof then is (z).

Thus, let A be a simple ring with unity e and suppose that A is an ideal of a ring K. Then we shall show that K is the direct sum of A and A^* and that $K/A^* \cong A$ is in M. For any x in K we write $x = xe + x - xe$. Then xe is in A and $x - xe$ is in A^*, for if $a \in A$, then

$$(x - xe)a = xa - x.ea = xa - xa = 0,$$

and $$a(x - xe) = ax - ax.e = ax - ax = 0,$$

since ax is in A. Thus $K = A + A^*$. To see that this sum is direct, suppose that $y \in A \cap A^*$. Then $y.e = 0$; but $ye = y$. Thus $y = 0$, $A \cap A^* = 0$, and $K = A \oplus A^*$. Then

$$K/A^* = (A + A^*)/A^* \cong A/(A \cap A^*) = A/0 \cong A.$$

This establishes (z) and proves the theorem.

From Theorem 45 we already know that the Brown–McCoy radical $\mathscr{G}$ is the upper radical determined by this special class, and thus we have:

Corollary. *The Brown–McCoy radical is a special radical.*

We know, therefore, that the Brown–McCoy radical is hereditary. It is interesting that any class of simple rings with unity is special, for in the proof, $K/A^* \cong A$. Thus any subset (containing, of course, any rings isomorphic to any of its members) of the class of all simple rings with unity is also special. The curious thing is that no special class of simple rings exists if a member does not have a unity.

Lemma 84. *If a class M of simple rings is a special class of rings, then every ring in M has a unity element.*

Proof. Suppose that B is a ring in M, and let K be any proper extension ring of B. Then, from (z), K/B^* must be in M, i.e. K/B^* is a simple ring and therefore B^* must be a maximal ideal of K. Now $B \cap B^* = 0$, for it is an ideal of B and thus is either B or 0. If $B \cap B^* = B$, then $B \subseteq B^*$ and $BB \subseteq BB^* = 0$. However, all the rings in M are prime and therefore $B^2 \neq 0$. Thus $B \cap B^* = 0$. Then $K = B + B^*$ and, in fact, $K = B \oplus B^*$, a direct sum. This is true for any proper extension ring K. If B does not have a unity, let K be the ring obtained by adjoining a unity to B, in the usual pair-taking manner. Then K/B^* has a unity element. However, $K/B^* \cong B$, and thus B must have had a unity to begin with.

Corollary. *A class of simple rings is special if and only if every ring in the class has a unity element.*

This is, of course, related to Theorem 46.

Theorem 63. *The class of all simple matrix rings over division rings is special.*

Proof. Since every member of this class is simple with unity, the theorem follows from the corollary to Theorem 62.

Thus $\mathcal{T}$, the upper radical defined by all $\mathcal{M} \times \mathcal{D}$, is a special radical.

Since β, the Baer lower radical, is the smallest possible special radical, it is clear that $\mathcal{S}$, and $\mathcal{D}$, the two radicals in our list smaller than β, cannot be special radicals. But what about $\mathcal{L}$, the Levitzki radical, and $\mathcal{N}$, the nil radical? Are they also special radicals?

Theorem 64. *The Levitzki radical is special.*

Proof. Let M be the class of all prime rings which are $\mathcal{L}$-semi-simple, where $\mathcal{L}$ is the Levitzki radical. Then, clearly, M has property (x). Lemma 70 tells us that every subring, and, in particular, every ideal of a locally nilpotent ring, is itself locally nilpotent. Thus, $\mathcal{L}$ is hereditary (Theorem 48) and (Theorem 47, Corollary 2), every ideal of an $\mathcal{L}$-semi-simple ring is itself $\mathcal{L}$-semi-simple. Then, any non-zero ideal of a ring of M is itself $\mathcal{L}$-semi-simple and it is certainly prime (Theorem 58). Thus, M satisfies property (y). To establish property (z) for M, suppose that A is a ring in M and that A is an ideal of a ring K. Then we know (Theorem 58) that K/A^* is prime. All we must show then is that K/A^* is $\mathcal{L}$-semi-simple.

Suppose, then, that B/A^* is a non-zero locally nilpotent ideal of K/A^*. If $A \cap B = 0$, then AB and BA are both 0, for they are both contained in $A \cap B$. In this case $B \subseteq A^*$ and B/A^* is 0. Thus $A \cap B \neq 0$. Now $A \cap B$ is an ideal of A. If we take any finite set of elements in $A \cap B$ and let W be the subring they generate, then, since B/A^* is locally nilpotent, $W^n \subseteq A^*$ for some positive integer n. For any finite set of elements in B/A^*, generate a nilpotent subring, and this means that a power of the subring lies in A^*. Since elements of $A \cap B$. are in B, we must have $(W + A^*)/A^*$ nilpotent, and thus $W^n \subseteq A^*$ for some n. However, $W \subseteq A$ as well, and thus $W^n \subseteq A$. But $A \cap A^* = 0$ because A is a prime ring and has no non-zero nilpotent ideals. If $A \cap A^* \neq 0$, then $(A \cap A^*)^2 = 0$ and thus $A \cap A^* = 0$. Consequently, $W^n \subseteq A \cap A^* = 0$. Therefore, any finite set of elements from $A \cap B$ generates a nilpotent subring and thus $A \cap B$ is a locally nilpotent ideal of A. Since A is $\mathcal{L}$ semi-simple, $A \cap B = 0$ and thus B/A^* must be 0. Therefore, K/A^* is a prime ring which is $\mathcal{L}$-semi-simple.

Therefore, this class M is a special class of rings. The special radical it determines is, by Lemma 80, the intersection of all ideals T_α of a ring K for which K/T_α is a prime $\mathcal{L}$-semi-simple ring. By Theorem 51 this is precisely the Levitzki radical.

Theorem 65. *The nil radical $\mathcal{N}$ is a special radical.*

Proof. Let M be the set of all prime rings which are nil semi-simple. Clearly

M has (x). Lemma 6 tells us that the nil radical is hereditary and (Theorem 47, Corollary 2) every non-zero ideal of a nil semi-simple ring is itself semi-simple. Since every non-zero ideal of a ring of M is prime (Theorem 58), M has (y). To establish (z), let A be a prime, nil semi-simple ring and suppose that A is an ideal of K. By Theorem 58 we know that K/A^* is prime and all we must then show is that K/A^* is nil semi-simple. The proof is very much like the corresponding one in Theorem 64. Suppose that B/A^* is a nil ideal of K/A^*. If $A \cap B = 0$, then $AB = BA = 0$, $B \subseteq A^*$, and B/A^* is zero. If $A \cap B \neq 0$, then it is an ideal of A. Take any x in $A \cap B$. Since it is in B and B/A^* is nil, x^n is in A^* for some integral power n. Since x is in A, x^n is in A, and thus $x^n \in A \cap A^*$. However, $A \cap A^* = 0$, for it is a nilpotent ideal of A and A is prime. Thus, $x^n = 0$. Therefore, $A \cap B$ is a nil ideal of A. Since A is nil semi-simple, $A \cap B = 0$ and therefore B/A^* is zero and K/A^* is nil semi-simple. Thus, M is a special class of rings.

The special radical determined by M is $\cap T_\alpha$, for all ideals T_α of K for which K/T_α is a prime, nil semi-simple ring (Lemma 80). We must merely show that the nil radical N of K is equal to $\cap T_\alpha$.

Since K/T_α is nil semi-simple, $N \subseteq T_\alpha$ for every α and thus $N \subseteq \cap T_\alpha$.

Let us put $\cap T_\alpha = T$. If $T \nsubseteq N$, take an element $b \in T$ such that b is not in N. Then b itself may be a nilpotent element but (b), the ideal generated by b, is not a nil ideal (if it were, b would be in N). Thus, there must exist an element x in (b) such that x is not nilpotent. Thus, x is in T and $x^n \neq 0$ for every positive integer n. In particular, x^n is not in N, for any positive n. By Zorn's Lemma select an ideal V which is maximal with respect to excluding all powers of x and including N.

Then K/V is prime, for if $C . D \subseteq V$ for ideals C, D of K, which contain V, then if $C \supset V$ and $D \supset V$, C and D must each contain a power of x, by the maximality of V. Say $x^m \in C$, $x^n \in D$. Then $x^{m+n} \in CD \subseteq V$. However V does not contain any power of x and thus either $C \subseteq V$ or $D \subseteq V$, and K/V is prime.

Furthermore, K/V is nil semi-simple, for if G/V is a nil ideal of K/V and $G \supset V$, then G must contain some power of x, say x^t. Since G/V is nil, some power of x^t, say $(x^t)^r$, must be in V. Thus $x^{tr} \in V$. Since V does not contain any powers of x, $G \subseteq V$ and K/V is nil semi-simple.

Therefore, V is one of the ideals T_α. Therefore $b \in V$ for $b \in \cap T_\alpha$. Then $x \in (b) \subseteq V$. However, V has no powers of x. This contradiction proves that $T = \cap T_\alpha \subseteq N$ and thus $N = \cap T_\alpha$. Therefore, the nil radical is a special radical.

Thus, all the supernilpotent radicals we have studied, $\mathscr{B}, \mathscr{L}, \mathscr{N}, J, \mathscr{G}, \mathscr{T}$, are special radicals. This adds point to the question asked earlier: Are there any supernilpotent radicals that are not special?

7.6. Embedding supernilpotent radicals in special radicals. If there exist supernilpotent radicals that are not special radicals, we can embed them in special radicals in a tight-fitting fashion.

Let R be any supernilpotent radical property and let S be the class of all R semi-simple rings. Let M be the class of all prime R semi-simple rings. Then $M \subseteq S$ and, in fact, $M \neq S$ for S contains direct sums of rings from M and direct sums are not prime. The class S has properties (E) and (F) (see Theorem 2).

Lemma 85. M, *the class of all prime R-semi-simple rings, is a special class of rings.*

Proof. Clearly M has (x). Since R is supernilpotent, it is hereditary, and by Theorem 47, Corollary 2, every non-zero ideal of an R-semi-simple ring is itself R-semi-simple. Since every non-zero ideal of a prime ring is prime (Theorem 58), the class M has (y).

To establish (z), let A be a prime R-semi-simple ring and suppose that A is an ideal of a ring K. From Theorem 58 we know that K/A^* is prime. Thus, all we must show is that K/A^* is R-semi-simple. To do this, consider $(A + A^*)/A^* \cong A/(A \cap A^*)$. However, $A \cap A^*$ is a nilpotent ideal of A and A is prime. Thus $A \cap A^* = 0$, and therefore $(A + A^*)/A^* \cong A$. Thus K/A^* contains a non-zero ideal, $(A + A^*)/A^*$, which is R-semi-simple. That is, $R((A+A^*)/A^*) = 0$. Since R is hereditary,

$$R((A + A^*)/A^*) = R(K/A^*) \cap (A + A^*)/A^*.$$

Thus $R(K/A^*) \cap (A + A^*)/A^* = 0$. Therefore, $R(K/A^*).(A + A^*)/A^* = 0$. However, K/A^* is prime and since $(A + A^*)/A^*$ is not zero, we must have $R(K/A^*) = 0$. That is, K/A^* is R-semi-simple. This establishes (z) and proves the lemma.

Let S_M be the upper radical determined by M. Then, of course, $R \leqslant S_M$. Thus, in this sense, we have embedded the supernilpotent radical R in a special radical, S_M. However, we can also prove:

Theorem 66. *For any supernilpotent radical R, the special radical S_M determined by the class M of all prime R-semi-simple rings is the smallest special radical such that $R \leqslant S_M$.*

Proof. Suppose that Q is a special radical property determined by some special class N, and that $R \leqslant Q$. This means that every R-radical ring is Q-radical and thus that every Q-semi-simple ring is R-semi-simple. Suppose, then, that P is a prime ring and is Q-semi-simple. Then P is R-semi-simple, and since it is prime, P must belong to the class M. Now the class N consists entirely of prime Q-semi-simple rings, and each one of them is in M. Thus $N \leqslant M$. Since Q is the upper radical determined by N, or the largest radical for which all rings in N are semi-simple, $Q \geqslant S_M$, for all the rings in N are S_M-semi-simple. This proves that S_M is the smallest special radical $\geqslant R$.

Corollary. *A supernilpotent radical R is special if and only if it is equal to S_M, where S_M is the upper radical property determined by the class of all prime R-semi-simple rings.*

Remark. It is interesting to note that if M is a special class of rings and S_M is its associated special radical, then there may be prime rings which are S_M-semi-simple and which do not belong to M. Thus, if M_1 is the class of all prime S_M-semi-simple rings, then it is possible to have $M \subset M_1$. The class M has property (E). As in Section 1.2, we construct $\bar{M}$ from M, where $\bar{M}$ has (E) and (F), where $M \subseteq \bar{M}$, and where $\bar{M}$ is the class of all S_M-semi-simple rings. It is quite possible for prime rings which are not in M to creep into $\bar{M}$. The class M_1 is the set of all prime rings in $\bar{M}$.

However, the radical determined by M_1 is the same as S_M; since $M_1 \subseteq \bar{M}$, we must have $\bar{M}_1 \subseteq \bar{M}$, and since $M \subseteq M_1$, $\bar{M} \subseteq \bar{M}_1$.

Problems.

1. If M is a special class of rings with associated special radical S_M, if M_1 is the class of all prime S_M-semi-simple rings, and if a ring K in M_1 has a minimal ideal, prove that K must be in M.

2. Prove that every supernilpotent radical is special on rings with D.C.C. on ideals.

3. Prove that every supernilpotent radical is special on rings with A.C.C. on ideals.

7.7. Dual radicals: The anti-simple radical. Let R be an arbitrary supernilpotent radical property. Let M be the class of all subdirectly irreducible rings with R-semi-simple hearts. Since R is supernilpotent, an R-semi-simple heart must be a simple non-trivial ring (Lemma 75), and, in particular, indempotent. Furthermore, if K is a subdirectly irreducible ring with heart C and C is isomorphic to a heart of a ring in M, then C is R-semi-simple, and thus K is in M. Thus, M satisfies the conditions discussed just prior to Lemma 76, and we may think of M as a class M_φ. By Theorem 56, M_φ is a special class of rings, and the upper radical R_φ determined by M_φ is a special radical.

Since all the rings in M_φ are R-semi-simple (Lemma 74), and since R_φ is the upper radical with respect to M_φ, we must have $R \leqslant R_\varphi$. In general, $R \neq R_\varphi$. We shall call a supernilpotent radical *dual* if $R = R_\varphi$, i.e. if R is the upper radical property determined by the class of all subdirectly irreducible rings with R-semi-simple hearts.

Our final programme is to take the radicals we know, say R, and consider R_φ for each one. Of course, if a radical is dual, $R = R_\varphi$, we get nothing new.

However, not all of our radicals are dual. Lemma 74 and the definition of R_φ tell us that such a process cannot be continued, that is, R_φ is itself dual. Thus, if a given radical is not dual, $R < R_\varphi$, we do get something new in R_φ. However, $(R_\varphi)_\varphi = R_\varphi$ and we cannot get anything more.

Let us then begin with the Baer lower radical β and consider β_φ. This is the upper radical property determined by the class M_φ of all subdirectly irreducible rings with β semi-simple hearts. If a heart is a zero ring, it is β-radical. If a heart is idempotent, and therefore simple, it is β-semi-simple. Thus M_φ is the class of all subdirectly irreducible rings with idempotent hearts. And, by Lemma 80, every β_φ-semi-simple ring is a subdirect sum of subdirectly irreducible rings with idempotent hearts. A β_φ-radical ring is one that cannot be mapped homomorphically onto a subdirectly irreducible ring with an idempotent heart.

The first question is naturally: Is $\beta \neq \beta_\varphi$? We know that $\beta \leqslant \beta_\varphi$.

We can actually show that the Levitzki radical $\mathscr{L} \leqslant \beta_\varphi$. Let T be an $\mathscr{L}$-radical ring. Suppose that T can be mapped homomorphically on a subdirectly irreducible ring W with an idempotent heart C. By Lemma 70, W is $\mathscr{L}$-radical and C is $\mathscr{L}$-radical. By Lemma 75 we know that C is a simple nontrivial ring. However, Theorem 55 tells us that there does not exist a simple non-trivial ring which is $\mathscr{L}$-radical. Therefore, T cannot be mapped homomorphically onto such a ring W and thus, by definition, T is β_φ-radical. Thus, every $\mathscr{L}$-radical ring is β_φ-radical, and $\mathscr{L} \leqslant \beta_\varphi$.

In particular, since $\beta < \mathscr{L} \leqslant \beta_\varphi$, we know that $\beta < \beta_\varphi$ and thus β is not a dual radical.

Therefore, not every special radical is dual. This may seem surprising at first, but if V is the class of all subdirectly irreducible rings which are, say, β-semi-simple, and we expand V to $\overline{V}$, a class having both (E) and (F), then it is not too difficult to see that $\overline{V}$ may not fill out all of $\overline{M}$, the class of all β-semi-simple rings.

We shall call β_φ the *anti-simple radical*.

Theorem 67.

1. *The anti-simple radical β_φ, determined by the class of all subdirectly irreducible rings with idempotent hearts, is a dual, special radical.*

2. *Every β_φ-semi-simple ring is isomorphic to a subdirect sum of subdirectly irreducible rings with idempotent hearts.*

3. *The Levitzki radical $\mathscr{L} < \beta_\varphi < \mathscr{G}$, the Brown–McCoy radical.*

Proof. Parts 1 and 2 have already been established, and we know that $\mathscr{L} \leqslant \beta_\varphi$. Thus, all we must show is that $\mathscr{L} \neq \beta_\varphi$ and that $\beta_\varphi < \mathscr{G}$.

Since every simple ring with unity is subdirectly irreducible with idempotent heart, and since $\mathscr{G}$ is the upper radical with respect to such rings,

$\beta_\varphi \leqslant \mathscr{G}$. On the other hand, Example 11 is a simple non-trivial ring, without a unity. It is $\mathscr{G}$-radical, but it is β_φ-semi-simple, for it is a subdirectly irreducible ring with an idempotent heart. Therefore, $\beta_\varphi < \mathscr{G}$.

To show that $\mathscr{L} \neq \beta_\varphi$, we consider Example 10. It is nil semi-simple and therefore $\mathscr{L}$-semi-simple. Suppose that it could be mapped homomorphically onto a subdirectly irreducible ring W with an idempotent heart C. Since Example 10 is commutative, and Jacobson radical, W would have to be commutative and Jacobson radical. Then C would be commutative and Jacobson radical (for J is hereditary). Thus C would be a simple, non-trivial, commutative, J-radical ring.

However, every commutative non-trivial simple ring is a field. For if $B = \{x \in C : xC = 0\}$, then B is an ideal and $B \neq C$ for $C^2 \neq 0$. Thus $B = 0$. Therefore, $xC = C$ for every $x \neq 0$ in C, for xC is a non-zero ideal. Thus, for any $x \neq 0$ and any y in C, there exists a z in C such that $xz = y$. Thus, the non-zero elements form a group and C is a field.

In particular, C has a unity element and cannot be J-radical.

Thus, Example 10 cannot be mapped homomorphically onto a subdirectly irreducible ring with idempotent heart. By definition then, it is β_φ-radical. Therefore, $\mathscr{L} < \beta_\varphi$. This ends the proof of Theorem 67.

It would seem that since $\mathscr{L} < \beta_\varphi < \mathscr{G}$, there should be an intimate connection between $\mathscr{N}$, the nil radical, and β_φ, as well as between the Jacobson radical J and β_φ.

The relationship between $\mathscr{N}$ and β_φ is not clear. Example 10 is $\mathscr{N}$-semi-simple and β_φ-radical and thus, in any case, $\mathscr{N} \neq \beta_\varphi$. If there is any relationship, then, it would be $\mathscr{N} < \beta_\varphi$. This all seems to hinge on the existence of a simple non-trivial nil ring (which is highly unlikely but still an open question). If a simple non-trivial nil ring did exist, it would be $\mathscr{N}$ radical but β_φ-semi-simple, for it would be subdirectly irreducible with idempotent heart. In this case, $\mathscr{N}$ and β_φ would be independent radical properties. If we knew definitely that no such simple non-trivial nil ring existed, then we could say that $\mathscr{N} < \beta_\varphi$. For, in that case, a nil ring could not be mapped homomorphically on a subdirectly irreducible ring with idempotent heart because the heart would then have to be a simple non-trivial nil ring. Thus, every nil ring would be β_φ-radical, by definition, and $\mathscr{N} \leqslant \beta_\varphi$. Since we know that $\mathscr{N} \neq \beta_\varphi$, we would have $\mathscr{N} < \beta_\varphi$.

Since we are almost certain that no simple non-trivial nil ring exists, we feel strongly that $\mathscr{N} < \beta_\varphi$. However, mathematics is constantly full of surprises!

The relationship between β_φ and J is much clearer, as indicated in the following lemma.

Lemma 86. *The radicals J and β_φ are independent, i.e. they are different and neither one is bigger than the other.*

Proof. Example 12 is J-radical but β_φ-semi-simple because it is simple non-trivial and therefore subdirectly irreducible with idempotent heart.

The ring T of Example 13 is J-semi-simple but it is β_φ-radical. To see that it is β_φ-radical, we first note that T itself is not subdirectly irreducible because it contains ideals $z^2R \supset z^3R \supset \ldots$ and there is no unique non-zero minimal ideal of T. On the other hand, every homomorphic image of T with non-zero kernel is nilpotent. Thus, no image of T can be subdirectly irreducible with idempotent heart, for the heart would have to be nilpotent. Thus, T is β_φ-radical

What we can prove is:

Lemma 87. *For commutative rings,* $\beta_\varphi = J = \mathscr{G} = \mathscr{T}$.

Proof. Every commutative primitive ring is a field. For, let R be such a ring. Then it must contain a maximal right ideal M (which is then a two-sided ideal) such that $\{x : Rx \subseteq M\} = 0$. But $R.M \subseteq M$ and therefore $M = 0$. Since 0 is a maximal ideal, R must be simple. And $R^2 \neq 0$, for if $R^2 = 0$, then $R \subseteq M = 0$. Thus, R is a simple non-trivial commutative ring and R is a field (see proof of Theorem 67). Thus, J is the upper radical property determined by the class of all fields and $J = \mathscr{G} = \mathscr{T}$.

On the other hand, let R be a commutative subdirectly irreducible ring with an idempotent heart C. Then C is a commutative non-trivial simple ring; C is a field. In particular, C has a unity element e. Consider $I = \{x - xe\}$, as x ranges over R. Then I is an ideal of R and if $I \neq 0$, $C \subseteq I$. However, if there exists an element x such that $e = x - xe$, then $e^2 = xe - xe^2$, and since $e^2 = e$, we have $e = xe - xe = 0$, a contradiction. Therefore, $I = 0$, and e is a unity element for R. Since e is in C, C must be all of R and thus R is a field. See [20, 41].

Thus, β_φ is the upper radical with respect to the class of all fields and $\beta_\varphi = J = \mathscr{G} = \mathscr{T}$.

It is curious to observe that β_φ corresponds to the same partition of the simple rings that $\mathscr{L}$, β, $\mathscr{D}$, and $\mathscr{S}$ do. Every simple non-trivial ring is subdirectly irreducible with idempotent heart and is therefore β_φ-semi-simple, while the trivial simple rings are clearly β_φ-radical. An interesting question is the relationship between β_φ and the upper radical property $\mathscr{U}$ determined by the class of all simple non-trivial rings. Of course, $\beta_\varphi \leqslant \mathscr{U}$ and probably $\beta_\varphi < \mathscr{U}$.

This anti-simple radical β_φ may prove to be useful to an extent depending upon how much knowledge future mathematicians can gain about subdirectly irreducible rings with idempotent hearts.

Since taking the dual of β provided interesting information, we should consider the duals of the other radicals.

Since both $\mathscr{G}$ and $\mathscr{T}$ are defined as upper radical properties determined by certain classes of simple non-trivial, and thus subdirectly irreducible with idempotent heart, rings, it is clear that they are both dual. Thus, $\mathcal{G}_\varphi = \mathcal{G}$, $\mathcal{T}_\varphi = \mathcal{T}$, and we obtain nothing new from them.

As for $\mathcal{L}_\varphi$, it is precisely β_φ because any idempotent heart is $\mathcal{L}$-semi-simple and any nilpotent heart is $\mathcal{L}$-radical. Thus, the class of all subdirectly irreducible rings with $\mathcal{L}$-semi-simple hearts is precisely the class of all subdirectly irreducible rings with idempotent hearts, and thus $\mathcal{L}_\varphi = \beta_\varphi$.

It is likely that $\mathcal{N}_\varphi = \mathcal{L}_\varphi = \beta_\varphi$. This will be so if every simple non-trivial ring is not nil. However, we do not know. If a nil simple non-trivial ring exists, then $\mathcal{N}$ corresponds to a different partition of the simple rings than do $\beta, \mathcal{L}, \beta_\varphi, \mathcal{D}$, and $\mathcal{S}$. And in this case $\mathcal{N}_\varphi$ will be a new radical property.

Finally, we should consider J_φ, the upper radical property determined by the class of all subdirectly irreducible rings with J-semi-simple hearts, i.e. with hearts that are simple non-trivial rings with maximal right ideals. It is clear that $J_\varphi \leqslant \mathcal{G}$, because every simple ring with unity is J-semi-simple, and is its own heart. Since Example 11 is J-semi-simple, it is J_φ-semi-simple, but $\mathcal{G}$-radical and therefore $J_\varphi < \mathcal{G}$. Professor Sulinski has recently pointed out to us that Example 13 is J-semi-simple but J_φ-radical, for it is not subdirectly irreducible, and since every non-trivial homomorphic image of it is nilpotent, it cannot be mapped homomorphically onto a subdirectly irreducible ring with J-semi-simple heart. Therefore, $J < J_\varphi$ and the Jacobson radical is not a dual radical. It would be interesting to study the properties of J_φ.

7.8. The generalized nil radical.

Let M be the class of all non-zero rings without zero divisors. Clearly, every ring in M is prime and every ideal of a ring in M is also zero-divisor-free and thus in M. To show that M is a special class of rings, it is therefore sufficient to establish property (z).

Suppose, then, that A is a ring without zero divisors, and that A is an ideal of a ring K. Consider K/A^*, where, as before, $A^* = \{x \in K : Ax = xA = 0\}$. We wish to show that K/A^* has no zero divisors. Suppose, then, that $x.y$ is in A^* and that x is not in A^*.

If $w.A = 0$, then $aw.aw = 0$ and since aw is in A and A is zero-divisor-free, $aw = 0$ for every a. Thus $A.w = 0$. Similarly, if $Aw = 0$, then $wA = 0$. Thus, an element is in A^* if it annihilates A on any one side.

Since x is not in A^*, there must exist an element b in A such that $bx \neq 0$. Then for any a in A we have $bxya = 0$, for xy is in A^*. Then $bx.ya = 0$ and since both bx and ya are in A, and A is zero-divisor-free, one of them is 0. Since $bx \neq 0$, we must have $ya = 0$. This holds for any a in A, and thus $yA = 0$ and y is in A^*. Therefore, K/A^* has no zero divisors and (z) is established. We thus have:

Theorem 68. *The class of all non-zero rings without zero divisors is a special class of rings.*

Let $\mathcal{N}_g$ be the special radical determined by this class. We shall call $\mathcal{N}_g$ the generalized nil radical. This was introduced simultaneously by Andrunakievic and by Thierrin [48]. Thierrin calls it the compressive radical.

Lemma 80 tells us that an $\mathcal{N}_g$-semi-simple ring is isomorphic to a subdirect sum of rings without zero divisors. Theorem 57 tells us that $\mathcal{N}_g$ is supernilpotent, but we actually say more.

First we observe that the nil radical $\mathcal{N} \leqslant \mathcal{N}_g$, for any nil ring has zero divisors and every non-zero homomorphic image of a nil ring is nil and thus has zero divisors. Consequently, a nil ring cannot be mapped homomorphically onto a non-zero ring without zero divisors, and thus every nil ring is $\mathcal{N}_g$ radical, by definition. Therefore, $\mathcal{N} \leqslant \mathcal{N}_g$.

However, the ring of 2×2 matrices over a field is simple and is nil semisimple. But it has zero divisors. Since every non-zero homomorphic image of a simple ring is isomorphic to it, the ring of 2×2 matrices cannot be mapped homomorphically on a non-zero ring without zero divisors. Thus, the ring of 2×2 matrices is $\mathcal{N}_g$ radical. This proves that $\mathcal{N} < \mathcal{N}_g$.

This also proves that $\mathcal{N}_g \not\leqslant \mathcal{T}$, and thus $\mathcal{N}_g$ does not, in general, coincide with the classical nil radical on rings with D.C.C. Thus, $\mathcal{N}_g$ loses much of its appeal for us. However, it does contain all the nil one-sided ideals, and, in fact, it contains all nilpotent elements of a ring.

If K is a commutative prime ring and $xy = 0$, then $xRy = Rxy = 0$ and (Lemma 34) either $x = 0$ or $y = 0$. Thus, a commutative prime ring is zero-divisor-free. Thus, for commutative rings, prime rings are identical with zero-divisor-free rings and thus $\mathcal{N}_g = \beta$ and $\mathcal{N}_g = \mathcal{N} = \mathcal{L} = \beta$.

Lemma 88. *For commutative rings, $\mathcal{N}_g = \mathcal{N} = \mathcal{L} = \beta$.*

The generalized nil radical is associated with the concept of completely prime rings (see the discussion following Lemma 34).

We observe that in the commutative case the two families $\mathcal{N}_g = \mathcal{N} = \mathcal{L} = \beta$ and $\beta_\varphi = J = \mathcal{G} = \mathcal{T}$ are still distinct, for Example 10 is semi-simple with respect to β but radical with respect to J and it *is* commutative.

7.9. Summary. Before we conclude, we shall mention two other radicals. The first one is the Behrens radical [14]. Let M be the class of all subdirectly irreducible rings with idempotent hearts such that the heart contains an idempotent element. Theorem 56 tells us that M is a special class of rings.

Let J_B be the special radical determined by this class. Clearly $J_B \leqslant \mathcal{G}$ because all simple rings with unity belong to this special class. Also, $\beta_\varphi \leqslant J_B$ from the comparison of their special classes. However, $J \leqslant J_B$ because a simple ring with an idempotent e cannot be J-radical, since the element $-e$

cannot be quasi-regular. Thus, every heart with an idempotent element is a J-semi-simple ring. In fact, $J_\varphi \leqslant J_B$. We know that β_φ and J are independent (Lemma 86) and therefore $J < J_B$ and $\beta_\varphi < J_B$.

Furthermore, Example 11, which was $\mathscr{G}$-radical and J-semi-simple, is also J_B-semi-simple, because it contains idempotent elements, and is thus a subdirectly irreducible ring with idempotent heart and the heart has an idempotent. Thus $J_B < \mathscr{G}$.

Lemma 89. *The Behrens radical J_B contains J, β_φ, and J_φ, and $J_B < \mathscr{G}$.*

From Lemma 80 we know that every J_B-semi-simple ring is isomorphic to a subdirect sum of subdirectly irreducible rings with idempotent hearts such that each heart contains an idempotent element.

To connect up the generalized nil radical with the other radicals a little more precisely, we shall consider one more special radical. Let M be the class of all fields. These are all subdirectly irreducible with idempotent hearts and, by Theorem 56, we can conclude that this is a special class of rings. The special radical F associated with this special class is clearly the largest radical we have considered. It is immediate that both $\mathscr{T} < F$ and $\mathscr{N}_g < F$. Of course, F does not coincide with the classical radical on rings with D.C.C.

We can then make the following list (see [10] for another view of β):

Lower re all zero simple rings:
  $\mathscr{S}$
Lower re all nilpotent rings, nil radicals of D.C.C. rings:
  $\mathscr{D}$
Lower re all nilpotent rings:
  β (Baer lower) $=$ Upper re all prime rings
Lower re all locally nilpotent rings:
  $\mathscr{L}$ (Levitzki) $=$ Upper re all prime $\mathscr{L}$-semi-simple rings
Lower re all nil rings:
  $\mathscr{N}$ (Koethe) $=$ Upper re all prime $\mathscr{N}$-semi-simple rings
  β_φ (anti-simple) $=$ Upper re all subdirectly irreducible rings with idempotent hearts
  $\mathscr{N}_\varphi =$ Upper re all subdirectly irreducible rings with nil semi-simple hearts
  J (Jacobson) $=$ Upper re all primitive rings
  $J_\varphi =$ Upper re all subdirectly irreducible rings with J-semi-simple hearts
  J_B (Behrens) $=$ Upper re all subdirectly irreducible rings with idempotent hearts with idempotent elements
  $\mathscr{G}$ (Brown–McCoy) $=$ Upper re all simple rings with unity
  $\mathscr{T} =$ Upper re all matrix rings over division rings
  $\mathscr{N}_g$ (Generalized nil) $=$ Upper re all non-zero rings without zero divisors
  $F =$ Upper re all fields

The relationship between them is as follows:

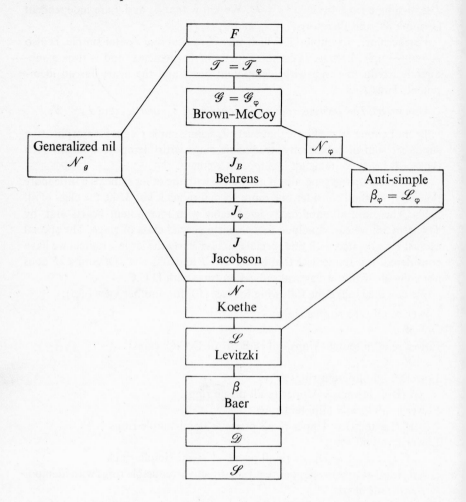

BIBLIOGRAPHY

[1] A. A. ALBERT, *Modern higher algebra* (University of Chicago Science Series, 1937).
[2] —— "Structure of algebras," *Am. Math. Soc. Coll. Publ.*, **24** (1939).
[3] S. AMITSUR, "A general theory of radicals, I," *Am. J. Math.*, **74**, 774–86 (1952); "A general theory of radicals, II," *Am. J. Math.*, **76**, 100–25 (1954); "A general theory of radicals, III," *Am. J. Math.*, **76**, 126–36 (1954).
[4] —— "On rings with identities," *J. London Math. Soc.*, **30**, 464–70 (1955).
[5] —— "Algebras over infinite fields," *Proc. Am. Math. Soc.*, **7**, 35–48 (1956).
[6] V. ANDRUNAKIEVIC, "Modular ideals, radicals and semi-simplicity of rings," *Usp. Mat. Nauk SSSR*, **12**, no. 3 (75), 133–9 (1957).
[7] —— "Anti-simple and strong idempotent rings," *Akad. Nauk SSSR, Mat. Ser.*, **21**, 125–44 (1957).
[8] —— "Radicals in associative rings I," *Mat. Sb.*, **44**, 179–212 (1958). (See p. 186.)
[9] —— "Radicals in associative rings II," *Mat. Sb.*, **55**, no. 3 (97), 329–46 (1961).
[10] —— "Prime modules and the Baer radical," *Sibirsk. Mat. Zh.*, **2**, 801–6 (1961).
[11] E. ARTIN, C. J. NESBITT, and R. M. THRALL, *Rings with minimum condition* (University of Michigan Publications in Mathematics, no. 1, 1944).
[12] A. M. BABIC, "The Levitzki radical," *Dokl. Akad. Nauk SSSR*, **126**, no. 2. 242–3 (1959).
[13] R. BAER, "Radical ideals," *Am. J. Math.*, **65**, 537–68 (1943).
[14] E. A. BEHRENS, "Nichtassoziative Ringe," *Math. Ann.*, **127**, 441–52 (1954).
[15] E. W. BETH, *The foundations of mathematics* (Amsterdam: North Holland Pub, Co., 1959).
[16] G. BIRKHOFF and S. MACLANE, *A survey of modern algebra* (New York: MacMillan Co., 1953).
[17] B. BROWN and N. H. MCCOY, "Radicals and subdirect sums," *Am. J. Math.*, **69**, 46–58 (1947).
[18] —— "The radical of a ring," *Duke Math. J.*, **15**, 495–9 (1948).
[19] —— "Some theorems on groups with application to ring theory," *Trans. Am. Math. Soc.*, **69**, 302–11 (1950).
[20] N. DIVINSKY, "Commutative subdirectly irreducible rings," *Proc. Am. Math. Soc.*, **8**, 642–8 (1957).
[21] —— "General radicals that coincide with the classical radical on rings with D.C.C.," *Can. J. Math.*, **13**, 639–44 (1961).
[22] N. DIVINSKY and A. SULINSKI, "Kurosh radicals of rings with operators," to appear in *Can. J. Math.*
[23] G. D. FINDLAY and J. LAMBEK, "A generalized ring of quotients, I and II," *Can. Math. Bull.*, **1** (1958).
[24] A. W. GOLDIE, "The structure of prime rings under ascending chain conditions," *Proc. London Math. Soc.*, **8**, no. 3, 589–608 (1958).
[25] —— "Semi-prime rings with maximum condition," *Proc. London Math. Soc.*, **10**, no. 38, 201–20 (1960).
[26] I. N. HERSTEIN, "Theory of rings," University of Chicago Math. Lecture Notes, Spring 1961.

[27] —— "A theorem of Levitzki," *Proc. Am. Math. Soc.*, **13**, 213–14 (1962).

[28] C. HOPKINS, "Rings with minimum condition," *Ann. Math.*, 712–30 (1939).

[29] N. JACOBSON, *The theory of rings* (Am. Math. Soc. Math. Surveys 1943).

[30] —— "The radical and semi-simplicity for arbitrary rings," *Am. J. Math.*, **67**, 300–20 (1945).

[31] —— "Structure of rings," *Am. Math. Soc. Coll. Publ.*, **37** (1956).

[32] E. KAMKE, *Theory of sets*, translated from German by F. Bagemihl (The Dover Series in Mathematics and Physics, 1950).

[33] I. KAPLANSKY, "Rings with a polynomial identity," *Bull. Am. Math. Soc.*, **54**, 575–80 (1948).

[34] —— *Infinite Abelian groups* (University of Michigan Publications in Mathematics, no. 2, 1954).

[35] G. KOETHE, "Schiefkorper unendlichen Ranges über dem Zentrum," *Math. Ann.*, **105**, 15–39 (1931).

[36] A. KUROSH, "Radicals of rings and algebras," *Mat. Sb.*, **33**, 13–26 (1953).

[37] J. LAMBEK, "On the structure of semi-prime rings and their rings of quotients," *Can. J. Math.*, **13**, no. 3, 392–417 (1961).

[38] L. LESIEUR and R. CROISOT, "Anneaux premiers noetheriens à gauche," *Ann. Sci. Ecole Norm. Super.* (3), **76**, 161–83 (1959).

[39] J. LEVITZKI, "On the radical of a general ring," *Bull. Am. Math. Soc.*, **49**, 462–6 (1943).

[40] —— "On multiplicative systems," *Composito Math.*, **8**, 76–80 (1950).

[41] N. McCOY, "Subdirectly irreducible commutative rings," *Duke Math. J.*, **12**, 381–7 (1945).

[42] —— *Rings and ideals* (Carus Monograph no. 8, 1948).

[43] S. PERLIS, "A characterization of the radical of an algebra," *Bull. Am. Math. Soc.*, **48**, 128–32 (1942).

[44] H. PRÜFER, "Untersuchungen über die Zerlegbarkeit der abzahlbaren primaren abelschen Gruppen," *Math. Z.*, **17**, 35–61 (1923).

[45] E. SASIADA and A. SULINSKI, "A note on the Jacobson radical," *Bull. Acad. Polon. Sci., Ser. Sci., Math., Astron., Phys.*, **10**, 421–3 (1962).

[46] M. SION and R. WILLMOTT, "On a definition of ordinal numbers," *Am. Math. Monthly*, **69**, no. 5, 381–6 (1962).

[47] A. SULINSKI, "Certain questions in the general theory of radicals," *Mat. Sb.*, **44**, 273–86 (1958).

[48] G. THIERRIN, "Sur les ideaux completement premiers d'un anneau quelconque," *Bull. Acad. Roy. Belg.*, **43**, 124–32 (1957).

[49] Y. UTUMI, "On quotient rings," *Osaka Math. J.*, **8**, no. 1, 1–18 (1956).

[50] B. L. VAN DER WAERDEN, *Modern algebra*, vols. I and II (New York: F. Ungar Pub. Co., 1949).

51] J. H. M. WEDDERBURN, "On hypercomplex numbers," *Proc. London Math. Soc.*, **6**, 77–117 (1908).

[52] O. ZARISKI and P. SAMUEL, *Commutative algebra* (Princeton, N.J.: Van Nostrand, 1958).

INDEX

ALGEBRA IDEAL, 38
Algebraic algebra, 105
Algebraic element, 105
Amitsur, 106
Andrunakievic, 107, 134
Anti-simple radical property, 150
Ascending chain condition, 47
Axiom of Choice, 11

BAER LOWER RADICAL PROPERTY, 44, 56, 59, 62, 63, 88, 89, 128, 140, 141
Basic left ideal, 83
Behren's radical property, 154
Brown–McCoy radical property, 63, 116

C^∞, the zero ring on the infinite additive cyclic group, 16
Cardinal number, 8
Central idempotent, 26
Centre of a ring, 24
Chain: 8, 61; similar, 8; well-ordered, 8
Closed left ideal, 75
Common left multiple property, 66
Complement, 79
Complete direct sum, 63
Completely prime ideal, 60
Composition series, 36
Compressive radical property, 154

DENSE RING OF LINEAR TRANSFORMATIONS, 100
Descending chain condition, 21
Direct sum, 26
Discrete direct sum, 63
Dual radical property, 149

EQUIVALENT SETS, 8
Examples: (1) p^∞, 14; (2) C^∞, 16; (3) nil but not nilpotent, 19; (4) non-associative, 20; (5) D.C.C. on right but not on left ideals, 37; (6) nil radical but $\mathscr{S}$-semi-simple, 41; (7) nil radical but not β-radical, 46; (8) A.C.C., simple but not $\mathscr{M}XD$, 55; (9) with right but not left quotient ring, 71; (10) even over odd; Jacobson radical but nil semi-simple, 103; (11) Jacobson semi-simple but $\mathscr{T}$-radical, 109; (12) simple Jacobson non-trivial radical ring, 112; (13) not Jacobson radical but radical re the upper radical property determined by all simple primitive rings, 113

G REGULAR IDEAL, 116
G regularity, 116
Generalized nil radical property, 154
Goldie, 74

HEART OF A RING, 63, 135
Hereditary radical property, 125, 134, 135
Herstein, 53, 131, 132

IDEAL: algebra, 38; basic left, 83; closed left, 75; completely prime, 60; G regular, 116; prime, 59, 61; regular right, 95; right primitive, 96; right quasi-regular right, 92; simple, 26; uniform left, 82
Idempotent: 21; central, 26; orthogonal, 26; pairwise orthogonal, 26; primitive, 29; semi-primitive, 26
Initial ordinal, 11

JACOBSON, 51, 91
Jacobson radical property, 93
Jordan–Hölder theorem, 35, 36, 50

KOETHE, 21
Kurosh, 113

L-RING, 57
Least upper bound, 61
Left quasi-regularity, 94
Left quotient ring, 66, 75, 87
Lesieur and Croisot, 74
Levitzki, 51, 62, 127, 128
Levitzki radical property, 127, 128
Limit ordinal, 10
Locally nilpotent, 21, 126
Lower class of a partition, 14
Lower radical property: 13; determined by all nilpotent rings, 43, 58, 59; determined by all nilpotent rings which are nil radicals of rings with D.C.C. on left ideals, 43, 44; determined by all zero simple rings, 40; of a partition, 14

M-SEQUENCE, 62
McCoy, 62
Modularity, 78

NIL RADICAL PROPERTY, 40
Nil ring, 18
Nilpotent element, 18
Nilpotent ring, 18